FORGED BY FIRE

FORGED BY FIRE

HOW TO DEVELOP AN UNSTOPPABLE PERSONAL BRAND

MILA GRIGG

LIONCREST
PUBLISHING

FORGED BY FIRE
How to Develop an Unstoppable Personal Brand

FIRST EDITION

ISBN   978-1-5445-3042-0 *Hardcover*
         978-1-5445-3041-3 *Paperback*
         978-1-5445-3043-7 *Ebook*
         978-1-5445-3044-4 *Audiobook*

For my girls, Sophia and Aleksandra.

Trials in life will come, and some will make you feel like you are on fire. Remember, Jesus will never leave you or forsake you. Your value comes from who you are in the Lord...nothing else matters.

Contents

Introduction

My personal brand was built during the most arduous trial of my life. I was forged by fire, and made stronger by all the elements that combined during that incredibly difficult time—and if I can do it, so can you. I'm living proof of the amazing things you can accomplish despite the fires you may be facing.

The abbreviated version of the story goes like this: I was a newly married, young entrepreneur trying to balance the needs of my husband, four new stepchildren, and a growing business when the US Attorney called. I gave the phone to Gordon and watched as the blood drained from his face.

He hung up and told me, "I'm going downtown today, and I'm probably not going to be coming back."

I started crying and yelled, "What did you do?" My husband being questioned for some unknown misdeed was not part of any future I'd ever envisioned.

Building an entrepreneurial brand is hard on a good day, but trying to do it with a husband facing criminal charges was going to be damn near impossible. Still, I put my head down and worked as hard as I possibly could. At the time, I was starting to make a name for myself in the business world and had been featured in several publications and magazines through sheer tenacity. My work focused on helping executives at all levels, businesspeople, and entrepreneurs build, revamp, or upgrade their image. Many of them were unhappy with what they saw in the mirror. They felt their image wasn't reflective of who they really were—often not inspiring, current, confident, or polished enough. I didn't try to change who they were; instead, I helped them change how they saw themselves and have an image that reflected who they really were.

Although survival was the only thing on my mind when Gordon was sent to prison nine months later, I ended up positively THRIVING. I soon realized my passion and calling went far beyond image and fashion—my God-given gifting was to help people find their purpose and help them to share their stories so that they would be seen, valued, heard. Through guts, grit, and determination, I grew my business and began coaching executives on branding. From there, it expanded to include companies and marketing teams. Then keynotes and employee training and coaching sessions. What a ride.

I was eventually tapped to give a series of keynotes for a Fortune 500 company in Tennessee. It was a huge opportunity at the time, and one of my first few at a business of that size and caliber. That I had been able to build my brand to a place where a Fortune 500 company was trusting me to train their executives felt like a huge success given everything that had transpired. It still blows my mind. To this day, I never take for granted the blessing of any client and am overwhelmed with gratitude.

That day, I was greeted by over a hundred faces in the audience. When I started talking about how to build personal brand and how to get recognized for your value, I realized the only way I could truly make my point was by sharing some key pieces of my story. I was as authentic as I've ever been in a corporate environment that day, and I figured either I'd get fired or it was going to be great.

After my presentation, I was met with a long line of people waiting to talk to me. Some people told me about their own fires. Others thanked me for sharing my heart. Most seemed moved and motivated by my message, and were fortified by the expression of faith I gave in response to some of their personal questions. Authenticity, as well as some courage, had won the day. There would be no firing, and lots more hiring.

I'll never forget sitting in my car after that keynote and realizing how the trials in my life had come together to help me deliver on my own purpose. I was grateful and completely overwhelmed by God's blessings. If I hadn't been tested, I'd never know how strong I—and my brand—could become, or how absolute and determined I could be. Fires have a strange way of leading you to your true reason for being on this earth if you continue to focus on the purpose of the fire versus the pain of it.

People have told me that watching me go through the fire changed their lives. They admire the way I never wavered in my resolve, my faith, or who I was. I had moments to be sure, but I was resolute in my conviction of faith, family, and growing my company, come what may. I want to instill in you the same kind of steadfast faith and strength with regard to your personal brand and yourself. That way, if the bottom ever falls out—which it absolutely will at some point—you're going to land on a solid foundation. You only fall as far as your brand allows you to fall. More on that later.

THE SPARK: YOU

Whether you realize it or not, you already have a brand. In fact, you are one.

Your brand is *you*. It's WHO you really are. It's what you say and do, who and what you associate yourself with, and the way you show up in the world. It is how people describe you and it matters.

How well you cultivate brand YOU determines whether you nail that hard-earned promotion or get passed over for it. Whether you're recognized and sought after for your talents or remain invisible to others. Whether the CEO of your company greets you in the elevator or stares at their feet, watch, or phone—anything but start a conversation with you. Whether you land that board position. Whether you are given the opportunity you deserve. And so much more.

Because let's get real here: you can be incredibly smart. Dress well. Communicate effectively. Have high emotional intelligence. Be a purposeful and inspiring leader. Know how to share on social media. But if you're missing one element of an unstoppable personal brand like those I mentioned and more—and you're making the same mistakes over and over without even realizing it—you're never going to get where you want to go or reach your purpose.

Brand-stoppers can be as small as the look on your face when people come to you with a business challenge, the way you acknowledge—or don't—your colleagues when you walk into a meeting, or your fashion choices. Often, we don't even know we're doing these things, or that anyone might possibly think what we're doing is ineffective, a turn-off, or even offensive. So many seemingly minor missteps can put the brakes on getting ahead.

After helping thousands of clients—from freshly-minted graduates to high-powered CEOs—further refine (or fully repair!) the image they're projecting into the world, I am now more convinced than ever that today's fast-moving, technologically-advanced, socially-connected world demands presenting the best of who you are at all times—in person and online. The only way to do that is by taking control of your own narrative. If you can't share your story, you will be left behind and lose out to someone who can. Especially when you're competing, growing, or transitioning jobs, the last thing you want is to unintentionally send the wrong message or turn off the connections you're hoping to attract.

Now I want you to get brutally honest with yourself: as it stands today, are the values and qualities your brand represents truly aligned with everything you are and aspire to be? Have you shared your authentic self and story so other people are seeing you in the best light? Or are you letting others take and shift your stories, goals, and dreams into something unrecognizable, throwing you off your God-given path?

If you're now realizing you might need to take better control of your personal brand, never fear. The spark is already inside you to successfully relaunch the new and improved brand YOU. I'll be right here with you to show you how.

THE FUEL: THIS BOOK

This book is designed to help you build your personal brand—step by step, brick by brick, leaving no stone unturned—so you won't ever have to wonder where you took a wrong turn or why you've found yourself at yet another dead end again. None of this is fluff. I hate when consultants or coaches offer fluff and motivation without tactical advice based on experience. Do you want more opportunities? This is how it happens.

It starts from square one and moves forward in a progressive, actionable manner. Every chapter increases your understanding and knowledge, offering tools and tips on how to develop, improve, or fix elements of your personal brand. By the time you're finished reading, you'll have the full facts on how all the pieces work together and what you need to do to create the strongest, most authentic and effective personal brand possible.

Of course, there are many other great books out there. I give them prominent shout-outs throughout these pages, find them incredibly aspirational and inspirational, and admire their authors. I consider many of those brand leaders to be my mentors, whether I know them personally or simply because their work resonated so highly with me.

I always recommend reading as widely as you can, because it's crucial to keep learning, growing, and exposing yourself to new ways of thinking and ideas. But when it comes to personal branding, my advice is to START HERE. While other books deconstruct personal branding into individual parts, focusing intently on singular aspects of it, this is the only one to my knowledge that brings all of those pieces together in one place.

THE FIRE: MY TRIAL

Right now you might be thinking, How on earth does this woman expect me to build a brand and be my best self every single day despite everything else going on in my life? I expect it from you because I know it's possible and worth it. I successfully built my brand even as my husband was serving a prison term. Now allow me to expand that story a bit further, because while it was not pretty, it also wasn't as heinous as people tried to make it out to be and it's a crucial part of how my experience will help you.

After the phone call that changed my life, Gordon quickly confessed to both me and the government, sparing no detail and taking full responsibility for his actions. He hid nothing and held nothing back. The 2008 crash had hit his company hard, especially the money management side of it, and eventually he'd found himself unable to make payments on his corporate debentures. He then made the life-changing, monumentally horrible decision to not share the truth with his clients concerning their financial accounts and his ability to make payment. Desperation and pride can make a person do terribly misguided things that have lifelong consequences for so many.

Pride is the worst brand attribute.

Since Gordon was being charged with a financial crime, all of his accounts were frozen. There wasn't any money for living expenses. We had no idea how we were going to pay for groceries or gas, and were forced to move in with my mother. A friend from our church offered Gordon a job digging ditches and doing odd home-building jobs while he awaited sentencing. Thank God for friends who get into the mud with you, even when you've created the mud yourself. Meanwhile, I was digging through old purses, the couch, my car, and every crevice of my office, hoping to find anything I could that would help.

Although we trusted and believed in Gordon's big-time, hot-shot lawyer, he did not represent my husband well. Essentially, the lawyer shared nothing, and his case went straight to sentencing. The sentencing guidelines for a federal case like Gordon's is generally six to eight years. His lawyer told him to expect one or two years, tops.

The judge gave him 120 months.

It took a minute to do the math in my head while sitting in the courtroom that day. Ten years. My husband was going to jail for the next decade. I put my head down and sobbed. I couldn't walk. I had to pray to even breathe.

I was six months pregnant at the time. Even though we'd been trying to have a baby for quite a while with no luck, the Lord works in mysterious ways. Now I was facing birthing and raising our child—my firstborn—alone.

While we hoped Gordon might be sent to a prison camp, which are a little less restrictive than penitentiaries and don't require living alone in a locked cell, we soon learned he was going to a federal penitentiary with a reputation for being nearly as bad as Alcatraz. Not only that, but he would have to stay in the main prison for a while to process before being sent to the federal prison camp. We drove to Atlanta the night before to ensure he was on time to begin his sentence. By the time we arrived back at the hotel after dinner, I couldn't keep it together anymore.

I told him, "I need God to show me that it's not going to be ten years. I need Him to write something in the SKY." I would never ask anything like that under normal circumstances, as I don't believe in signs or demanding anything from the Lord, but I was desperate. My husband said years later that in that moment he simply prayed for the Lord to give me a sense of peace, because I clearly needed it.

Our hotel was located in the Buckhead area of Atlanta. I opened the curtains and saw three telephone towers in the sky. Somehow, among all the tall buildings, that view was what greeted me. I took it as a sign and in that moment, I knew God hadn't abandoned me. Three years was long, but far less than ten. God's amazing grace and undeserved mercy.

The next morning, I dropped Gordon off at what looked like Castle Grayskull from the He-Man cartoon. It was dark, looming, and foreboding, and I drove up so fast I threw the car into park before it had even stopped. I barely remember the four-hour drive home.

Gordon's impropriety was big news, especially since Bernie Madoff had just been sentenced. It appeared in the newspaper, on television, and even reached as far as a London newspaper. The entire world knew his sin, and I was guilty by association.

God bless my mother, who was the only person to remain standing by my side during that time. People stopped calling. Women I thought were my friends shunned me. Many in my church didn't support me. Only a single family—who were clients at the time—wrote me a note, which I have to this day and still greatly appreciate. I felt more alone than I ever knew possible.

Although I'd been building my business for several years by this point, we'd certainly never had to rely on my income to survive. Now, I had been unceremoniously thrust into the role of sole breadwinner. The pressure to succeed was enormous, and I had to do it with a public scandal hanging over my head.

I was on a stage unlike any I had been on before. There were so many eyes on me. So many people waiting for me to fail. Some actually WANTING me to fail, as they told me years later through apologies.

Funny how things come full circle. I became hyper-aware of everything everyone did, because I was always trying to read them. Did they know? If yes, how could I mitigate the damage?

Soon after the news hit, I had a meeting scheduled with a publisher who wanted to talk to me about writing a column on business image, personal branding, and fashion. Although he could not have been more gracious about it, he quickly rescinded his offer. I felt like I was damaged goods as far as the business community was concerned.

I dug in my heels and went to work. I had developed a close working relationship with Dillard's, and even though the store manager knew what was going on in my life, he promoted and supported me anyhow. He let me take over the store for shows, where I would present about brand and image and invite hundreds of women. (Note: If you are ever in the position to aid others in need, please do. You never know how much you might change someone's life with one small act of kindness. His changed mine and I will be grateful forever.)

Sometimes, Gordon would call when I was shopping for an executive. Inmates in federal prison have only ten minutes a day on the phone, so I would run to find an open dressing room, shut the door, and talk to my husband there. Because the pain was so raw, I had to pray to the Lord to pull me together afterward so I could continue my day. I needed His help to allow me to offer the best of myself to the client I'd been given the honor of serving.

I'm reminded of the scripture that says God grants us a peace that transcends all understanding. By any stretch, I should have been broken into pieces, but the strength He gave me in those moments was so incredibly powerful. The Bible came to life as God and I walked through that fire together. And on the days I couldn't walk myself, the Holy Spirit pushed me forward.

The Lord gave me glimpses along the way of why and where my life would go because of the fire. As it turns out, the very thing that I'd been doing for an executive's wardrobe was actually connected to helping people find their purpose, which in turn walked me into my own purpose. Once I realized my true gifting, I began communicating my shift in business model to others.

I started blogging. I joined every networking group I could find. I went to chamber and rotary meetings. I spent a crazy amount of time with my feet on the pavement every day, doing the hard work of sharing who I was so people could begin to see what I had to offer.

> Trials don't define you—and neither do mistakes—so keep moving forward.

I became part of a group that builds women in the community at that time. I volunteered to head up PR for their biggest annual event, and when I called a woman I knew through an alumni group for my sorority to discuss it, she literally said to me, "I wish you the best of luck," and hung up the phone. My only comfort in that moment was knowing who I was in God's eyes. I was valuable. I was created for a purpose—and that purpose wasn't to be shunned by judgmental fools.

Thankfully, not everyone was so disparaging and dismissive. Another prominent businesswoman who knew me from the work I had done with her nonprofit began to promote my brand. Her word was so strong that people would look past what they thought they knew about me to start giving me a chance. My brand grew exponentially through her and others. That is called co-branding—when you have a personal brand so strong that you are able to lift others.

When I thanked her for having faith in me in spite of all that had happened, she said, "If I judged all my friends by what their husbands did, you can bet I wouldn't have one friend left." Soon, people in the groups and organizations I'd joined began to rally around me versus against me, and those who had shunned me were reaching out.

The morning of my big keynote at that Fortune 500, right before I was about to walk through the doors of a giant, multinational corporation, I received a phone call from prison. I was told my husband was being transferred to a maximum-security facility full of murderers, gang members, and lifers—a place even worse than the Alcatraz rival he was already in.

Through God's grace, I experienced a huge breakthrough in my career by mustering up the courage to be open, honest, and truly authentic that day during my keynote despite this grim news being front and center on my mind—and after a year, he secured a capable new lawyer who was eventually able to present his full case through an appeal. As a result, my business grew and my husband was released in a little over four years after his sentence began. Just when you think you've fallen too far to get back up, God Himself shows up.

If God could take me back twenty years and change the past, I'd grab a glass of whiskey and still say, "Nah, let's do it." I would never be the woman I am today or have the business or brand I've built if I hadn't gone through that fire. As Charles Spurgeon once said, "Trials teach us what we are; they dig up the soil and let us see what we are made of."

Don't hide from your mistakes and never let anyone hold you to your past—ever. Nobody has that right and you are not alone. Those who have fallen the furthest can lead better than many who haven't known a tough day in their entire lives.

THE HEAT: MY KNOWLEDGE + YOUR HARD WORK

So now you understand: the information I offer in this book is not only based on process, facts, data, and statistics, but on my life experience as well. I've lived this, and I've also worked with thousands of people to implement these same steps to build an unstoppable personal brand. It worked for me, it worked for them, and it will work for you, too.

Regardless of where you are in your life right now—whether you are starting out or at the peak of your career, want more money or already have financial stability, are looking to create a legacy or still trying to find a purpose at work—there is hope for you to get to where you want to go. It doesn't matter how old you are, what industry you're in, or where you are on the corporate ladder. If you want to get off the proverbial hamster wheel of working only to work, you are not alone. Even as a C-Suite leader, this book can help you grow as well as to see your teams differently and lead them differently.

People tend to worry that one moment, one disappointment, one terrible fire can dismantle and discredit them forever. But you are created for a purpose that is more than one client or colleague loving you or hating you, a few bad days at work, or a job that isn't a good fit. Any trial that has come or is yet to come will pass. This chapter isn't your last.

I also hope you take heart in the fact that EVERYONE is trying to reinvent themselves. We're all trying to find purpose and meaning. I've had the privilege of helping many people who had settled for being where they thought they should be. Many had forgotten their dreams or never dared to dream at all. Some of you simply haven't shared your story, either in person or online. It's time.

The great news in all of this is that you, too, can live your life out in a different way. Maybe this book will inspire you to start a business, change industries, or live the dream you've pushed down for years.

UNLESS YOU'RE LYING ON YOUR DEATHBED, IT'S NEVER TOO LATE.

THE LIGHT: THE BRAND-NEW BRAND YOU

This book is for you if:

- You want to ensure you are marketing yourself and sharing your value
- You have no idea how to be on LinkedIn
- You lead a large company or firm
- You are an entrepreneur or want to be one
- You are in leadership and you want to ensure your workforce is representing themselves and your company brand
- You need to learn one of the brand topics in this book
  - Grow your emotional intelligence
  - Communicate with truth and grace
  - Lead with wisdom
  - Create an authentic image
- You have no idea how to share your value or your story (in person or online)
- You are job hunting
- You want to be on a board
- You feel misunderstood at work
- You are a new leader
- You are trying to shift culture in your company
- You want to grow as a leader
- You can't figure out why you are not being promoted
- You want to hone your skills and learn to share your story
- You want to become CEO of your company, start your own business, or move into the C-Suite
- You are starting out and have no idea what to do
- You have missed opportunities you were totally qualified for and wondered why
- You have ever looked at yourself in the mirror and thought, Why am I going to work today? I don't even know why I do this. I don't really like the company. I don't like the culture, and people aren't like me. What am I doing with my life?
- You think you don't have the confidence to do any of this
- You wonder if you still have purpose in life, regardless of work, or even if you ever did at all

You're in the right place if you want to build your brand in a world that's moving at the speed of light. If you're ready to develop a plan to share who you are with the world. If you don't want anything to get in the way of where you'd like to go, regardless of your goal.

Everything I'm asking you to do here already exists within you—nothing is made up or inauthentic. Together, let's build your brand based on WHO you are and WHY you do what you do. Let's confirm your gifting and purpose, and then discover how to live and share it most effectively. By the time we're done here, your brand will be real, honest, and true to you—and I'll be by your side the entire way to inspire, motivate, and give you hope.

This book is structured in a way that allows you to read, digest, and revisit the information, lessons, and exercises it contains in bite-sized portions. Each section features:

The Spark, a flash of insight illuminating essential concepts and goals

The Fuel, the tinder you need to ignite your personal brand journey

The Fire, shining examples to light your path

The Heat, where simmering ideas get forged into rock-solid brand attributes

The Light, a "lite" recap of main messages and key takeaways

Brand YOU is ready to be born. Everything is about to change, and it all starts now. Let's get fired up!

Part One

BRAND DNA

*"Your brand is what people say about you
when you're not in the room."*

—JEFF BEZOS, FOUNDER AND CEO OF AMAZON

You're One in a Billion!

There are almost eight billion people in the world, and then there's YOU. You were born with a unique gift. A God-given purpose. This is the very reason you were created.

Every time I say this during speaking engagements, someone in the audience stares back at me with eyes that tell me they don't believe it and it's also incredibly "fluffy." I typically ask them to stick with me, because this is the most important thing I want them—and you—to know.

You were made for more than you think—created for a purpose. I don't want you to miss it.

Many of the so-called experts talk about personal branding only from the perspective of how to share who they "think" they are, or from a marketing-only filter. I will show you how to market yourself, but brand is so much more than marketing.

Other experts want to talk about hope. Hope in what? You must have a foundation first. What they're missing is the heart of a personal brand, which is your unique purpose and gifting. Before you ever walk into a networking room, go to an interview, develop a plan, create a social media calendar or elevator pitch, you must discover what that gifting is.

Simply working isn't good enough anymore. The world is full of noise, social media is crowded, and it is becoming harder and harder to be seen or stand out from your peer group. You don't have a LinkedIn? You need one and there is a chapter dedicated to just that. Before you do that though, you have to show people the value you offer beyond only doing the job. And here's the deal—you have great value. You were created for a purpose that nobody else has.

So, what sets you apart from the competition in your market or field? What differentiates you from the crowd? Perhaps you have the gift of compassion or empathy. Maybe you possess the ability to bring teams together. Maybe you see the information faster than anyone in the room and can put the pieces together while other people are still unpacking their laptops. Whatever your gifting is, it's what makes you more than what you do regardless of what you "do" for a living. Many people try to hide their gifting for various reasons. DON'T DO THAT. Let it shine through in everything you do.

Consider this: over the course of his lifetime, Luigi Tarisio sought out and purchased instruments of only the finest quality. After he passed, it was discovered he had an unused 1716 Stradivarius among his vast and valuable collection. Imagine all the incredible music that could have been made on that priceless violin in the 147 years it was stashed away, all the joy it could have brought to musicians putting bow to strings and audiences listening in rapt wonder. Yet the gift and purpose of one of the greatest instruments ever created was kept from the world for more than a century.

My greatest hope is that you discover, develop, and use your gifting to bless the world with your own music. This is a one-time show here on earth—you don't get another chance. Who cares what people say?

Your gift is YOUR gift, given to you by God Himself. No one wants to look back at ninety years old and wonder if they wasted their gifting.

Entrepreneur and communications guru Gary Vaynerchuk says if you don't want to regret your life, go to an old person's home. When you see regret in someone's eyes there, it will make you work harder than you've ever worked before. It will make you forget the fear that you have of what other people might think of you.

Shout-out to Gary Vee: Thanks for being such an inspiring mentor. I hope you are enjoying the advance copy of this book. I would love to be on your speaking tour or a part of your speakers bureau, and I will join you anytime (or, I'll fly to NY for coffee, lunch, whatever—let me know)! For anyone in business that doesn't know Gary Vee, you need to follow him on all his social media. He is the guru.

THE FUEL

Curate the Experience

Imagine walking into your favorite store. How does it smell? How are products placed on the floor? How are you greeted? Do the employees help you or leave you alone? Are you able to easily find things you love? How are you checked out? How clean are the bathrooms? All of that, from A to Z, makes up the brand.

When brands provide a memorable experience, they immediately stand out—like Target. It was renamed Tar-jay by its own audience. They lifted the company up without even being asked to because they loved the brand experience! Are people lifting you and your brand?

Although there are many definitions of personal branding, the one I live, breathe, and die by is this: the total experience of you. Your brand is not only what you say or what you share online—it's also how you walk into a room, carry yourself, speak, and engage. It encompasses every phone call, email, text, and social media post. It is what you think, how you grow, and how you're encouraged to rise when you're feeling weak. It is how you respond to criticism. It is what reminds you of who you are when it seems there is no hope.

Your task is to share this total experience of you with the world.

People need to know WHO you are, WHY you do what you do, and WHAT you do—and they need to hear it consistently over time. They must know where to find you when they need your gifting.

Personal branding is becoming less of a competitive edge and more of a requirement for anyone looking to grow their business, lead teams, build their company brands, land their dream job, or take their career to the next level. Some companies are never going back to working in an office environment, so personal branding may be the only way to share your gifts, talent, ability, and passion for work in the future. In fact, it may mean the difference between getting a new job or promotion in months rather than years—if at all!

Staying mindful of how others are experiencing you helps ensure that it matches what you want them to experience both in person and online. When you know how to live and manage your personal brand, you earn respect. Your brand helps others be aware and take notice of your value and what you bring to the table. It isn't fluffy in the least bit, but rather the most genuine way to share your gifts. It is truly the thread that binds your life together.

WHAT A PERSONAL BRAND IS—AND ISN'T

What it is: The process by which you share who you are on your best day with the world.

What it isn't: A logo, color scheme, or marketing materials.

CONTROL THE NARRATIVE

Whether you realize it or not, you already have a brand right now. People are already talking about it and describing you to others. What are they saying? Don't know? That is a problem. They are already trying to associate or disassociate with you, co-brand or not co-brand with you.

Your brand is interpreted by other people on impact. Many people believe they own their brand, but that's simply not true. For example, after reading this book I want you to believe I've taught you many valuable things about branding. I'd also love it if you recommended it to all your friends and became a brand ambassador of mine. But while I am hopeful you will do all this, I also know you might not. I can't control what you're thinking about me, only how I share my gifts, stories, and value with you.

A friend recently shared this description of me that she had texted to some friends she wanted me to meet: "Christian. Executive. Entrepreneur. Smart. Drinks. Cusses. Normal and reasonable. Stunningly beautiful. Loyal, honest, and just a good friend and person."

I cried. Nicest compliment ever and captures most of me. And I'll take the beautiful comment any day at my age! There were so many years I tried to fit a mold for other people—to be quieter and a bit meeker to fit in. Especially after my husband went to prison, I tried even harder at first to be perfect until I realized that people needed the real ME. I cuss occasionally and I'm working on it, but when I'm in a state of frustration it can fly out in Serbian or in English. I like whiskey. I laugh loudly and it takes me just a few minutes to feel like I'm part of a team at any company. I'm professional and hardcore, but I'm also loving and love to laugh with those I'm working with and coaching. I'm not a quiet and perfect person. You must be who you are and find the tribe that supports ALL of you.

When I'm working with companies, I often have people break into groups of three or four. Then I ask the group to give me the words they would use to describe one of the participants. One group kept describing this woman as happy, bubbly, and kind. You'd think this would be a great moment for her, but I could see she was incredibly mad and frustrated by it. I asked her what was wrong, and she said in a louder voice that surprised us all, "I am decisive. I am efficient. I get things done." One of my all-time favorite coaching moments.

This is a prime example of someone who needed to take control of her narrative. I reminded her that people were describing her in a positive way, even though that may not have been the first, second, or even third thing she wanted people to think about her. To change that perception, she was going to have to start sharing different stories whenever she was describing herself or things she was working on as well as allowing her real personality to show.

You, too, have the power to craft your own narrative. Don't let your brand languish and become an uninspiring story out there for all to see. You simply must take control, or other people will do it for you.

And remember this: not everyone will like you. Now believe this: who cares? MUCH more on this later.

When people told me I was crazy for staying married, building a business, and not working for a company to be "safe," I knew who I was and what my purpose was. If they didn't like me because I stayed married and fought for my family, I didn't care then and I still don't care today. I followed my path. I was obedient to the Lord and followed His wisdom, not the wisdom of fools. You must have a strong brand, have courage in your conviction, know your values, and use them daily to make decisions. Keep it going!

> Remember: GREAT BRANDS ARE BUILT. THEY DO NOT SIMPLY HAPPEN.

STAY STRONG AND STEADY

Once you discover and believe you have a unique purpose meant only for you, your brand is being built on a rock-solid foundation. It will bring you opportunities over and over and over again. But when people don't know exactly who they are and haven't yet established a purpose, their brand is built on sinking sand. It is ever shifting and will eventually collapse under the weight of their uncertainty. You make terrible decisions when they are based on what others think about you and your life—your brand values and purpose are what matter. Know those and you win every time.

So which would you rather be? Right! Unshakeable. Unflappable. UNSTOPPABLE.

When fires come, you only fall as far as your brand allows you to fall. A solid brand sustains you in the bad times and steadies you in any storm. If you make a mistake—and God knows we all do, nobody is perfect—your brand holds you up because people already know you. Your brand ambassadors, people who know you and who you really are, will be there to vouch for you.

When the fire came in my life, almost everything was taken away: my husband, money, and material things. All I had left was my personal brand and Jesus, and that was more than enough. I wanted to put up a facade, a wall—getting vulnerable felt too risky, like I might fall apart. But because I knew who I was, who I was created by, and why I do what I do, I made a decision to share unreservedly and with passion instead. After a moment of hesitation, I was me and let the cards fall where they may.

By being intentional, transparent, and consistent about sharing my story, I had ambassadors who not only spoke for me, but also stood with me. They let the people who were trying to hold me guilty by association know that simply wasn't who I was. And it brought the people who needed my gifting right to me. I learned to love the gossiper and the naysayer. Still do. And I feel bad for that gossiper—they are in more pain than I am if they need to gossip about others. They are also that person in my mental rolodex I pull out when I am tired and need inspiration, whether I'm on the treadmill or putting together a proposal.

Recognizing you have a God-given purpose, making that purpose the basis of your brand, and always using your brand as a filter allows you to be your best self, even on your worst day. When the fires come, your brand helps you stay strong, consistent, and authentically you. It won't let you fail, and it won't let you fall too far. If you don't have a strong brand foundation, you will keep falling and nothing is there to stop you.

THE FIRE

Characteristics of Great Brands

So, what do all great brands have in common? All these things and more! Great brands:

INSPIRE OTHERS

Good brands inspire people because they're sharing, leading, and guiding. You don't need to be in the C-suite of a company to lead. On a visit to NASA, President Kennedy noticed a janitor. When he asked him what he was doing, the janitor responded, "I'm helping put a man on the moon!"

Everybody is in a leadership role. No matter what your job, make it your business to inspire those around you. And if you are already leading, or at the pinnacle of leadership success, the questions become, *Am I still doing it well? Am I bringing up others into leadership positions? How can I continue to improve?* Don't fall into the trap of resting on what you know about leading. You can always improve.

ALWAYS USE THEIR BRAND FILTER

We often wonder how some people get so lucky in their lives and careers, but what we're not acknowledging is the twenty years that "lucky" person has spent sharing their brand story and narrative. Nobody is an overnight success.

Your brand is the filter that reminds you of who you are on your best day. It's the thing that you'll always turn to. It is there to guide every decision you make. It is the thread that binds your life together.

I have five words to describe who I am and what my brand is, the most of which is faith. I know regardless of any fire or challenge that may come, faith is my foundation. It is who I really am.

In the next chapter, we're going to start finding the words that best describe you and using them to define your personal brand. Get excited!

ARE KNOWN OUTSIDE THEIR CIRCLE

I've worked with a lot of executives who are incredibly well-regarded and respected within their company. But on the outside, nobody knows them. So what happens then if the company fails?

Many people were caught off guard during the pandemic. High-powered executives were furloughed and had no idea how to get their next position. But there were also people who made life-changing career moves despite COVID.

I worked with one client to help build his brand, raise self-awareness, interview well, and share the right stories in person and online. He left one hospital system and started a new chapter in his life as CEO of another. Another client was let go because her entire department was eliminated. Several weeks after we began working together to build and share her personal brand, she was named head of an entire department at a Fortune 500 company.

The most exciting changes can happen any time—even during a pandemic! But to do that, you must share who you are and consistently build your brand. You need to give people the opportunity to know who you are. That means networking online. That means being a thought leader in your industry.

Don't get caught flatfooted. If you're building your brand and you're intentional about it, people will know you and where to find you. It won't matter what is going on. Your brand will always come out of the fire stronger than it was prior. Fires refine strong brands, and crush the weak ones.

The goal is to build a personal, professional, and corporate brand that thrives versus dies during an economic downturn or market correction. Build a strong foundation now so you are prepared, ensure your relationships are solid, and rely on your brand to create success. Give yourself every opportunity for success. Your online brand should work for you while you are sleeping. Much more on this later.

There will be more pandemics and trials. More fires personally, professionally, and globally. Building an unstoppable personal brand means you won't be caught off guard.

GET MENTORED

Has anyone ever asked you to mentor them? Has anyone ever mentored you? If not, it's most likely your fault—not because you don't deserve to mentor or to be mentored, but because you haven't shared a story that inspires people to connect with you.

Sometimes we believe we live in a world where nobody is willing to lend us a hand, but that's not the case at all. People *want* to reach out and offer assistance—but they need to know who you are and what your goals are to do that.

When you build a strong personal brand, people can see who you are.

They know where you're going because you've set a clear direction. What you're telling them allows them to come into your life and into your circle.

Start sharing yourself with the world and watch how many people want to share their talents and expertise with you.

DRESS THE PART

Colin Powell said that Margaret Thatcher "exuded influence and power. The hair style, the dress, her manner, the way in which she carried that handbag—when she walked into a room, you knew that somebody had arrived, and you'd better be careful." What do people think when they see you?

It takes less than a second to make your first impression. According to 2011 research by Harvard Medical School and Massachusetts General Hospital, people assess your competence and trustworthiness in only a quarter of a second, based solely on how you look. (Clearly, a professional image matters because your brand begins on impact!) I know this isn't fair, but if you control your narrative and take hold of building your brand authentically, the sky's the limit. Other studies show it takes a quarter of a second to make a first impression and up to five years to fix a poor one. I'm in the business of fixing poor impressions, quickly and honestly. If this statistic creates fear, don't let it—together, we will ensure we begin building the real message of who you are and fixing poor first impressions!

Like it or not, brand is visual. Yes, God sees you on the inside. We are all fearfully and wonderfully made. I'm not trying to "fix" anything, or make you cuter, prettier, or more handsome. Those words are silly. Still, your visual presentation needs to always reflect your best self on your best day. When you get dressed every morning, remember that image matters.

SPEAK INTENTIONALLY

If somebody were to break into your cell phone, print every single text message off of it, and post them on the web for the world to see, would you be terrified or not worried at all?

During the 2016 election year, Colin Powell's email was hacked. Regardless of what you think about him, he has a very strong brand based in strength, integrity, and honesty. People on both sides of the aisle—CNN and Fox—commented nobody else could have had their email hacked and come out smelling like roses like Colin Powell. He was the same person in his written word as his brand would have you believe. He didn't go, *Oh no, what are people going to say?* He said, *Have at it!*

Word choice is so important to your brand. Are you intentional about the words that you're using every single day? Are you specific? Speaking to a child is obviously very different from speaking to your boss. A strong brand changes the narrative, story, tone of voice, and words it uses based on the audience.

ARE ALWAYS PREPARED

A solar energy company sent a young, relatively inexperienced representative to an event where they thought he would simply be listening to the President speak. On the contrary, he was led into a conference room that held a senator, a congressman—and the President! And what was he wearing? A white wrinkled polo! He wasn't dressed appropriately.

Here is the headline to one of the many news articles: "A little under-dressed? Engineer wears polo shirt to meeting with a 'government official'...only to find it's PRESIDENT OBAMA."

The CEO later explained that he did not think they would be given a chance to meet the President. They could have received incredible press from the experience. Instead, they ended up looking stupid.

Good brands are always prepared. Remember that no matter where you are, opportunity can strike. Be ready for it!

This story and so many more will be featured in the *Forged by Fire* Facebook group (https://www.facebook.com/groups/milagriggforgedbyfire). Join today!

LIFT UP OTHER BRANDS

Everyone knows who Peyton Manning is. Even if they didn't like his team, they generally have a positive feeling toward him. It's hard not to be a Peyton Manning fan given the integrity with which he's conducted his career and life. What he's done on the field plays into that, of course—he's a winner with an incredible work ethic. But he's also a top earner off the field, garnering hundreds of millions between salary, bonuses, endorsements, and licensing.

Companies know co-branding with him lifts their brand even higher. It brings them the right kind of visibility. Gatorade, Papa John's, and Nationwide have paid him top dollar because his brand is worth it. (*Nationwide is...*You sang the song, didn't you?!) Good brands are memorable, and Peyton continues to solidify brands and their messaging.

So why do companies pay certain executives more to do the same thing? Brand. And why are some executives paid less? Because they haven't shared their brand, or their brand is weak. (They themselves aren't weak—their brand simply hasn't been intentionally developed or shared in an effective way yet.)

Brand is about so much more than making money, but if that is something you're concerned with—and I know we all are; it's okay to want to be financially successful—you have to build your brand so people can buy into you and quickly see the value you offer. When you have a brand that can lift the company because of who you are, why you do what you do, they'll give you more because you offer more value to them. The sky's the limit.

Always make sure you Peyton Manning yourself around the office and online.

LEAVE A LEGACY

Most of the time, people don't think about their legacy until it's too late.

I want you to know what you want your legacy to be. Every single day, you're building a legacy for your family, community, coworkers, colleagues, and people you don't even know. It may change and shift and update over time, but one of the most important pieces in life in general is to know the legacy you're leaving behind.

I know exactly what I want people to say about me after I'm gone. I want my children to say my mom led us to the Lord. I want my clients to say she helped me to discover my purpose and gifting, and helped me to build a brand that others saw and allowed me to live my purpose. I want my community to say she was kind and strong and she led—she not only talked about helping, but she actually did. Knowing what my legacy is allows me to have a strong brand filter which helps me to remember who I am. This allows me to quickly make the right decision toward my legacy with each choice in front of me.

I often use Nelson Mandela as an example of a great brand that left a great legacy. When I put his picture on the screen during my keynotes or employee coaching seminars, I often hear a collective sigh of positive emotion. When he passed, influential leaders from all over the world attended his funeral. Under any other circumstances, many would not have been in the same place at the same time. But Mandela's legacy (and brand) was so strong, there they all were, shaking each other's hands. It was as if he came back to life during the funeral and told them to shake hands—and though some didn't want to, they still did it. Legacy moments like that come after years of building a consistent brand.

Of course, you don't have to die to know you have a strong brand. Have you ever had a colleague leave the company and people still think about them positively for days, weeks, or even months after? That's a sure sign of a really good brand. If you've ever done something in honor of someone, that's another perfect example of a person who has built a strong brand by practicing what they preach, living with integrity, and being consistent. If you left your company today, what would people remember you for?

Planning your legacy is an important piece of this journey for you. You must develop a path for your future that includes a plan for your career, personal growth, and relationships. Without one, you're working to nothing,

Every day you're leaving a legacy behind. When you build a great one like Mandela, it lasts beyond any position at a company and even life here on earth.

THE HEAT

Get Ready for Opportunity!

My heart's purpose for this book is to help you acquire the knowledge you need to be ready for opportunities. If you're not prepared, those opportunities will pass you by and go to other people that may not deserve them as much as you. This world is so full of fake and fluff, but people crave authenticity. Have confidence, give them the real you, and opportunity will follow.

Let's start getting you ready for the opportunities about to come your way by delving more into how your brand makes people feel as it stands today. Your answers will help drive the work we do in upcoming chapters, so think carefully about each question.

HOW DO YOU MAKE PEOPLE FEEL?

Do you know what people REALLY think about you?

Maybe, maybe not. I can't tell you how many clients I've worked with who think their employees and colleagues love them and other leaders in the company value what they have to say, but then the feedback process reveals the exact opposite to be the case. This holds true whether someone is right out of college or the CEO of a major company.

Knowing how you make other people feel allows you to control your narrative. If you don't know what others are thinking and saying about you, there's no opportunity to change a narrative that might be wrong.

One way to learn how others perceive you is to listen carefully to how you're being introduced via email or in person. Those words tell you deliberately, directly, and without any reservation what people think about you. When people introduce me, I try to be very aware of the stories and words they use to describe me to ensure they accurately reflect my brand. If they don't, I know I haven't communicated my brand message, narrative, and brand story in a way that resonates and is worth remembering.

Another clue comes from the emotions you elicit in others. When your name pops up in someone's email, are people excited to hear from you, or do they feel overwhelmed or anxious? Do they think *I'm going to need eight more cups of coffee before I can deal with this* or *I'm happy to open it and respond quickly*?

Ask yourself: what is the total experience of having a relationship with me like? Write down the top five things that come to mind. Now ask a close friend the same thing. Are your answers the same or similar in meaning? If they are, good for you! If not, you have some work to do. (Keep your answers close at hand—we'll be using them in Chapter 3.)

ARE YOUR ACTIONS ALIGNED WITH YOUR BRAND?

Branding is all about authentic emotion. All your behaviors are either going to endorse and create authenticity in your brand, or they're going to destroy it. As Warren Buffet said, "It takes twenty years to build a reputation and five minutes to ruin it. If you think about that you'll do things differently."

Integrity is measured by what you do, so your actions must be aligned with your brand for people to trust you. You either are who you say you are or you're not. A lot of brands try to fake it, like the CEO of Enron—and look where they ended up.

If you're saying to yourself, *I don't like to brag and all of this "branding stuff" is a bunch of mumbo jumbo,* know that I don't like to brag either—but I do share my story and my brand. I am not afraid of naysayers, doubters, or gossipers anymore.

Without a strong personal brand, you might be highly qualified but be stagnant at your job and invisible to those who need to know you. You might be highly gifted, but your gifts go unused. You might be talented, but nobody knows it. You simply cannot wait for people to notice you. The world is rapidly changing, and brand is your only security system.

Have you ever known someone who walks into a networking room and starts handing out their card to everybody and telling them what they do like a chicken with their head cut off? The difference between that person—the one who is obviously desperate for work, opportunity, and attention—and someone with a strong brand is enormous. Great brands eliminate competition and open doors. They bring vast opportunity in times when other people are drowning in zero opportunity.

A strong brand walks into the room before you even arrive. It stands out from the crowd because you know your gifts, are living your purpose, and are using the right tools to share your stories. People know who you are because you've communicated consistently.

Ask yourself: Am I being authentic in work and life? Do my actions reflect my values? If not, how might I be able to bring those into better alignment?

WHO WOULD WEAR YOUR JERSEY?

If you were a professional athlete, you would most likely have a jersey. And on that jersey would be a number accompanied by your last name. Your jersey would represent you—your brand and the emotion people felt when they thought of you.

When others choose to wear your jersey, it means they want to be associated with your personal brand. That you inspire creativity, teamwork, and excellence. That you have integrity.

One of the things I often ask the executives and groups I work with is: Who would wear your jersey? Would they wear it because they thought they had to or because they wanted to? Would they wear it because they wanted to co-brand with you?

Ask yourself: Would my children wear my jersey? My clients? Company? Colleagues? Community? Why or why not?

THE LIGHT: BRAND DNA RECAP

You were created for more than you may think—you have a unique gift and God-given purpose like no one else.

There's so much hope and opportunity for you when you know who you are and you have a personal brand.

When you take the experiences you've had—good, bad, and ugly—and start using them for good, it helps others see there's more to you than what you do.

When fires come, your brand will hold you strong.

Part Two

BRAND PURPOSE

"People don't buy what you do; they buy why you do it. And what you do simply proves what you believe."
—SIMON SINEK, *START WITH WHY: HOW GREAT LEADERS INSPIRE EVERYONE TO TAKE ACTION*

THE SPARK

Your WHY Is Why You're Here

Your brand is your map to getting where you want to go in your career and life. It helps you to know what's right and wrong for you. It makes decisions come much faster and easier.

The person with the plan is the one with the power. Any time you shoot from the hip, you increase your margin of error. You cannot shoot from the hip!

A lot of people are still navigating their careers without a map and making decisions based on what looks good or feels good in the moment—which may not always be the next best step. (I hardly ever feel like working out in the morning, but I still get up to exercise because I know it's good for me. If I followed my feelings, I'd never get out of bed!) On days I didn't want to work during the fire because I was feeling weighed down by my fear and sadness, I remembered my WHY.

Now is the time to get introspective, find the answers that lie within you, and start sharing you, your gifts, and your value with the world.

What drives you? What inspires you? What moves you? What brings you joy? The answers will help you get to the why of your brand. This is how you start living your true purpose—the one God intended for you.

In case you haven't taken this to heart yet: God created you for a special purpose greater than what you "do" for a living. You were meant to change the world in some way, shape, or form, even if it's only a small part of the world. This is your WHY. It is the very reason you are on the planet today. Don't miss it!

I've had many clients try to skip the whole "finding your why" part of brand-building and jump ahead into more comfortable and familiar territory: defining core attributes, values, descriptors, and mission. I'm excited about all that too—and promise we'll get to them in the next chapter—but believe me when I tell you, without a WHY, none of that matters.

Your why is absolutely the foundational piece of your story you need to know, because it is the very essence and core of your brand. It is why you keep going. It is what inspires, encourages, and motivates you. It provides a rock-solid foundation in good times and ensures your brand does not collapse under the weight of any trials that may come.

Other people need to know your why as well. It's what attracts others to want to hire, work, and associate with you. We're all inspired by those who truly know their purpose in life and share it freely—and you will notice when they talk about it because it comes so easily.

I'm not a motivational coach or an inspirational speaker, but one of my biggest hopes and goals for this book is that it will inspire you to start the journey toward uncovering your why. Finding your true purpose takes time—sometimes, even years of exploration and trial and error—so I'm not expecting many of you to exclaim, *I found my ultimate purpose in life!* once you're done reading. But I do hope to help you realize you absolutely, 100 percent have a why, give you better clarity about the path to discovering what that is, and offer the understanding of why it matters so much.

Your why forges the path you need to follow—and that is so much different than working only for money.

Throughout this book, I use the words *why* and *purpose* interchangeably. They are one and the same in my book.

THE FUEL

Why Your WHY Matters

I worked with a woman who had been at the same healthcare company for thirty-three years. One day I said to her, "Thirty-three years at one firm is unheard of nowadays! You must really love what you do."

You know what she told me?

She said, "I majored in art in college. I only started in this job because it was financially the right thing to do at the time. I thought I'd eventually leave, but year after year, I simply kept working—the job kept me so busy, I never really lifted my head up. Now thirty years later, I'm realizing this is not why I was put on this earth. I'm not better for it. NOBODY'S better for it. I haven't used my gifting. My purpose has been completely lost in translation."

I asked her what advice she might give to others who find themselves in a similar position, having said yes to a job that doesn't necessarily align with their why. She replied, "I would tell everybody to check in with themselves at least once a year and see what's in their heart." All the experts in the world—myself included—try to explain the importance of having a why in a statistical, data-driven way, but her response really came down to brass tacks: if you're not doing what's in your heart, you're doing it wrong.

I share this story because I don't want you to be in the same position my client found herself in—or if you already are, to climb your way out of it. I don't want you to have missed using your gifting. I want you to use your why and your purpose to lead you to doing what God put you on this earth to do.

Your why is literally why you are on earth. It is your very purpose. It is why you were born.

If your why has eluded you up until now, have faith that it exists and you simply haven't discovered it yet. I want you to be hopeful as you walk this path. There are many people who have never thought about where they want to be in life, or considered what brings them joy, inspires them, or drives them. It's okay if you find yourself in that same position. I am here to help!

I often liken your why to a map. Knowing your why helps you to take the right turns so you can be led to the right experiences. It helps keep you on track and headed in the best direction. Not knowing your why is like getting in a car and driving without having any clue where you're going. You're along for the ride, but you're definitely not in the driver's seat.

If you're reading this thinking, *I start working at nine a.m. and I don't look up again until six because I love what I do*, great! You're on the right track. But if your work isn't inspiring and you can't get lost in what you do for even forty-five minutes, that's a red flag. Most people see these kinds of red flags pop up in their lives and they keep driving right past them. I encourage you to stop and look around instead. Without a why, you have no reason to want to improve your life.

YOUR WHY KEEPS YOU FOCUSED

When I was starting to build my business, I often thought any client was a good client. The entrepreneurs reading this right now might even be thinking, *Yes, that's exactly right*. But I want to encourage you NOT to take any old business that comes your way. Sometimes taking on a "just another" client is the very thing that completely shoots you off your purpose, your why, and where you should be heading.

Several years ago, I had a great contract working with a top company doing branding, coaching, and restructuring for them. Because I'd been so successful doing those things—which are the core of my business—they asked if I'd be interested in taking on their public relations as well. Doing so would have tripled my income on an already lucrative contract, and I love doing PR. (In fact, I would have done it for free—another sign you're doing what you should be doing.)

But I also knew these additional responsibilities would take a great deal of time, and I would have to bring on another employee to help me manage the increased workflow. My business would have morphed into a full-service firm versus a specialty practice focused on what I do best—consulting, teaching, and coaching. It would have limited my ability to work with more companies and meet more people, which are among the things I love most about what I do. The financial success would have been great, but probably not the "life success."

So was it hard for me to say no? Absolutely. But did it take me longer than a minute to know it was the wrong thing to do? Not at all. I knew taking that assignment would have completely veered me off course. I immediately told the client, "That's not what we do, but we can certainly help you hire, train, and coach the right person for the job."

Afterwards, I told a friend about the offer. He exclaimed, "But you absolutely could have done that job!" I thought, *Sure, I could have. But that's not why I'm here.*

Knowing your why helps you make the right decisions. You're able to turn down offers that would bring in more money but put you off your path. It's what allows you to do things other people might say are crazy, like quit an executive position to start a shoe company in your garage if that's your passion.

Following your why lights you up in every way. It gets you up early. It keeps you going on your worst day. It reminds you of who you are on your BEST day.

When you combine something you love doing plus your sense of purpose, that often equals your why. What you do and why you do it are 100 percent connected. By finding your why, I want to help you show people your value, make the right friends, have the right experiences, and grow into the person you're meant to be.

YOUR WHY FILTERS OUT NEGATIVITY

Buster Douglas was a fighter whose why was to become boxing's heavyweight champion, though people doubted he could ever back up his claims. Buster told his mom he was absolutely going to reach his goal, but she passed away right before he went into the ring with Mike Tyson. Although there were many times in that fight when Buster was down for the count, he always fought his way back. His why was greater than the pain. Eventually, against all odds, he knocked Mike Tyson out. I, for one, think Buster's surprise win came from knowing and being so focused on his purpose. His why was greater than his opponent's in that moment. When you get knocked down, sometimes the only rope to help you climb up and out is your why.

Without a well-defined why, you can't completely fulfill your personal and professional dreams. You fall prey to the naysayers. People thought Columbus was nuts. The experts looked at his travel plans and said his journey was impossible. Imagine if Columbus had looked at them and said, "Well, I guess you're right," and walked away from his plans!

All of which is to say: Be careful who you listen to. Use your why as a filter to tune out negativity. Especially while my husband was in prison, there were so many people who looked at me and said, "I can't even believe you think you're going to do that." I'd simply look back and think, "Watch me." They didn't know better than God what my purpose was! No one is greater than the Lord.

Someone is always waiting for you to fall. When you're challenged by life, remember you were created by a Creator for a purpose not to only live—but with a purpose to *do*. No matter how many times life knocks you down, that's the reason you keep going for your dreams.

A saying I randomly found online works well for me: *Kill them with success and bury them with a smile*. Screw the naysayer and let them be part of your fuel. Long game perspective, hard work, and patience win every time.

Tune out the negativity. Stay tuned into your why.

YOUR WHY HAS FAITH

When Michael Jordan was cut from his high school team, lost over 300 games, and missed the game-winning shot twenty-six times during the course of his NBA career, he didn't give up. He knew his why, he knew what he loved, he knew what brought him the most joy—and he kept at it. He says the key to his success has been failing over and over and over.

People who don't have a why give up after failing once or twice because they think, *This is not what I'm supposed to be doing*. But those who have reached the pinnacle of success have failed more times than anybody else because they have absolute faith they are living their purpose.

Purpose keeps you grounded. It is what allows you to be okay and find joy even on the toughest days, because you aren't simply working for a check or a job. Your life has more meaning, and a life of meaning is one that can find joy in any situation. You may lose a million battles, but if you're fighting for your purpose, your why, you can't lose.

Though the road might be treacherous, your purpose is the North Star. Don't think about how fearful you are. Let your purpose be greater than the fear.

Back when I was transitioning from strictly fashion to coaching, I had to find a way to offer my new services when I saw I could be of greater assistance. I needed to be brave enough to say, "I know we're working on clothing and personal brand image, but I see there are other ways I can help you." I had to be unconcerned if people brushed me off as not having the skillset to do more. I had to push forward and keep going.

If I hadn't recognized my why, or been too timid to let my why shine, I would probably still be in closets working with people. I wouldn't have started coaching individuals and companies. I wouldn't have ever been able to walk confidently into a conference room filled with executives who were, at that time, almost twice my age. But knowing why I did what I did, and that my gifting was given to me for a reason, gave me the courage to believe in myself. Side note: I also back up my why with an incredible amount of learning, reading, and growing. More on that in later chapters!

Chadwick Boseman, star of the movie *Black Panther*, was remarkable, and his legacy will live on. He said it best in his speech at Howard University: "Purpose is an essential element of you. It is the reason you are on the planet at this particular time in history, your very existence is wrapped up in the things you are here to fulfill. Whatever you choose for a career path, remember the struggles along the way are only meant to shape you for your purpose. I don't know what your future is, but if you are willing to take the harder way, the more complicated one, the one with more failures at first than successes, the one that has ultimately proven to have more meaning, more victory, more glory—then you will not regret it."

I want to encourage you to step into your power. When you know why you do what you do, you take more risks and achieve more success. For me, the question of why I stayed with my husband could always be answered with my why (more on that later). Follow your why come hell or high water. When you are grounded in your purpose and your foundation is secure, failure isn't an option.

YOUR WHY IS YOUR COMPASS

I love the *Pirates of the Caribbean* franchise. In it, Jack Sparrow, the renegade pirate, has a compass everyone thinks is broken. But it's actually working perfectly—it always points to what his heart wants most.

Let your why be the same kind of compass for you, pointing you to your mission and goals in life. Trust that it won't lead you in a direction other than the one that helps you to fulfill your very purpose in life.

A steadfast why is Southwest saying no to raising prices in order to serve meals on the plane because it's not what they do—they're focused on customer service and value first and foremost. It's an athlete refusing to represent a sugary beverage because they don't want to take any endorsement that will pollute or dilute their brand. It's the man standing in front of the tanks as they approached Tiananmen Square on June 5th, 1989. It's Rosa Parks refusing to sit in the back of the bus.

> If you don't know who these people are, you need to. Knowing history is the sign of a well-rounded brand that cares and has experience.

Knowing you have a purpose and why you do what you do may sound superficial or look like another exercise to check off a list, but this is a life-builder if you do it correctly. This can absolutely build your dream, lead you to the roads worth taking, and keep you focused in the right direction.

Your why is your differentiator and super power. When you connect WHY you do what you do, who you are, how you do what you do, and your goals, you are limitless.

YOUR WHY LEADS EFFECTIVELY

If you're reading this thinking right now, *I don't really know how any of this relates to me,* allow me to share another example that may resonate. I worked for several years with a company whose CEO led with true heart. This leader knew the why of the organization, and always inspired and encouraged people using that.

When that person retired, it was like the heart of the organization stopped beating. Unfortunately, the new CEO was not a great fit and did not have the same style of leadership. While the why of the company remained the same, the leader who'd always kept it top of mind was no longer there to do so.

Without that inspiration, employees began to grow dissatisfied in a way they never had before. Their desire to keep going, work harder, and at times even stay later because they knew what they were doing was creating an incredible legacy above and beyond pushing paper— that started to fade. The organization started to flail.

I imagine many of you are reading this book to become a better leader. One way to do that is to know without a doubt your why, the why of your company, the why of your teams, and the why of the individuals on your team. As Tony Robbins says, "In order to influence somebody, you must know what already influences them." When you know somebody's why and use it as a filter for the things you ask them to do, people will naturally follow you because they trust you're guiding them to their purpose.

Great leadership leads with the why, and great leaders embody, exude, and encourage a sense of purpose that inspires everyone around them. If you think you're a great leader because you walk into a company with a title, you've lost the battle before the war has even started. No one will follow a leader whose why isn't obvious.

When companies grow to a different level of success, they often become less concerned with their why. It's easy to veer off purpose as more money, fame, and status start rolling in.

A recent study showed that consumers in the US are 89 percent more likely to have a positive image of brands with a purpose. They are also 86 percent more likely to trust those brands and are 83 percent more loyal to them. Nearly eight out of ten people surveyed (79 percent) said they feel a deeper personal connection when companies have similar values to their own, and 72 percent find it more important now than ever to buy from companies that hold similar values. That's a pretty compelling argument for keeping an eye on your why! (Source: Cone/ Porter Novelli, 2019 https://www.businessofpurpose.com/statistics)

Companies that sell the same services or products but know their why work differently. They're more efficient. There's more joy. They gain more loyalty. They aren't concerned with competition because they know their purpose is different from someone who is perceived to do the same thing. It's the same thing with people who know their why.

I've worked with so many executives who say their lives were most exciting when they were starting out, because they very clearly knew their passion and purpose. Building that business in their garage or whatever project they were working to bring to market is what kept them going. When they reached the pinnacle of success, they forgot that why and that's when work became a job, not a joy.

Shout-out to Jeff Bezos: I hope you love the book. Thank you for continuing to inspire despite your mistakes. Keep pushing!

YOUR WHY IS WAITING FOR YOU

I once coached a client who was a healthcare executive (Nashville, where I live, is the healthcare capital of the world, so many people end up in the industry even if they didn't intend to). When I asked him, "Why are you doing this?" he replied, "I'm divorced and I have children. I'm financially responsible for them, and need to pay for their college education. I would eat dirt to be able to do that."

He was working for his daughters and his son, and that is an amazing why—but I didn't want his own purpose to get lost in that. I didn't want him to skip his gifting because he thought money should be the driving force of his why. I needed him to know there was more to him than simply working to ensure his kids get through college. There's more to you, too.

As the saying goes, "It's never too late to be who you might have been." I assured that man he could still live his purpose in the same way I assured the client who had been working in the "wrong" job for the past thirty-three years that once she truly discovered her why, she could potentially do more in a year than she had in the past three decades. All her hard work had not been in vain, and there was still time to find and unleash her why on the world. The same holds true for you!

I've worked with so many people who aren't living a life that reflects who they truly are or utilizes their gifting, and I don't want them—or you—to waste another minute that way. So if you're reading this at seventy, eighty, or ninety years old and thinking, *I'm way past that point*, I'm here to tell you, no, you're not.

I don't care where you are, where you've been, what you've done, or the mistakes that you've made, *you can still live your purpose.*

YOUR WHY IS YOUR LEGACY

Executives who wave their big titles around—*I'm CEO! I'm COO! I'm the Chief Big Time Officer!*—are totally missing the point. They're relying on the weight of their status and title to impress everyone. They're so busy telling everybody what they do, they often neglect to do anything that helps others—which is what is impressive in this world.

A friend of mine recently passed away from colon cancer at forty years old. She was beautiful inside and out; her death was unbelievably tragic. At her funeral, no one ever said, *This woman was the COO of a company.* It wasn't about that at all.

Everybody who spoke about her—both her family and her colleagues—mentioned how she always saw the best in people. She had the uncanny ability to build others up, encourage them, and get to know their gifting so she could guide them to where they wanted to go. That was 100 percent why she was on this planet. It's what she loved to do.

People who never lose sight of their why—no matter what they achieve—leave a great legacy. They're doing what they do because they know it's what God put in their heart. They're following His lead. Sometimes that inspires millions, like Mother Teresa did. Other times, it impacts a smaller number of people but reverberates forever nonetheless, as with my friend who died too soon.

I want the story of my friend who passed away far too early to inspire you. What mattered in the end wasn't her title. It was who she was and how she helped make the world a better place.

Even if you're at a large corporation, know that like her, you can still live your why and purpose. Maybe you have an amazing gift of bringing people together. Perhaps you are emotionally intelligent. Or you might be a natural cheerleader.

You can still have status, especially if that's part of what you want (she certainly did—everybody looked up to her). But her legacy lies in how she helped encourage and lead others to their very purpose. Similarly, I want you to work towards a legacy that lies in your why, not what you do on a daily basis.

THE FIRE

The Why of Great Leaders

Tony Robbins, top life coach and business strategist as well as one of my biggest mentors, was the first coach I ever heard emphasizing the importance of knowing your why—but he certainly didn't originate the idea. Every leader in history has had a clearly defined why, from Abraham Lincoln to Martin Luther King. It's what propelled them forward, gave them courage and strength, and helped them lift their heads on their darkest days.

The most effective and successful leaders we follow, presidents we love, and titans of business we want to emulate all have a why that pushes them out of bed every day. The greatest of the greats know exactly what their why is.

Oprah Winfrey's why is to be a teacher. Her purpose is to inspire her students to be more than they thought they could be. I admire her ability to focus so intently on that calling and continually use it to serve the world.

Sir Richard Branson says his why is to have fun on his journey through life and to learn from his mistakes along the way. Nowhere in that statement does it say become founder of the Virgin Group, go to the moon, or become one of the greatest entrepreneurs on the face of the planet. His why isn't focused on the things he's going to *do*—it's the way in which he is going to do them.

Mother Teresa's why was to serve and use the gifting she knew God had given her. It wasn't, *I want my legacy to change the world* or *I want to be remembered forever*. Like Mother Teresa, your why doesn't have to be financially- or status-oriented, either. It can certainly be found in serving others if that's what speaks most to you.

It's been shown that companies with core values based on their purpose have consistently outpaced others in the stock market by 15 percent and exist for an average of one hundred years. When the authors of the book *Built to Last* examined pairs of similar companies, they found that in seventeen out of eighteen cases the higher-performing company—which included luminaries like Disney, Sony, Walmart—had a stronger why, identity, and sense of purpose than the lower-performing one. The conclusion they came to was that strong foundations create a sense of community and continuity for employees, which then translates into greater business success for the company.

So why wouldn't we as humans do the exact same thing?

> When Satan came to Jesus at the top of the mountain and said, "I can give you all of this," Jesus, of course, declined. The very fact that Satan thought he could give Jesus something more than he already had was ridiculous. Jesus was here for the ultimate purpose—his why was to save, not to rule.

Don't be deceived when someone tries to sell you their why and change yours.

HOW I DISCOVERED MY WHY

As I mentioned earlier, I began my career as a fashion and image consultant. I have been in thousands of closets with thousands of executives. To this day I still think it's wild I get to say that! (And so incredibly humbling that so many would trust me in that way.)

Fashion consultation is not something I regularly practice today personally, but I still do it every so often because I believe image and fashion are an enormous part of your brand (which I'm excited to talk about in later chapters). I cut my teeth doing this kind of work, and I love it.

Being in a closet with people is an intimate experience. I have been welcomed into their homes, and inevitably, we start talking about things that wouldn't be spoken of in a boardroom, office, or networking event. I have been told about aches, pains, trials, and fires, the likes of which you would not believe, by people the world would say had already reached the pinnacle of success.

This only goes to show that money is not the thread that brings joy. In my experience, joy is directly tied to purpose. Joy comes from having a mission, something you know you were born to do.

One day—this was almost twenty years ago now, but I will never forget it—a woman called me and said, "I'm not sure if I can afford you, but I really need your help. I need to move up in my career. I am the breadwinner for this family."

When I pulled up to her home, it was the size of a shoe box. She was living with her parents and had a beautiful daughter she was working for as hard as she could. She had been through many trials, including a chronic illness that had contributed to her becoming obese, but her hard work was finally paying off. She had landed a new job.

She explained she simply didn't know how to dress for the position. Finding clothes that fit correctly was difficult for her, but beyond that, she didn't feel worthy of getting dressed in the morning. She thought she wasn't worth spending money on clothing!

After hearing her story, I let her know she was created for a purpose and that God loved her. I talked about how there was a reason she was alive, and that her child not only needed her, but looked up to and adored her. I made her promise she wouldn't let the world break her down.

It was an incredible honor to sit and listen to her as we talked about image and clothing while she tried things on and saw there was hope. That experience brought me such joy that I didn't even charge her for my time. I couldn't. I knew in that moment my purpose was greater than money (even though Lord knows I really needed it back then).

After our meeting, I realized this would remain one of the greatest moments I'd ever experience. It wasn't that I had worked with the CEO of a Fortune 500 company. It wasn't that I was sitting in a board-room feeling important. It was that I had worked with a human being whose life was changed, all because God gave me the ability to walk into that house, that closet, and that woman's life to make a difference. I literally wept the whole way home. To this day, it still brings tears to my eyes thinking about it.

It was then I realized then my gifting went beyond simply being able to see what clothing to put on any body shape or type. Sure, I could easily look at someone and tell them, *This pant and that shirt in this line will look great on you. Go to Dillard's and get it in a size three X. I promise you, if it doesn't fit, I'll quit.* That's how confident I was in my abilities.

But now I understood what I had to offer was far more than that: It was to share my experience and offer hope. It was to help people see that God knows who they are, loves them, and wants the best for them. It was to encourage others to see they were created for something special.

Recently—nearly twenty years after that experience—a woman at a Chamber of Commerce I love working with announced in front of a large group of people that anytime she needs inspiration or hope, she simply goes to my Instagram. All I could think in that moment was, "There it is again. The common thread. My why is to help people to be the best that they can be."

People sometimes smirk when I tell them this. They look at me like, *Is that really what you said? Can you possibly get any cheesier?* But I have such confidence in my why, I smile back at them. The truth is the truth. There's no denying it, "cheesy" or not.

THE HEAT

Finding Your Why

I want you to be on the lookout for those times in life when your why hits you. It's a different journey for everybody, but there may come a day you find yourself blindsided by it. Welcome and embrace it however it comes!

But how do you find your why if it DOESN'T hit you?

WHAT WOULD YOU DO FOR FREE?

That day in the closet with the woman who had received a promotion, I didn't think, Well, shoot, I drove two hours on a Saturday, I need to get paid. Instead, I thought, I would do this for the rest of my life without payment to have this feeling. I absolutely knew I was doing what I was supposed to be doing and I didn't feel bad about not being somewhere else.

God put me there, and it didn't matter what else was going on in the world. I should not have been with my children or my husband in that moment. I shouldn't have been working somewhere else, or on some island drinking a margarita. I needed to be right there, on a Saturday, in that little house out in the country, helping someone who was in pain.

Ask yourself: what would I happily do for free—no paycheck required?

WHY DO YOU DO WHAT YOU DO?

A question I pose to all my clients when I first start working with them is: have you ever thought about what your purpose here is, and why you do what you do? More often than not, people answer with a resounding no. I want you to know it's okay if, like many of my clients, you haven't started to discover your purpose yet.

In fact, you might even be thinking to yourself right now, I really only work for money. I have bills to pay and I need a home. I have an electric bill. I have kids in college. I want to retire one day. Of course, all those more practical reasons can factor into this process. Eventually, though, you're going to want to start thriving instead of simply surviving.

Believe me, I understand the need to survive from experience. During my trial, I didn't have a penny or a pot to put it in. I literally had to sell my wedding ring to pay the bills. Certainly, there were days I didn't want to get out of bed. The fire was so hot, I didn't think I could take another step. But having everything stripped away from me (with the exception of my children and my health) is also what allowed me to discover not only my gifting, but also why I did what I did.

If I'm having a hard day at work, or I'm frustrated or worried, I think about my kids and their smiling faces. That pushes me to be better. It doesn't allow me to give up. I know I'm working not only to inspire my clients, but to inspire my children as well. I'm here to show them they can do anything they set their minds to, regardless of the trials that may come.

Ask yourself: Why do I do what I do? Why do I get out of bed every morning? And why should anybody care?

If you haven't already, I highly recommend reading Simon Sinek's book *Start with the Why: How Great Leaders Inspire Everyone to Take Action*. It focuses on the concept of how a well-defined purpose is key to developing a strong brand. More importantly, it offers readers a path to finding their purpose by questioning their motives.

WHAT BRINGS YOU JOY?

Transformational speaker Jack Canfield encourages people to complete a "joy review" to help discover their purpose. I recommend doing this at least once a quarter.

When I refer to joy, I'm talking about so much more than those happy-yet-fleeting moments—like when you buy a new purse or a new car and love it for all of about an hour before you start thinking, *Oh no, what have I done?* Joy fills you from your toes to the crown of your head. Joy is when your whole being knows *this* is exactly where you should be in this moment. It comes from God, not a new BMW.

Joy was what I experienced with the woman who needed help dressing for her new position. Or what my client, a high-level executive I adore, feels when she brings her therapy dog to help calm and raise the spirits of patients in the local hospital on the weekends.

I want you to think about the things in your life right now that bring you joy—the kind that's visible on your face, in your body, or in your energy. Maybe that comes from telling jokes. Inspiring someone. Driving a race car. Pretty soon, you'll start to see a common thread—it never fails. That thread is what drives you. It is part of why you are here on earth.

Ask yourself: what sparks joy in me? Take a couple hours, go to a place where you won't be interrupted, and get quiet. Look back on your experiences and determine the ones that have hit you the hardest. DIG DEEP. Whatever it is, write it down. There are so many studies that show when we commit our goals to paper, we see things more clearly and our intentions stick with us.

Don't know where to begin? Try anything and everything: acting, business, entrepreneurship, sports. What sparks those moments of total joy? You have to take the first step. Purpose is not something that is magically revealed to you at a certain age. You find it step by step.

IS THIS PART OF YOUR PURPOSE?

Asking the right questions and using your answers as a filter helps you discover what fills your life with passion, purpose, and direction. From now on, whenever you get an opportunity, request, or a project coming across your desk, I want you to question whether it relates to your purpose or not. I know you can't necessarily say no to your boss, but you can have a clear vision of whether your current job is fully aligned—or aligned at all—with what you were put on this earth to do.

When God puts a vision and dreams in front of you about where you're going to go in life, how you're supposed to live, and the impact that you're intended to have in the world, He's not kidding. He doesn't change his mind. He doesn't teach you to swim only to let you drown.

Ask yourself: Is this part of who I am? Is this who I am working to become? Is this part of my purpose in life?

IS THIS YOUR CALLING?

Don't look for a career before you focus on your calling. If you are already in your career, your purpose can become a part of it! Don't simply check off boxes. College, check. Marriage, check. Kids, check. Save for retirement, check. Next...

Your purpose eclipses all of these.

To find your calling, ask yourself:

- What is it that I would do if money wasn't an issue?
- When I wanted to go in one direction, but people talked me out of it, what did I want to do?
- What do I think I'd be good at?
- What do I love doing (i.e., when I do this, I don't watch the clock)?
- What do I believe strongly in?
- What would I do if I knew I couldn't fail?

Do you have an inkling of what your why is yet? Try to write some statements that encompass what you love doing, brings you joy, and focuses on your strengths.

ARE YOU PUTTING IN THE ENERGY?

Andrew Carnegie once said, "The average person puts only 25 percent of his energy and ability into his work. The world takes off its hat to those who put in more than 50 percent of their capacity, and stands on its head for those few and far between souls who devote 100 percent."

The reason most people don't get the promotion, visibility, loyalty, or following they want is due to a lack of energy. And most of the time, they're not expending enough energy because they don't know what their purpose is, or the job they currently have is not bringing them closer to what that purpose is.

When you truly know your purpose, you automatically bring 100 percent of your energy to it. You do everything with a passion because you're headed in the right direction. You know you're doing what God put you here to do.

Ask yourself: How much energy am I putting into my work? Am I one of the rare souls who gives 100 percent? Are people standing on their heads for me? Or am I stuck down there with all the average Joes giving a mere 25 percent? Do I need to put in more energy?

THE LIGHT: BRAND PURPOSE RECAP

Your WHY is why you are here on earth.

Knowing your why is what sustains you and leads you to your purpose.

On your worst day, your why is what keeps you going.

You're living your why when you do what you love, and love what you do.

When your purpose and why come together, you are unstoppable!

Part Three

BRAND VALUES

"Your core values are the deeply held beliefs that authentically describe your soul."

—JOHN C. MAXWELL, AUTHOR OF MANY BOOKS INCLUDING ONE OF MY FAVORITES OF ALL TIME, *THE FIVE LEVELS OF LEADERSHIP*

THE SPARK

Getting Down to the Very Core

Core values give you the strength to speak the truth from the very core of who you are. They allow you to pause in conversations before making big decisions. They remind you of your value and who you are on your best day. They help you command the right attention, from the right people, at the right time, for the right reasons.

Some people will say, *I'm simply a bank teller* or *I only work at a shoe store*, but you can demonstrate and live your core values in ANY position. It isn't what you do, it's why you do it. This is how you step out of your job and show your purpose.

For example, we recently employed a man to help resurface our kitchen cabinets. It was uniquely refreshing to see how he so faithfully followed his core values in his everyday life.

He was a talkative, gregarious guy, and if you live in the South, you know the conversation will eventually turn to: *where do you go to church?* When he asked, I told him where we like to worship, how long we'd been there, and how much we love it. We knew some of the same people.

During this conversation, my then ten-year-old daughter emerged from her room. He stopped what he was doing and said, "Young lady, I have a story to tell you." She looked at Gordon and I to make sure it was okay to engage in this conversation. We nodded yes.

"Do you know who created you?" he asked her.

"God," she replied, in the most childlike, innocent way. "God created me."

"That's right," he said. "And do you how valuable you are to God?"

She hesitated. "I *think* so."

"And do you know who Leonardo da Vinci is?" When he saw she may not, he continued, "He's the artist who created the most expensive painting in the world. It sold for hundreds of millions at auction. Do you know why it's so valuable?"

"Well, I'm not exactly sure," my daughter replied.

He told her, "Because of the creator. Anyone can paint a picture of Jesus. But that painting is so valuable because of who created it, in the same way you are valuable because you were created by the Creator."

He went on. "God went to the depths of the ocean, and saw all these creatures that He had created. He looked at them and then He looked at you, and He said, 'You're still more valuable than they are.' Then God traveled around tasting the best food, drinking the best wine, and listening to the most amazing music, and He said, 'Nope, you're still more valuable than all that.' And then He looked at all His angels glorifying Him and He looked at you and He said, 'You're *still* more valuable than them.' And then He looked at his Son and he looked at you and He said, 'You're so valuable that my son died on the cross for you.' And THAT is how valuable you are to your creator."

By the end of his story, I was weeping. My husband, who doesn't EVER cry, was tearing up. The man's assistant was even dabbing at her eyes. It completely caught us all off guard.

When I was able to compose myself again, I said, "Thank you. That is so meaningful to us."

He replied, "If I came here but for that one purpose today, it would be worth it."

This is a perfect example of a person knowing who they are and why they are here, and being willing to show that regardless of the potential consequences. This man knew his why, which was to glorify God in all that he does, and He showed that in every interaction. He was the living embodiment of his core values. (And the fact that he happens to be a carpenter is insanely ironic!)

Even if I'd looked at that man and said, "Get out of my house! You're crazy. You're never coming back," I don't feel like it would have affected him at all. He knew what he was saying was true, and he also somehow knew my daughter needed to hear his message from someone other than her mom and dad.

For him, living his purpose was following the nudges of the Holy Spirit. It worked out well in this case, but it might not in the future. And that's okay, because he was being led by his core values.

Let your core values be your guide in everything you do, too. Fear somehow flies out the window when you do.

THE FUEL

Why Your Core Values Matter

Brands can often seem far away and so unrelated to us—a type of cereal, logo on a shoe, or something only large corporations do—but that's not the case. Being mindful in creating your personal brand ensures that people can see you, hear you, read what you've written, and count on you to make them feel a certain way. It's what makes people want to befriend, work with, and co-brand with you.

You can think of the individual elements comprising your personal brand as resembling the Target logo. The bullseye is your why—the very heart of you and why you do what you do. The next ring contains your core values, words derived from your why that represent the unique qualities you bring to the table. The next circle is your value statement, which is the distillation of your core values into a few short, punchy sentences, and the very outside ring demonstrates the reflection of those in your everyday work and life. Taken together, your "target" creates a unified personal brand that represents you on your very best day.

Having strongly held core values are as important to you as they are to the most successful corporate brands like Target. They are foundational to everything you do. If you're going through a trial in life, your core values are there to lean on and walk you through it.

The individual words you choose to represent your core values—which we'll get to deciding later in this chapter—determine how you speak, think, prioritize, engage in conversation and conflict, share your message and your company's message, and come home after a hard day at work. What you fill your mind with is where you'll go, so choose and use them wisely.

> Foundational words, branding words, brand attributes, core values, unique selling propositions—all these terms are interchangeable. I most often refer to them as core values, though, because they're at the very core of who we are.

CONSISTENCY IS KEY

Have you ever worked with someone who is happy one day, sad the next, mean the next? Then the next week they're kind, then frustrated, then arrogant? It feels like a tornado whipping around the office, and makes everyone around them think, *Who the heck are you, anyway?*

People want to know what to expect from you. They don't want to be hit with a different person, with different values, who needs a different kind of interaction every day. While we all have hard days and even hard years (believe me, I know), core values are what keep us consistent.

When Gordon left for prison, I was six months pregnant. His story was all over the papers, so it wasn't a secret. I knew the road would be difficult and on my worst day, I would have to remember who I was.

Throughout that trial, I never once said Gordon didn't do something wrong. I never once tried to hide it. I never once tried to cover it up.

I always held him accountable for his wrongdoing. I knew integrity was a big deal for me, and Gordon's breach of integrity was going to be difficult for me to accept.

Yet everyone also knew I was fighting for my family to stay together, I wasn't going to leave my husband, and this decision was based on my core values. When I stood in front of God and my family and said *for better or for worse, till death do us part*, I meant it. Though the waters may be rough, I was going to make good on my promise to the Lord and trust Him through my obedience.

So when people started to say, *If that's the choice you're going to make, then I can't be your friend* or *I'm going to choose not to talk to you*, I decided the covenant I made that day in front of God was more important than anything else. I knew the consequences would be lost friendships and relationships, but I couldn't have known how much loss would come. The flip side of that over a long time was new friends who became family as well as increased business opportunities because I kept pushing forward daily. Staying consistently faithful to my core values, even when it felt the hardest, was key to my success.

I often share that story in hopes of inspiring you to stick to what you know is right, especially in moments of tribulation. During my trial, I needed my core values in front of me at all times. They really enabled me to stick to my guns and keep going in the right direction. They can do the same for you.

Most of us *know* what to do when we get up every day: eat a good breakfast, work out, read to grow our minds, stay true to our values at work and at home. We WANT to do the right things. But few people actually DO them, and even fewer do them EVERY SINGLE DAY.

You can't say *I have empathy* and leave it at that. You must actually act in an empathetic manner. So for instance, even though you may look down at your phone when it rings and think, *I don't want to talk to this rude person,* your core value of empathy is going to make you answer that call in your best voice, as your best self, and with a mind that's right because you know who you are.

Or if you want to be known as someone who works hard, you're going to stay later than everyone else on certain days. You're going to do things to the best of your ability at all times, not only when someone is looking. And you'll always persevere, even when times get tough.

Or if you want to be seen as having integrity, you'll listen to others first. Your body language will show you're present. When it's your turn to speak, your filter will be in front of you and your communications will reflect that. If you're on a conference call, you'll go into a separate space to get away from regular distractions.

Really think about that last point: have you ever been on a Zoom call and realized someone doesn't have their video turned on? And then when they get asked a direct question, they quickly reappear, saying, *Oh sorry! I was in the bathroom.* It's like, *No you weren't. You were working. This clearly isn't important to you.* The takeaway is you're not listening. You're all about yourself. That's not integrity, or any other worthwhile core value!

Sometimes we focus so much on the big things—not cheating, lying, or stealing—we forget about common courtesy every day. That shows up in all sorts of behaviors, like not listening on a call, acting distracted during conversations, walking into a room and not looking everyone in the eye, or forgetting to follow up after meetings. Those little hits can become the biggest cracks in how others perceive you.

Consistency is the key to success. People who are consistent in action, behavior, words, and thoughts are the ones who succeed because they're a known quantity. And it's not enough to talk the talk—you have to walk the walk, too.

CORE VALUES ARE YOUR FILTER

One of my greatest mentors, Tony Robbins, talks about Constant and Never-Ending Improvement (CANI), a concept I hold near and dear. Keeping my core values in front of me helps me strive to be my best at all times. They were an absolute life-saver during my greatest trial, and act as my North Star daily.

My core values are faith, integrity, empathy, fight, and passion. These words get me out of bed in the morning. They are inscribed in my journals and posted prominently on my phone and desk. Whenever I'm faced with a tough decision, all I have to do is look at them to remind myself of who I am.

Because I've come to know my core values so well, it's often a gut feeling guiding me these days. Something inside of me will say, *Don't do that. You're getting caught in the moment. You do not want to gossip.* If I'm not edifying someone, I'm not going to say it. And I fall—but I always rise.

It's so easy to forget ourselves in this pressure-filled world. I've seen many executives make the wrong choices because they forget to use their core values as a filter. Oftentimes, the easier path is the wrong path, and knowing no one will be the wiser makes that even easier to choose.

This is why you always need to go back to your words when you're faced with a challenging choice. It can even be helpful to envision your words as being written on the wall in front of you, each with a mouth that can talk. If one of your words is integrity, imagine it telling you, *At your core, you have integrity. There is no gray area when it comes to making the right decision. The correct choice here is the one with the most integrity. It might be the toughest road—but it's going to be the right road.*

As much as you might want to feel like a part of something at your company, fight the urge to join in on gossip to achieve that. By doing the right thing, you may find yourself being ostracized. But what would you rather have: someone using the words loyalty, honesty, integrity, compassion to describe you, or ones like self-righteous, greedy, callous, cold, or condescending? It all comes down to how you want to be known.

It's easy to get flustered and go in the wrong direction when you forget to use your core values as a filter because your decision-making is based on the wrong things. Very few things can shake you when you unequivocally know who you are and what you stand for in life. For example, if someone tries to attack or say something negative about me now because of my husband's history, I am not rattled in the slightest. I say, "Yes, that's right. That's exactly what he did. But that was many years ago." I don't battle back anymore because I've already been through that fire, and I'm very secure in knowing who I am in any given moment. I do, however, speak the truth and I am not afraid in the slightest to have a direct conversation with anyone—especially on that topic.

The cream always rises to the top. Take the high road, but be direct.

VALUES FIRST—NOT FEELINGS

While feelings are important, they should never be the first thing you listen to. Why? Because feelings are often wrong.

Like I've mentioned before, I certainly don't FEEL like working out every day. In fact, my feelings often tell me, *Don't work out. Don't get in the garage. Don't sweat it out. Don't lift that weight. Don't get on that treadmill.* However, I know the right thoughts on this subject are: *I want to be healthy for my family, myself, and my clients. I want to be able to fit into my favorite pair of jeans. I want a strong heart.* Those statements align with my values, not my feelings.

Or another example: when my husband was in a federal prison, there were days I didn't FEEL like being married to him anymore. I didn't FEEL like visiting him in such an awful place. I didn't FEEL like getting out of bed, hustling, and trying to share my value with the world. But my core values told me, *Faith is my foundation, and I know who I am. I know that in the Lord, all things are possible.* My feelings wanted to drag me down into the dirt, but my core values lifted me up and kept me soaring. Sometimes you just have to say screw my feelings, they are lying.

When you're going through a trial in particular, it's easy to make poor decisions based on feelings. During COVID-19, many business owners and executives panicked, making hasty choices that did not lead to great outcomes. As a result, some even lost their businesses. But especially in a pandemic or other trying times, try to remind yourself that decisions based on reality, facts, and values versus emotions, panic, and fear are the smarter options.

Let's say you're feeling afraid because you don't have eighty clients knocking down your door at the moment. Or you haven't sold a hundred million widgets this month. Or you have two employees leaving. Or you have a supply chain problem. Or you are not bringing the sales into your company or firm the way you used to. Whatever the issue and emotion might be, go back to your core values. Let them help you remember your value, why, and purpose, and get you back into the right mindset quickly. Knowing these will help you write your narrative in the moment (much more on storytelling later).

Or let's say you're writing an email while you're angry. Your immediate reaction might be to respond, *You're so rude. Why would you say that?* But always having your core values in front of you makes you realize you should respond based on your filter, not your feelings. (Waiting until your emotions have subsided before you hit reply is always a good idea, too.) You can be direct and kind—those two things don't have to be independent of one another.

The battle isn't at work. The battle is for the mind, and core values keep your mind right. Remember, emotions are fleeting but your filter is forever.

MISTAKES HAPPEN—FIX THEM

For those of you out there who have made mistakes, welcome to the club! We've all failed at one time or another.

I emphasize the need to play offense in situations like this. The only way to control your narrative is by owning your mistakes. I've had to tell many executives, "Explain what happened. You didn't mean to do it. You're keeping the story alive by not approaching it and bringing it into the light. You don't know what's being said about you in the dark."

When you've made a mistake, you must re-engineer those moments. Reflect on your actions, decide what you will do differently in the future, and then move forward. Next time, you'll be more aware of the look on your face, tone of voice, or body language that have in the past affected other people's perceptions of you.

I don't want your mistakes to hold you back from choosing the words you aspire to as your core values. These are meant to be part of who you are, and part of who you're growing into. We're all always growing (and if we're not growing, we're dying).

You're never stuck with an unwanted legacy. You can work your way out of it. So if you've breached loyalty in the past and think it can't be one of your core value words as a result—even though it reflects who you really are deep down inside—forget about it. I know you can be loyal. You can aspire to that.

I want you to write down the mistakes you've made, either accidentally or on purpose. Talk to yourself about how people may perceive those mistakes. Fix what you can. Own up to and apologize for past behavior. If people have the situation wrong say, "This is the perception, but this is what really happened."

But what if it's someone else who has made a mistake? In that case, I want you to be willing to stick your neck out—even if it's your boss or someone higher up than that.

I know we all make mistakes—I love someone dearly who made a huge mistake—and I am a big believer in second chances. Lord knows my husband had a lot of grace bestowed on him that he didn't deserve, and isn't that what grace is? It's undeserved and given freely, but met with truth and accountability. I forgive the inexcusable because God has forgiven the inexcusable in all of us. That's why Christ died on the cross for us.

When I'm coaching someone who has done something bordering on a gray area, I always approach that person with compassion and an incredible amount of empathy. I walk in with a lot of grace. But because my value of integrity is so rock solid, I also demand accountability.

I once said to a CFO who had told me about a wrongdoing, "Look, I understand what's going on here. You decided to make that decision and I am so sorry, but this is how it is going to affect you and your family. I'm not going to leave you in this fire alone, but you have to do the right thing."

If I had never walked through a fire myself, would I ever have been able to give a high-powered CFO in his late fifties that message in my late thirties? I'm sure part of me would have thought, *What the heck do I know?* But because I've lived through trials, know who I am and what my values are because those attributes stay in front of me at all times, and understand how painful the consequences can be when the wrong choices are made, I was able to gather the strength, confidence, and wherewithal to say, "I know what is right in this moment."

Without your core values in front of you, some people might decide to run from a moment like that. They might be told a secret and hold onto it instead. They might think, *I don't want to be a part of this.* But the truth is that integrity ALWAYS matters.

If you're ever unsure of how to handle this type of situation, simply ask yourself, *What is the next best step?* In scripture, it says the Lord will light the next best step. You don't have to see the path all at once. Your core values will help you get where you need to go.

THE VALUE IN VALUE STATEMENTS

The *Harvard Business Review* defines a mission statement as describing what business an organization is in as well as what it isn't, both now and projecting into the future. In short, it's what a company does. Similarly, your value statement takes your core values and puts them into a sentence or two explaining how you bring your gifting to the world to positively impact your company, employees, customers, and community.

Having a personal value statement is no longer optional. You must solidify yours and promote it to be successful in today's competitive business climate. At minimum, you need it prominently displayed in your LinkedIn profile.

Saying *I'm the VP of Organizational Development* isn't enough anymore. In every company, that could mean something entirely different. For instance, I often find the duties associated with the Chief Operating Officer role are like night and day from one company to the next. Sometimes it's part management. Sometimes it includes financial responsibilities. Sometimes business development falls under that title. You must clarify exactly what you bring to the table and what lights you up so there's no confusion.

Your value statement puts your core value words into action and gives you direction. It is not another flashy slogan, but an intrinsic motivator that shows what your values are. It also helps with your LinkedIn headline (more on that later).

THE FIRE

The Core of Corporations

Patrick Lencioni, one of the greatest thought leaders of our time, wrote, "Core values are the deeply ingrained principles that guide all of the company's actions. They serve as its cultural cornerstones... They are the source of a company's distinctiveness. Mission and values can even serve as an important point of differentiation and set a company apart from competition by clarifying its identity."

In other words, core values are the secret sauce. They indicate to the world what makes us different from everyone else. Core values showcase our superpowers!

Companies focused on core values are not only able to say who they are, but consistently ARE who they say they are over time. This consistency builds trust and breeds incredible loyalty. It's what contributes to these firms existing an entire century on average.

For example, the Ritz-Carlton's credo is: The Ritz-Carlton is a place where the genuine care and comfort of our guests is our highest mission. We pledge to provide the finest personal service and facilities for our guests who will always enjoy a warm, relaxed, yet refined ambience. The Ritz-Carlton experience enlivens the senses, instills well-being, and fulfills even the unexpressed wishes and needs of our guests. Their motto is: We are Ladies and Gentlemen serving Ladies and Gentlemen.

Because of these values, the Ritz offers an incredibly warm, personal, luxurious experience to all its guests. Everyone from the valet and bellhop to the concierge and housekeeping gives you a sincere greeting. They use your name. They anticipate your needs before you even have a need, and then fulfill that need. They pride themselves on preparation. When you leave, they give you a farewell that makes you feel like the most important person on earth.

You know you're always going to get honesty, respect, integrity, and commitment when you go to a Ritz. They ensure this experience by nurturing and maximizing their talent to the benefit of each individual. Companies that can deliver this kind of consistently top-notch service are completely crushing it in the world!

And the employees at the Ritz are not the only ones empowered to create memorable, personal, unique experiences through deeply instilled corporate values. Consider Chick-fil-A. You can go to one in Scottsdale, Arizona, or Augusta, Georgia, and get the exact same food, with the exact same smile, purpose, and kindness.

That's because Chick-fil-A lives and dies by their values, and all their employees buy into those values. They create consistency by incorporating them into everything they do, every single day. This is how they outperform all other fast-food chains despite being closed on Sundays. Pretty amazing!

Or how about Southwest Airlines? Their core values are to display a:

- Warrior Spirit—as shown through hard work, the desire to be the best, and demonstrating courage, a sense of urgency, perseverance, and innovation.
- Servant's Heart—by following the Golden Rule, treating others

with respect and putting them first, demonstrating proactive customer service, and embracing others at the company.

- Fun-LUVing Attitude—by having fun, not taking themselves too seriously, maintaining perspective, celebrating successes, enjoying their work, and being passionate team players.

If you've ever been on a Southwest flight, you've seen these core values in action. The announcements are often made with great humor. The flight attendants and pilot make you feel welcome and like part of the family. Even though you are on a cost-effective airline, traveling with Southwest is a fun and enjoyable experience rather than one that makes you feel undervalued, or worse, ignored, because you've paid less to fly with them.

> Shout-out to Patrick Lencioni: Thank you for all of the wisdom you have left us. I hope to meet you soon!
>
> For everyone reading this: In trying to recommend a book to read, it was hard to choose only one. I'd say start with *The Five Dysfunctions of a Team* first and go from there. I promise you won't regret it.

INDIVIDUAL CORE VALUES IN ACTION

I recently began working with a man who had his core values in front of him at all times. It was so inspiring to see him living out his authentic purpose in the world every single day. He had an incredible ability to lead with compassion, and fully embodied his faith. He has the greatest integrity.

Integrity is a part of most companies' value propositions, but very rarely do they actually demonstrate integrity in all things. Leadership says it's one way, and then they act a different way. Not with this man.

While working with his company, I gathered feedback from every level of employee about him. Each time I mentioned this man's name, people physically changed. They absolutely lit up. Everyone had a story about something he'd done without advertising or promoting how great he was, whether that was through encouraging words, other types of support, or a kind gesture. (I even experienced this firsthand when he gifted me a faith-based journal because he thought I would enjoy it. I now use that book every day, and think of him gratefully whenever I do.)

The entire company used the same two to three words to describe this man. They all said he was one of their favorites. The follow-up was always, *I hope he doesn't retire soon.* Now that's the kind of leader everyone wants and needs!

His consistency created a family environment full of trust, care, and compassion—he completely took fear out of the equation. His employees knew if they made a mistake, they were going to be held accountable, but they also knew they had a safe place to fall. As a result, they were more creative and prone to thinking outside the box.

These great rewards came because my client is who he is all the time. His values are always in front of him. He is always who he says he is.

SUPER SUCCESSFUL STATEMENTS

Let's take another look at Sir Richard Branson, founder of the Virgin Group, entrepreneur, author, philanthropist, and all-around cool dude as a great example of this. His personal brand is rock solid. In his Twitter bio, he describes himself as a "tie-loathing adventurer, philanthropist, and troublemaker who believes in turning ideas into reality. Otherwise known as Dr. Yes at Virgin." His statement is not only funny and engaging, but it tells you the type of professional he is. He's on a mission. He does things unconventionally. He's a go-getter. He thinks out of the box.

Tim Tebow gives us another great example to follow. His foundation's mission is "to bring Faith, Hope, and Love to those needing a brighter day in their darkest hour of need." He is someone who always stays true to his why, words, and value statement—very few people have lived their values as consistently as Tim Tebow always has. He is respectful, loves the Lord, and knows who he "reports" to in life. I like that he's a humble, understated young man who is now fighting sex trafficking after having been a successful athlete.

Or what about Netflix? Their mission is to entertain the world. They don't say to bring entertainment to users so they can watch things easily, even though that also describes what they do. Blockbuster offered a different kind of in-person experience, and they were absolutely crushed by Netflix. Different mission, different value statement, different core values—but the one that resonated most with people is the only company left standing.

THE HEAT

Defining Your Core Values

So how do you define your core values? Start by asking yourself, How do I want people to perceive me? How would I like them to describe me when they see me, hear me, or read something that I've written? Some of the ideas you come up with may not fully portray who you are now—they can be aspirational. You can certainly grow into your words!

These values then need to show up in all your actions, deeds, words. The more you use and demonstrate your words, the more people will start to associate them with you. Soon, even your aspirational words will describe you to a T, effectively building your brand and creating consistency in your narrative.

In past chapters, we've talked about how strong the personal brands of Colin Powell, Peyton Manning, Nelson Mandela, and Margaret Thatcher are. The words people use to describe them are strikingly similar no matter where you are in the world. You should aspire to the same.

No matter who you're interacting with, you want the impression to be consistent. Whether your words are honest, trustworthy, truthful, approachable, kind, or genuine, take care to act that way at all times. Your words are what make people say, "I've heard about so-and-so eight times, and I've heard the word empathy come up all eight times. I really want to meet this person!"

HOW DO OTHERS PERCEIVE YOU NOW?

When I first sit down with a client, I always say, "Tell me what you perceive other people think about you—your teams, colleagues, boss, friends, people from your past and those you've only known for five minutes, people in the community and those you've met at networking functions."

More often than not, their perceptions are not at all aligned with reality. There's a great cartoon I use to illustrate this point showing a little dog who sees his reflection as a lion. I'm forced to tell clients, "You're looking in a mirror and seeing someone different than everyone else is."

I recently worked with a man who was one of the smartest people I've ever met. He would describe himself as brilliant and a master communicator; a people-person with a gift for reading others; cordial, nice, and funny. But if you asked his boss, colleagues, teams, or even the community in which he served, you'd be more likely to hear the words arrogant, a gossiper, a jerk, rude, self-centered, and a culture-killer.

Underneath it all, I think he simply lacked self-confidence in his own value. I finally had to say to him, "This is how you see yourself, but it is not how others see you. Have you listened to how other people are describing you? They're describing you as smart, but not as a leader."

Yet regardless of how many times we had this conversation, or his boss gave him feedback, his behavior didn't change. He was always wondering, *Why aren't people listening to me? Why can't I get this pushed through?* At the end of the day, there was no need to wonder. His problem was the perception he had of himself versus what people actually thought of him. It was night and day.

This man was what John C. Maxwell would describe as a level one positional leader—someone who thinks they are a leader simply because they have a certain title. They walk into the office and think, *Everybody's going to follow me,* but then no one does because there's no guidance, inspiration, or motivation to do so.

In business and in life, it's incredibly important to know how people really perceive you. One way of finding out is to determine how you make people feel. My client who described himself as brilliant and a master communicator brought fear with him whenever he walked into a room.

Other clues can be found by listening carefully to how you are introduced in all types of situations—at a networking event or party, online, before giving a talk, in a conference room. What people say about you here is what they are seeing and feeling. These are the things they've grabbed onto and gravitated toward when they think about you.

Ask yourself: What emotions do I bring along with me—a sense of innovation? Inspiration? Creativity? Openness? Or do people hide when they see me? Clam up? Look away? What are the characteristics they've grabbed onto when they think about me? Noticing how people respond to your presence can give you important clues to how they are perceiving you.

WHAT FEEDBACK ARE YOU GETTING?

Of course, the best and most direct route is to simply ask others to give it to you straight. Direct feedback leaves nothing open to interpretation, especially when you ensure you have shared exactly what you want to happen—and you must be ready to hear it all: the good, bad, beautiful, and ugly.

Many companies rely on online tools to gather 360-degree feedback on their employees. While these assessments can be valuable, they also have their limitations. Many times, people are afraid to give their uncensored opinions because they worry about what might happen if they do. This is especially true if there's an uneven power balance in the relationship, like an employee giving feedback to their boss or a child to their parent.

This is why my suggestion is to always introduce the concept of feedback in an in-person conversation. Tell whoever you are asking that their honest answers truly matter to you, and you value their opinion. Explain your mission is to become the person you were born to be, and their input will help you achieve that goal.

My advice is always to ask several different people from different parts of your life to provide feedback. Including coworkers, bosses, friends, and family members as well as people you have longstanding and newer relationships with is more likely to give a well-rounded view of how you are being perceived in the world. This is the only way to truly know if you've taken control of your narrative and successfully launched brand YOU.

I then recommend following up this conversation with an email that includes the actual questions you want answered. (I like to ask people to respond with three to five words that describe me, looking for how similar the responses are to my core value words. I then make any necessary shifts if people are not seeing me accurately.) Allowing them to consider their responses gives the appropriate time and space for candor. You don't want to put people on the spot—it is much harder to give open feedback face-to-face.

Once you receive feedback and have time to digest the responses—which can be HARD—follow up with everyone who participated. Tell them you appreciate their honesty. Talk about the things you're working on as a result. Explain how you plan to use the information you uncovered to learn and grow into your best self.

Ask yourself: What kind of feedback are people giving me? Is it consistent? Does it match my perception of myself, or are people seeing me in a different light? If needed, how can I bring those two into better alignment?

HAVE YOU BEEN INCORRECTLY LABELED?

Your brand never sleeps. It is what you write on LinkedIn. What you say in line at the grocery store. That conversation you had at a networking event, or eye roll you hoped no one saw. It's the bad word that you said about somebody in the hallway, or the kind shout-out you gave a colleague on social media. In short, it is you and everything you do.

By reading this book, you are beginning to build your brand by design and take control of your narrative. But if up until now your brand has evolved by default—meaning you weren't necessarily mindful of the way you are being perceived—that may have resulted in getting labeled incorrectly.

As an example: I want everyone I meet to use integrity as a descriptor of me. It's the word I hold dear, because I understand what happens when there is a serious breach of integrity. I know firsthand the consequences of that kind of lapse don't typically fall on only one person—they also fall on their teams, company, and family. If someone were ever to say, "I don't think Mila Grigg has integrity," I would search to find out why. What had I done to show I don't have it? How had that perception come to life? If that person had gravitated toward the wrong things when thinking about me, I'd be sure to tell the right stories to help them see me in an honest light. (More importantly, if I had done something wrong, intentionally or unintentionally, I would work to fix it!)

I call it "taking a brand hit" when you've been labeled because of something you've chosen to do incorrectly. You said you stayed late, but you left early. You claimed to finish the project, but you had someone else complete it for you instead. You gossiped.

As the old saying goes, "A lie can travel halfway around the world before the truth puts its boots on." When a brand hit happens, you can be sure it's going to travel at lightspeed. The biggest problem comes when people assume your behavior is something you do all the time versus something that happened only once.

Whatever the situation—and whether you meant to do it or not— you're now labeled. If you've been conscientiously building a brand and people know who you are, it will help quell some of the rumors. For instance, during my fire if someone said, "Have you heard about what Mila Grigg's husband did? Why on earth would I hire her to help talk about integrity?" I knew I had people in the community— brand ambassadors—who knew and were ready to stand up for me. They'd respond, "Have you met her? Do you know her? Do you know how open she is about it? Do you know how she's held her husband accountable for what he did? Do you know what he is doing now? Do you know that she uses her experience to coach, teach, and keynote on integrity? This isn't a secret." More often than not, the person would think, *Maybe I should explore that.* Or, *Oops, maybe I spoke too soon.*

But if you haven't used your core values as that filter, it's going to be a problem. No one's going to back you up. No brand ambassador is going to step in and defend you. They're not going to say, *But I know this person has integrity.*

Ask yourself: Have I been labeled incorrectly? If so, why? What can I do differently to have a different impact on how people describe me? What stories can I tell to turn this misperception around? This doesn't mean hiding things or being inauthentic. You simply have to share different pieces of you at different times (which we'll talk about in more detail in the next storytelling chapter) and ensure everything you do goes through your core value words as a filter.

WHAT ARE YOUR WORDS?

Now for the exciting part: choosing your core value words!

My advice is to find a quiet place and carefully consider the following list of words. Think about what each means to you. Pray or meditate on them if that's something you practice in life.

Next, check off as many words relating to you as you possibly can. This could be as many as fifty or as few as five. Take your time—the goal isn't to pick your words in record time. Sometimes this exercise takes a day, sometimes it takes a week, sometimes it takes months. Discernment is what matters here, not speed.

Once you're done marking off every possible word, it's time to start winnowing down your larger list. By this point, you'll probably notice your words are beginning to umbrella beneath one another. Choose the ones that best describe you now, or as you want to be seen in the future.

Ray Dalio would call these words absolute principles. This is exactly what great companies do to build a winning culture. I recommend doing this exercise every quarter to ensure your words best describe who you are and who you aspire to be, because you'll use these words every single day to build a consistent brand.

Ask yourself: Why did I choose that word? Why is it important to me? Is it who I've always been or who I aspire to be? What stories can I share where I've demonstrated this quality? Keep questioning yourself until you can confidently pick the three to five attributes that speak most to you. Then, take out a sheet of paper and write each of your words down. Underneath every word, explain how and why the word has meaning for you. This is an important building block in brand-building so be thoughtful in your answers and keep them close at hand.

WHAT'S YOUR VALUE STATEMENT?

Now we're going to use your core value words to create a statement about who you are. You want this statement to be memorable and short—one to two sentences—and highlight what you do best. It needs to show people what differentiates you from everyone else and connect with your target audience in a matter of seconds.

In building my value statement, I took my why (*to live my purpose and be an example to/provide for my family and community*) and my purpose (*to help other people find their purposes*) and distilled how I utilize these in the world into two short, punchy sentences. That became: *I coach people to be the best that they can be and share their gifting. I lead companies to find their purpose, their brand, and their value, and then to market it and share it in a way that is unique to them.* This statement demonstrates exactly what I do and how I do it quickly and effectively.

In the same vein, your statement needs to encompass everything you offer both as a human and a personal brand. This is the place to showcase the skills and talents you possess that cannot be found in anyone else. People are waiting for your message the way in which only you can deliver it!

One way to begin this process is to think about individuals you admire. Who are they and what are their characteristics? What ideas of theirs are you connecting to? You want to find the people that reflect who you are on your best day, or who you would be if you had all the money in the world. You can then draw inspiration from their value statements in creating yours.

Another way is to look at the whys, words, and statements of people you seriously dislike. Their values compared to yours are likely night and day. Determine why you don't like what these people stand for, and ensure those qualities are not included in your value statement.

You might even want to try to emulate Apple's mission when writing your personal brand statement. It is by no means boring. They don't say, *We're a computer company.* They say, *Our mission is to bring the best user experience to customers.* In 2009, Tim Cook set Apple's vision as: *We believe that we are on the face of the earth to make great products and that's not changing.*

Your value is no less than Apple's, so what are you on the face of the earth to do? Don't say you can deliver a hundred widgets a day on a supply line at an auto company. People want to know, *How do you do it? Why do you do it? What are the things you do above and beyond putting widgets together?* That's your gifting. That's the value you bring to your work.

Ask yourself: What value do I bring and what differentiates it from the things other people bring to the table? What problems do I potentially solve? How do I do that in a unique way? What is my selling proposition? Who is my target audience? Answering these questions will lead you to discover your unique values and key attributes. Put those into one or two short, snappy sentences and voila! A value statement is born.

THE LIGHT: BRAND VALUES RECAP

Core values are foundational to everything you are.

These are the three to five words you want people to use when describing you.

Your core values then act as a filter for everything you do.

Consistency is the key.

Your core values are used to create a value statement to use on LinkedIn and beyond.

Mistakes happen—own up to them and move forward.

Hold others accountable with grace and empathy.

Part Four

BRAND STORIES

"Marketing is no longer about the stuff that you make, but about the stories you tell."

—SETH GODIN, AUTHOR, ENTREPRENEUR,
MARKETER, AND PUBLIC SPEAKER

THE SPARK

What's Your Story?

You were born for a purpose, and it wasn't to hide under a rock. You have a gift and experiences no one else has. Whether your story inspires a million people or only one, it is absolutely worth telling.

Because a strong personal brand is authentic, stories that allow others to connect to you, your experiences, and your character validate your brand's authenticity. Your stories show that you walk the walk, not only talk the talk.

As humans, we're emotional beings, and storytelling is the BEST way to garner an emotional response. People love putting themselves into a great story. Research has shown that messages delivered as stories can be up to twenty-two times more memorable than facts alone.

Even better, storytelling is effective for all types of learners. Paul Smith, in *Leader as Storyteller: Ten Reasons It Makes a Better Business Connection*, wrote:

> In any group, roughly 40 percent will be predominantly visual learners who learn best from videos, diagrams, or illustrations. Another 40 percent will be auditory, learning best through lectures and discussions.

The remaining 20 percent are kinesthetic learners, who learn best by doing, experiencing, or feeling.

Visual learners appreciate the mental pictures storytelling evokes. Auditory learners focus on the words and the storyteller's voice. Kinesthetic learners remember the emotional connections and feelings from the story. In other words, storytelling wins over your entire audience, every time.

Right now, some of you might be thinking, *I'm an introvert* or *You couldn't pay me to start telling stories*. I feel you and hear you. I'm also here to say it doesn't matter. Storytelling is not an option anymore, it's a must whether you are emailing, texting, on social media, or in person. Quite honestly, you will be left behind if you don't share your stories.

I can't even begin to count the number of clients who tell me that they don't have any stories worth telling or they don't have any to tell at all. This is a lie. You may not be a natural-born storyteller, but you certainly do have stories to tell. The other lie you may be telling yourself is that your stories aren't worth sharing. They are.

Telling your stories makes you more likable, relatable, and connected to others. Your stories make you memorable. They build incredible loyalty. This in turn makes your work and life more enjoyable. And the cherry on top is, your stories get you seen and provide entrée to better positions and more money. In a world that's currently so polarized, storytelling is a way to breach that divide.

So now you have a choice: you can keep telling yourself that your story isn't interesting, that it's too complicated, or that people wouldn't care—or you can choose to get into the driver's seat of your own story and turn it into a personal brand that attracts your ideal audience as well as increases your visibility, impact, and income.

Ready to start sharing now?

People often ask, "How do I get to know the Lord?" My answer is: read His words in the Bible, the greatest and truest story ever told. Listen to His stories. He is always the same. Once you hear His voice, you'll always be able to recognize it. And if you don't believe—ask Him to reveal Himself to you!

THE FUEL

Storytelling Isn't Bragging

In 2017, a team of psychology researchers from Harvard concluded we're screwing up small talk. Too many people think that quickly focusing the conversation on themselves and sharing impressive self-stories is how it's done. This is most definitely not the case. As the researchers noted, "Redirecting the topic of conversation to oneself, bragging, boasting, or dominating the conversation tends to decrease liking."

It's true that talking only about yourself and not listening to others makes people like you less, so I don't want you to do that. What I want you to do instead is SHARE.

A lot of people hide behind humility, and while there's something to be said for being humble—pride comes before the fall—it can also be a real career staller. But if no one knows your story, there's no reason for them to care about, sponsor, or mentor you. Keeping quiet about your story often means getting stuck, like a recent client of mine did.

They'd worked eight different jobs to pay for their college tuition, graduated magna cum laude, and went on to earn a doctorate degree. This is one of the smartest people I've ever met, as well as one of the least braggadocious—which was unfortunately why they didn't yet hold the type of position they deserved. I distinctly remember this person's boss saying to me, "I don't know if they're committed." I wanted to yell, "Are you kidding me? They were the first in their family to go to college. They worked multiple jobs to fund their education and now they're working their butt off for your company, and you're questioning their commitment?" But I also understood the boss's position. Because they hadn't shared their story, the boss knew none of what I knew. So I shared their story for them. Next up, raise and promotion.

This is also why you need brand ambassadors (more on this later). This is why I want you to be thinking, *How can I best share my story and hear others' stories in this moment?* Don't miss an opportunity.

Before you go to that meeting, lunch, or networking event, take a look at who else will be there and decide what information might be the most appropriate and relevant to share. Perhaps you grew up in the same state as another attendee, went to the same college, or were in the same fraternity or sorority. Maybe you share an interest in fly fishing or running marathons or both have kids who play competitive soccer. There's no need to blast your stories out in front of a huge group of people if that's not comfortable or appropriate. Often, you can share with one person as effectively. Again, the goal is not to dominate the conversation or brag, but to tell an appropriate story and then listen to other people's stories as they share in return.

Always be mindful of what you're sharing and when. Relationship building takes time. More importantly, it requires a great deal of authenticity. Storytelling doesn't reap an immediate reward, and people can tell when you are trying to hustle them.

For instance, it wouldn't be a successful strategy to tell your boss two stories in an effort to relate to them and then turn around and ask for a raise in the same conversation. Sharing correctly takes time, effort, and intentionality. It can't be rushed. It happens story by story, which builds your brand brick by brick.

The most important part of the story is that it fosters a connection. Sharing and listening appropriately shows you care for other people rather than seeing them as another sale or a stepping stone to a promotion or more money. I'm here to help you craft a story you're passionate about, serves a real purpose, and allows you to have a bigger impact on the world. And that is most definitely not bragging!

IT'S ALSO NOT SELLING

Personal branding is not about closing a deal. It is about engaging your audience, increasing influence and leadership, and creating real connection. It introduces you to new audiences who need to know your story, and creates brand ambassadors who help share your story.

Sharing means you're never selling because your stories have already shared your value for you. You don't have to feverishly work a room trying to sell yourself. You can be very calm. By building a brand, developing equity, and sharing stories the way I'm teaching you in this book, people will get to know you in a different way.

If you're reading this and thinking, *But I have to sell myself*—know that I understand being on high alert.

Still, I don't ever want you to walk into a room with the goal of telling everyone what you do. I want you to share a story, ask questions, and LISTEN. After you've made a connection, be sure to follow up. In that follow-up, share another story that demonstrates your value. Take your time. One strong connection is better than twenty poor ones.

Imagine every story you share as another brick that goes into building a strong personal brand. Sales will follow as a result of sharing your value—not from shoving your card in everyone's hand. Trust the process.

IT'S CONNECTING

Sharing our stories is one of the most powerful means we have to influence, teach, and inspire. What makes storytelling so effective? Connection. Our stories are truly the tie that binds. They are what bond us together.

A great story:

- is memorable
- connects people
- builds loyalty
- helps us relate to you
- stands out
- creates personality
- creates a visual landscape of who you are
- shares your value without you having to sell yourself

People pay attention to stories to learn vicariously through the experiences of others. If your audience learns from you, is inspired by you, or makes a connection by laughing with you, people get to know you. You become more memorable. You become more influential. You become more of a leader. Promotions come more easily because your stories have pre-sold your mindset, skills, and capabilities.

We've all heard the phrase, "It's not what you know, it's who you know." Ask yourself: who really knows me at work, in my industry, or in my business community? If you're a bigwig inside your company but unknown outside of it, no one will have any idea about your achievements, capabilities, or what you bring to the table in the event that your job is eliminated. They'll think, *Who are you?* And that's a problem.

It's even more of a problem now that many of us are not going back to working in an office post-pandemic. How on earth are you going to get your boss to know about you and your experience short of blurting it out in the middle of a Zoom meeting (which is not a great idea, by the way)? By sharing your stories and creating a connection.

Sharing your stories online has become as—if not more—important than sharing in person. You don't have the luxury of walking down the hall, bumping into someone, and having a laugh together anymore as a means of bonding. So if you're not sharing online, there's a distinct possibility you're going to get completely missed. More on this later!

I have a nonprofit client in Nashville that I love. They've raised money simply by sharing the stories of the people they benefit. I want you to start thinking of yourself as that nonprofit. You're trying to raise money for *yourself* at your company. Just like my client, your stories are what will help people recognize your value, experience, commitment, passion, empathy, innovation, and resilience. And those are the qualities that make companies willing to give you more money.

Bottom line: stories give you the upper hand. If you want to be successful, you have to connect with others through your stories.

Share your experience. Show value. Engage employees, inspire colleagues and clients, and rally the troops. This is how you win.

SHOW, DON'T TELL

In interviewing, winning jobs, and winning in the world of career advancement, you can't simply run around saying, "I AM INTELLIGENT, I AM INNOVATIVE, I AM COMPASSIONATE!" and expect it to clinch the deal. It's one thing to tell someone you can do something. It's quite another to show someone what you've done through an authentic story that resonates.

Your stories can highlight your humor, strategy decisions, brand development, how you think in a crisis, how you respond to criticism and setbacks—any quality you want someone to recognize in you. This is what allows you to break through the noise and get seen.

For example, I'm an extremely competitive person. But that word alone doesn't give you any idea the lengths I have gone through to win even the smallest of contests. If I show you how competitive I am through a story about my antics, on the other hand, you'll truly know what I'm talking about. Watch.

A few years ago I threw a great fall party—I'm nuts about the fall—that included a good old fashioned sack race. All the soccer kids were having a go at it, when one of the moms said, "I bet I could win that race." Not with me around she couldn't. Challenge on!

We each jumped into a burlap bag and started hopping down the course. We were neck and neck until the end, when I started thinking, *Oh no, she might actually win!* So I literally threw myself head first over the finish line into a front roll type of thing. I even have a picture and video to prove it.

My family thought I was insane. I told them, "I might be, but at least I didn't lose."

Now when I say I'm competitive, you know I'm not kidding!

You can also see how I'm sharing my story authentically here, but I'm doing it for a purpose. If you love fall, now we relate. If you're as competitive as I am, you're thinking we're two peas in a pod. If you're thinking of hiring me, you'll assume I'm going to do whatever it takes to win over your employees. You know all that not because I TOLD you—I demonstrated it through a story that illustrates those facts.

Remember when my client was being seen as bubbly but she wanted people to consider her decisive? Her problem was that she hadn't shared any stories showing how decisive she is. People needed to see it in action or hear a story to confirm that value in her.

Sometimes, it's a matter of putting all the pieces together. I once worked with a woman who wanted to be head of diversity and inclusion. She'd educated herself, hosted events, and been involved in the area for a long time. It was where her heart and passion were, but she felt she didn't have any stories to confirm this. (Side note: diversity and inclusion makes companies far better. Having more women on the board in particular is a game changer.)

As it turns out, she'd grown up in a small town that lacked diversity. But her parents worked at a university that attracted students from all over the world. They often lived with her family while going to school.

I looked at her and said, "You realize this is where your heart for this came from, right? THAT'S the story." I couldn't believe she'd totally missed the connection. Once I pointed it out, she couldn't either.

We went on to talk about the people she'd met and the friends she still has globally as a result. We discussed this as a means for how she came to truly know people of all different backgrounds are so important for creating success. Sharing this story with the people in her company—SHOWING them why she was so passionate and prepared for the job—helped propel her into her dream role.

Think of the storytelling process as laying bricks. Mention the professor you studied under in college during one meeting so people know your educational background. In the next, commiserate with the person whose teenager is going through a rough time by saying, "High school can be so tough. I was on the debate team with someone who constantly made fun of me, even heckled me from backstage. We were on the same team, but she bullied me that entire year." Now people know where you went to college, and that you were on the debate team in high school. Your goal is to take every opportunity to weave pieces of your story into normal conversation.

Many social platforms have a stories feature. Many of us eagerly await the stories of the people we're following, and as a result feel connected to people we don't even know—and I'm talking about *real* people, not the Kardashians. These are regular moms, dads, businesspeople, and organizations sharing their stories. These brief windows into who they are intrigue you, grab your interest, and create a connection. I recommend you give it a try, too.

For those of you who are thinking, *This is all so planned.* Yes, it absolutely is planned. Life is planned. To be successful, you must be very well-planned and structured, and that includes your stories. Authenticity is what makes them work.

Storytelling that is well-done and shared at the right moment, with the right person, in the right tone of voice, wearing the right kind of smile (or intentional facial expression) can win over anyone. One good story can break through all the noise and crush your competition. You can raise millions based on one powerful story.

Yes. You. CAN.

I threw myself over that finish line because I could not lose. I don't want you to lose either. Start winning by showing the world what you're made of. Do it through your stories.

CURATING YOUR STORIES

It is your responsibility to curate stories from your life—WHY you do what you do, WHY you started the business, WHY you love your customers, WHY you love your employees. WHY you keep going. These stories are the lifeblood of the growth of your brand, the strength of your business, and the connections you're developing.

Stories solidify your identity. They build confidence in who you are as much as why you do what you do. That kind of emotional connection is why we reach for brand-name products at the supermarket—we know what we're getting, no surprises. The product's value and selling points are proven and well-known. Your own personal brand should be as recognizable.

A strong identity is BUILT with stories. Acclaimed Pixar director Pete Docter puts it this way:

> What you're trying to do, when you tell a story, is to write about an event in your life that made you feel some particular way...and to get the audience to have that same feeling.

So, he asks:

- Why must you tell THIS story?
- What's the belief burning within you that your story feeds off of?
- What greater purpose does this serve? What does it teach?

This is the heart of great storytelling as well as deciding which stories to tell and when. You need to have a reason and an end goal when you share, and that goal needs to be related to why you do what you do. You can't share willy-nilly.

Remember, people connect over feelings. Always start at the heart of the matter, stay focused, and make it short and sweet. Don't start talking about how in junior high you began running track and then list every event you ever competed in—start with how you continued to run track in college despite the rigors of academia because you loved it so much. This shows your dedication, perseverance, and competitive spirit.

Applying Docter's points to why I'm writing this book:

- I must tell the story of how I was able to grow a successful business even as my husband was in prison to show that you can do the same despite whatever you are going through. Even though that makes me incredibly vulnerable, truth is truth.

- My burning belief is that my branding expertise as well as what I've walked through is well worth sharing, and will change your career trajectory and life if you follow the advice I am giving in this book.
- It teaches you to build an unstoppable brand by sharing authentically who you are, and the greater purpose it serves is helping you know you can get through anything.

All of this isn't as hard as you think. You have stories. You have value in those stories. These memories, experiences, moments, fires, trials, mistakes, and successes have shaped you. Your experience and value need to be seen.

WHEN IN DOUBT, BORROW OTHER PEOPLE'S STORIES

I was once on a panel where the introductory question was, *What was your worst moment and how did you get through it?*

I thought, I could talk about Gordon. I could say, "Hey, I'm finally seeing great success in my career, and P.S. my husband is still in prison." My worst moment was finding out what Gordon had done, followed by the moment when the judge said 120 months and I then had to do the math and divide by twelve before I realized that equaled ten years.

Of course, that's not what I actually said. The pain was still too raw and I wasn't sure how this particular audience would receive the message even if I could manage to choke it out without breaking down in tears. Instead, I talked about my grandfather, who was my hero, and in every way larger than life. He stood six foot six and had a booming voice that could shake the rafters.

My upbringing was a lot like the movie *My Big Fat Greek Wedding*, with one difference being that we're Serbian. Everybody's in everybody else's business, everyone knows everything about everyone, lots of laughter, and they're talking all at once. As such, my grandfather was always at my house to greet me after school, almost every single day.

Now, junior high was not the easiest thing in the world for me. (Can I get an amen about junior high?) When I was about eleven years old, I'd had a bad day and was moping around the house. My grandfather asked in his big, thick Serbian accent, "Why you have bad day?" I mentioned something about friends and boys, tears running down my cheeks the whole time.

My grandfather was always very loving to me, so I was expecting to fall into his arms and get a hug. Instead, he looked at me and said, "Running uphill without shoes on, being chased by Nazis shooting at you in the snow—that's a bad day. I was shot in the leg and I still ran six miles. Bad day, hah!" (Imagine this with a big Serbian accent.)

He was slightly irritated with me, because that really was his definition of a bad day. And unless that's what I had going on, the message was that I needed to stop complaining. My bad day was actually a pretty darn good day in comparison to his. Many times as I drove up to the prison in Atlanta that looked like Castle Grayskull from He-Man and She-Ra, I'd have to remind myself, *I don't see Nazis coming up this hill. They're not shooting at me. It's not snowing. Jesus is still on the throne. I'm going to be alright today.*

I ended my introduction with, "So now, I have a really high tolerance for a bad day and a really low tolerance for complaining. Things could always be worse, and if you're breathing and healthy, you really have every opportunity in the world."

I borrowed my grandfather's story for that panel discussion because sharing mine didn't quite feel appropriate at the time, and choosing that anecdote did a lot for me. My audience certainly thought I was funny—the story told with my grandfather's accent provided comic relief while still packing a punch with the truth. But they also heard the underlying message: This woman is strong. She's been through some things, but she does not complain. She probably works hard and has a very high level of integrity. She speaks another language. She has a larger worldly perspective.

Whenever you don't have an appropriate story from your own life, or don't want to discuss your own take on a particular situation, feel free to borrow away—especially from people close to you—to convey information about yourself. People still make that connection to you and your values, like they did with me through the story about my grandfather.

READ THE ROOM, LEARN TO PIVOT

Storytelling is as much about knowing your stories as it is about knowing your audience. You want to share stories based upon truth and authenticity, but you also need to be able to read a room and decide what someone needs to hear about you at any given time.

Whenever I'm in a session, seminar, keynote, networking event, or board meeting, I am hyper-aware of how people are walking in and greeting one another. I watch, listen, and wait for opportunities to share bits and pieces of myself and create connections with others. I always come prepared with stories that back up my position.

Recently, I was on a call with the Nashville Area Chamber of Commerce (shout-out to everybody there—they're such wonderful people!), where I'm humbled and honored to have been a part of the membership committee. We have to introduce ourselves before meetings. Elevator pitch time.

The trick about introductions? Don't be boring. Make people want to Google you afterward and connect on LinkedIn.

That means I don't always say, "Hi, my name is Mila Grigg, I'm the CEO of MODA Image and Brand Consulting, and this is what we do." Instead, people learn about different pieces of my life every meeting. During the pandemic, I once introduced myself by saying, "I'm Mila and I own MODA, but right now the most important thing going on in my world is that my children are finally back in school."

Now people know I'm a businesswoman and owner of a company

called MODA, but also that I'm a mom. I have more on my plate than work. If you're a parent, you can relate.

As I'm speaking, I always watch for people's reactions so I can pivot if necessary. I look to see if someone doesn't like a particular story, is not really hearing me, or isn't paying attention. I then file that away in my brain and know I need to ensure I capture them later with something else, like a follow-up note on LinkedIn.

Sometimes the elephant in the room is that we don't really know each other yet. In that case, you can simply say, "We've never had the chance to sit down and talk. Here are some things I think you need to know about me." Be forthright.

Some stories will connect and others will fall flat. Sometimes, even the same story told the same way works for one audience but not another. That's because THERE IS NO PERFECT STORY.

Instead of trying to guess what will work, try to think of what makes you great, what experiences in your life taught you most and inspired you. Chances are those stories will also inspire other people. Of course, you can keep testing them to see which ones are winning, and with plenty of stories to draw from you can be ready to change on a dime. This does not change your authenticity—it only changes HOW you tell your story so the person you are speaking with can relate to you. Don't worry if you don't get it right on the first try. It's your story, so you can rephrase it and change it any time if it doesn't work out.

Be very intentional with the stories you choose. You have to know who your audience is and be aware of their reactions. If you realize, *Oh, they're not tracking with me. They don't like what I'm saying. They did not think that joke was funny*, move on. Always have other options prepared. If not, you'll get caught off guard. Fear will creep in and you'll start thinking, *I didn't say what they needed to hear so I'll be quiet now*. No—keep going! Fix that moment.

At the end of the day, if you still don't think you've quite connected, say so. Acknowledge, "I don't think you liked that story." Maybe you'll get a laugh. Maybe you'll gain the audience's trust. Maybe not—it isn't always possible to capture your entire audience. The most important thing is to keep trying.

Knowing your stories allows you to pivot in those moments and be confident in who you are no matter what. The more stories that you have written down and reviewed, the more comfortable you will be in sharing them. Remember, all it takes is one good story to break through the noise and crush your competition.

BE SEEN AS A SPECIALIST

A specialist is someone who is sought after rather than shopped for a price—and no one wants to be shopped for a price. If you're an entrepreneur reading this, I know you're with me in this moment! If you're at a company, remember this: you get paid for your value, not your work on the job. What MORE do you offer the position and the company as a whole?

Sharing your story is sharing your value. And the more you share your value, the more that value rises. Raises, titles, lateral moves come more easily. People don't worry about how much they're paying you—they're more worried about keeping you on their team and in their company. If you're really known for your value, they will also ensure you're making sure you're doing what you love doing.

If you've shared the right stories about who you are and your area and level of expertise, this is the prize you win: people come looking for you because they need your skills. They are happy to invest in you and won't quibble on price knowing you'll deliver.

The flip side of this is if you haven't shared your story widely or effectively, no one will know what you bring to the table. They won't know where, when, or why to find you. They'll negotiate especially hard when talking salary because they're so busy wondering whether you're worth it or not.

So which sounds better? Being seen as a specialist, of course. And the way to do that is by finding and sharing your stories consistently and authentically.

> Shout-out to companies: Teach every single person in the company how to share your stories in person and online. Every value or value statement needs to have several stories to back it. Then create a social media toolbox so employees can pull those out and post them online. Don't make storytelling hard. Build a process and make it happen! We give this same advice to all our corporate clients—the more brand ambassadors you have, the better.

SPEAK UP FOR YOURSELF

Many clients tell me they've missed incredible opportunities and don't know why. But the thing is, I DO know why. It's one (or more) of several reasons: they aren't known, didn't share who they are, didn't know how to connect with others, gave off the wrong impression, or made a mistake. We all make mistakes—but fixing the brand hit is necessary. This is why my heart is so into writing this book. I don't want you to get missed!

I once worked with a woman who was pretty much unknown in her company. She was by all means worthy of a promotion, raise, and new title based on the quality of her work and strong work ethic, but no one knew about her efforts or the results she was producing for the company. I kept telling her, "If you don't share your strengths, education, and contributions that are far beyond what you're getting paid to do, no one will ever know or recognize your value."

I told leadership that she was one of the most passionate and hardest-working people at their company and that I felt she deserved more responsibility. Unfortunately, their impression of her was a rude, dispassionate person who never had much to say. I told them I understood she hadn't adequately shared herself or her stories with them, but the biggest thing I wanted them to know was how much she loved the company and what they were doing.

Working together, we were able to not only get her a raise—which changed her life—but also a promotion (the job responsibilities of which, by the way, she was already performing). Not everyone cares about titles, but she did. It was incredible to watch her start fulfilling the very purpose for which she was created.

I see people all the time who have missed opportunities when a simple story or emotional connection could have helped them be seen. When that happens, it's often because they haven't been able to capture AND PRACTICE their stories. If you're the last one in the office every night but you're not sharing that because you're humble, you need to. Drop it into conversation by mentioning, "The other night, when we were getting ready to leave around eight o'clock, I realized this report needed to be in by the next morning..." Notice you're not saying, *Hey, I'm a hard worker. I'm here late every night.* You're only telling a story.

People often tell me, "Oh, my boss is so mean. I've deserved this promotion for a long time and they don't really hear me." But then after coaching them, I come to find out they don't walk down the hallway to talk to the CEO. They don't go to lunch with anybody. They don't bond, share, or network. Whose fault is that? THEIRS.

Others don't think their boss has time to hear their stories. Fair enough. People are running a million miles a minute. The truth is, NOBODY has time to hear it. But when you know what your stories are and are confident in the successes you've had, you can drop those mentions in here and there so it doesn't impede on anyone's precious time. It's simply a casual conversation.

People can't read your mind so stop blaming them. Your boss can't promote you if they don't know better. That's your fault, not theirs. You simply MUST share.

You don't ever want to think, *My greatest regret is that I was prepared for that moment, but nobody knew.* My greatest fear isn't someone looking at me and thinking, *I hate your story.* It is dying, getting to heaven, and having the Lord show me all the things He meant for me to do in this life that I was too afraid to do. I'd hate to look back on my life and realize I was too afraid to share the experiences the Lord allowed me to walk through—good, bad, or ugly—because I was afraid of what other people were going to say. **Screw the naysayer. They don't pay your bills.**

I recently worked with a man who, by no stretch of anyone's imagination, should have already been in the C-suite at his company. In getting to know him, I thought, *You really love what you do. You're so passionate about the industry you're in and helping people and their communities.* He'd won awards and created immense change in his industry. His brand was literally holding his division up.

So why wasn't he sitting in the C-suite yet? How on earth was that even possible?

I started to dig and realized he hadn't ever shared his awards or achievements. He'd been at the company for a few decades without making what he should have financially, according to my assessment. I started to share his story, act as his brand ambassador, and advocate for him. I told the current C-suite, "I think you're making a big mistake. This person needs to be on more committees. He needs to be more of a face for the company. He has more integrity than the other leaders who are currently representing you."

This man ended up getting a HUNDRED THOUSAND DOLLAR raise and the promotion he so well deserved. It was clear he was ready for the role and should have been promoted to it ten years earlier. Which, by the way, means had he shared his story and been recognized for his contributions in a timely manner, he could have made an extra million dollars.

A million bucks is worth sharing your stories, right?

PLAY OFFENSE

When Gordon was in prison, it seemed to me that people were always looking at me and thinking, *That's the woman whose husband is in jail. I'm not sure I can trust or work with her.*

I knew at that point I could either hide or decide to rise above that tide. I chose the latter. I knew I had to play offense and control my own narrative by sharing my story. Truth is, I should have won wife of the century versus being judged. After I knew that truth, I ran with it.

I wanted to ensure people knew two things. The first was that I was staying married. If someone had a problem with that, tough. The second piece was that I held Gordon accountable as much or more than anyone else did. I wasn't a wife who said, "Oh, he didn't really do it. He didn't commit a crime." Yes, he did commit a crime. So, I would go into every situation ready to tell my story, tell his story, and diffuse any misconceptions.

Being upfront and honest about what happened helped others see my core values of integrity and faith. I may have been collateral damage, but I did not cause, support, or encourage what happened. I could be trusted and provide value despite the mistakes someone I loved dearly had made. In fact, anyone who looked at me sideways for staying married was the one who should have checked their core values.

Many of you reading this may be thinking, *People don't deserve to know my story. What businesses is it of theirs? Why should I have to talk about something like that?* Believe me, I understand your feelings. There are still times—and we're talking more than thirteen years after the fact now—when people ask me about Gordon's transgression. My initial reaction is always, *I don't ask you about your sins. I don't ask if you've had an affair. I don't ask if you've ever stolen money, and no one ever found out. I don't ask how often you lie or gossip. So why do I have to share my story?* Once that passes, though, I realize I still need to play offense. That story will always be out there, and how I respond needs to counteract whatever poor impression that has made on potential clients as well as friends. The story is so much more than a sentence. It is hard, but giving up is not an option.

Some of our stories are more "out there" than others. Some of us have things we've done or had happen to us that aren't going away. If you're in this same boat, the most important thing to do is get out in front of it.

The best way to do that? You guessed it. Through storytelling. Online storytelling is vital—don't miss this chapter ahead!

THE FIRE

The Great Communicator

I love Ronald Reagan, and so do a lot of people on both sides of the aisle.

One of Reagan's nicknames was the Great Communicator. He was incredibly prepared for all his speaking engagements. He notated his speeches with the stories he planned to share and sent them back to his writers so they were never surprised by his additions. The Great Communicator always had a joke ready when appropriate, a story ready when necessary, and a plan he always stuck to.

Remember his debate with Walter Mondale? At the time, Reagan was one of the oldest presidents to ever run for reelection. Mondale was hitting Reagan hard on this point. Eventually, the moderator even said, "Let's talk about age."

Reagan replied, "I will not bring age into this. I will not make it a part of the political process. I will not use it to share that my opponent is much younger and inexperienced."

Well, Walter Mondale couldn't help but burst out laughing. Reagan had completely flipped the table on him. He didn't have to defend himself. Instead, he told everyone, "I'm older and more experienced." Needless to say, Reagan won in a landslide.

Reagan never missed a chance to share a story or slay with a joke. Even his opponents couldn't help but like him. And while I'm certain some of Reagan's quips were spontaneous, it's interesting to note that most of his stories were written down in a journal that is now on display at his Presidential library. This prepared him for any situation that came along.

Follow Reagan's lead. Write your stories down. Be prepared. And leave your opponents surprised and laughing.

> For those of you too young to remember this moment in history, I want you to Google the debate where Reagan makes Mondale laugh. Watch the clip on YouTube. You need to know who these people are!

STORIES TRANSFORM COMPANIES

Steve Jobs was a great storyteller, and it is a big part of his legacy to this day.

As one larger-than-life story goes, when the engineers at Apple were working on the first iPod, they presented Jobs with a prototype. He looked at it and was not impressed, to say the least. He thought it was way too big.

His engineers tried to convince him it was impossible to make an iPod any smaller. So what did Jobs do? He dropped it in a fish tank and watched. Then he said, "There are air bubbles, which means there's still space to make it smaller."

What does this tell you about Steve Jobs? That he's innovative. He's always going to think outside the box. And he's certainly not going to take no for an answer.

It also shows you the power of stories and their ability to define a brand. Make sure your stories are saying the right thing about you.

TRANSPARENT SHARING

Successful businesses tell great stories—and the MOST successful businesses get their executives in on the action. Especially during trials, people want to know who's behind the curtain. They want to hear the personal brand stories of the people running the company.

During the pandemic, the head of GoodRx shot a commercial from what looked like his home office using his cell phone. In it, he talked about why he started the company. His message was, *Here's what happened. Here's where I am now. Here's why I care. Here's why I'm never going to stop.* It was not a huge production, but it was as authentic as it gets.

The CEO of Walmart did a similar video in the beginning of the pandemic when people were worried about not having food or supplies available. He shot it in one of the stores, and he thanked all the employees for working so hard to keep toilet paper, paper towels, and hand sanitizer on the shelves. Having the CEO share his gratitude with his sleeves rolled up and standing next to his employees was so impactful. His message was, *I'm in this fight with you, and I'm grateful for you.* He knew sharing a piece of his story would rally the troops and build emotional brand loyalty. And he did it by holding up his cell phone. Don't overcomplicate it.

Another great example of transparent sharing comes from the CEO of Tractor Supply, Hal Lawton. I believe he truly knows that stories matter. Soon after joining Tractor Supply, he posted videos and pictures to his LinkedIn that included references to core values and the faces of real employees. It is clear that he cares about people, shares their stories, and uses one of the greatest tools we have at our disposal to do it—social media. He is a leader who understands the power of communicating with employees, shareholders, and the communities the company serves in real-time. When you have a leader that actually cares about people and communicates through the company core values—it cements a legacy.

If you're a leader, telling personal brand stories is an absolute must. It is simply too easy these days for other companies to come into your market and win fast. Loyalty cannot be bought, but it can certainly be created quickly by telling your stories.

LEADERS TELL STORIES, LISTEN, AND LEARN

Stories help rally the troops and get people on the same page. As a leader, you need to know the stories of your team members. You must know what has influenced your people.

Stories tell you a lot about a person. You learn about their life experiences and come to understand why they might act a certain way in certain situations. Typically, there's a good reason. For instance, when it comes to my kids, I am a mama bear times a thousand.

My youngest was in pre-K when Gordon was still in prison, and sometimes when other moms found that out, they weren't as friendly or were big-time gossipers. Now they are as sweet as can be but I see you!

To this day, someone unfairly judging my child is a trigger. I can go from zero to a hundred because of what I've been through. I'll take anyone to the mat for my kids and my high level of emotional intelligence and self-awareness goes right out the window. Especially an adult who talks poorly about them. Side note: any adult who talks negatively about someone else's child needs therapy.

Stories help you figure out where and why people might overreact, so you don't turn around and overreact to their overreaction. Sharing a little bit about your own stories can help encourage people to share theirs with you, too. The power of story goes both ways!

THE HEAT

Discover Your Stories!

Storytelling works the same way for personal branding as it does in business. For example, if I say "favorite Super Bowl commercial," what's the first thing that pops into your head? Most likely a Budweiser ad featuring Clydesdale horses, a big emotional connection, and quite possibly a few tears. Remember their 9/11 commercial? It was shown only once. But it resonated so strongly and was so touching, people never forgot it. Budweiser as a brand is authentic and true to itself. That's how you have to be, too.

Your experiences have led you where you are today, and how you share them with the world will have a direct impact on the types of people and opportunities you attract into your life. Resist the temptation to embellish, or you will experience a loss of integrity.

A good story isn't only entertaining, it's scientifically proven to be more effective in helping people remember critical information. Cognitive research shows the reason people pay attention to stories is to learn vicariously through other people's experiences. Your stories grab interest and make people intrigued enough to want to meet you, get to know you, and work with you. You might even become a real-life, up-close hero to one person—someone they can touch and feel and see versus a story on a large screen at home or in the movie theater.

Your competitive advantage isn't necessarily your skillset, it is the value that you bring above and beyond what you do at work. I'd rather hire someone who does the job well and understands culture than a jerk who is great at, say, analyzing data or lobbying. So the next time someone says, "Tell me about yourself," I want you to have a few compelling stories that help you answer this effortlessly, because even recruiters are tired of hearing the same old thing. Remember, stories are twenty-two times more memorable than facts.

So how do you start building your narrative? How do you start the storytelling process? Never fear—it isn't rocket science. There's no need to overcomplicate the process.

We've already talked about how your core values are the foundational piece for building your brand. I hope you've thought, prayed, and meditated about the three to five words that resonate with who you really are, because now is the building block moment where we pinpoint up to twenty stories from your life to confirm how these core values represent the best of you or who you are striving to be. These are the things you want to be actively telling the world!

To determine what stories might be worth sharing, it can be helpful to start thinking about your life in buckets. Start as far back as you can remember. What are your first memories? Why do you think those stuck with you?

Next, move on to elementary school. Did a teacher say or do something particularly horrible or wonderful that changed your life forever? Is that why you're so successful now? To prove them right or wrong?

Then do the same for junior high, high school, college, young adulthood, and so on, reflecting on those times that have impacted your life negatively and positively. We go through trials in life so we can help others go through theirs. Your stories, whether they're good or bad, are meant to be shared.

Now I want you to go through the following questions and think of stories from your life that relate to each. Make sure the stories you choose uphold your core values and you know why that is. Write these stories down and start using them in conversation whenever appropriate and the opportunity arises.

Everyone has a story. Yours is the movie of your life put into words and actions.

HOW WERE YOU RAISED?

My heritage is Serbian (formerly part of Yugoslavia). I was born in Southern California, but I'm first generation on one side and second on the other.

When the Serbs immigrated to the US after World War II, they used to say, "I came to this country with only my underwear on a stick." It doesn't translate well, but it's really funny to think of my ancestors seeing the Statue of Liberty with their underwear hanging off a stick. That's the American Dream—to come here with nothing, work extraordinarily hard, and become successful. I share their stories constantly.

Sebastian Maniscalco, one of the funniest comedians ever, who also grew up in an immigrant family, says in one of his stand-up routines: "My father walks into the room and he's like, 'Go start a business.' I looked at him and said, 'Dad, I'm eight years old. I'm watching cartoons.'" This is exactly how I grew up! You must work hard, have a visible work ethic, and bust your ass. We're going to live the American Dream. This is why I often talk about my Serbian heritage. We're a strong-willed people with a great tradition and impeccable work ethic.

Things you may think are benign can become a big part of your story.

Your upbringing is part of who you are. It can be a great starting point for conversation because it is something everyone shares. We're not all comics, but I emotionally connect to Sebastian because of that story.

Ask yourself: Who raised me—mom and dad, single parent, grandparents, other relatives, foster parents? What's my heritage? What languages do I speak? Was I rich or poor growing up? Was I raised in confidence that I was safe, or was I scared bullets were going to hit me? How did these circumstances affect me? Did I work harder? Did I give up? Did I hide? Did I become bolder? Did I learn martial arts to protect myself?

> Shout-out to Sebastian Maniscalco: You are hilarious! Thanks for always keeping me laughing. Everyone, go watch him on YouTube!

WHAT FACT ABOUT YOU MOST SURPRISES OTHERS?

For me, the answer is that I speak Serbian. People don't often look at me and think my second language might be Eastern European.

Ask yourself: What is a fact not many people know about me that is unusual or unexpected? Why would people not think this was part of my life or in my wheelhouse?

WHAT ENERGIZES YOU? WHAT GETS YOU EXCITED?

Whatever excites and energizes you is an important facet of your storytelling. The answer might be hobbies and special interests—those things you do whenever you grab a spare moment. It could be alumni gatherings or networking associations. Perhaps it is being around a certain group of people.

For instance, do you enjoy helping others? Creating and being creative? Building things? Working with your hands? Influencing communities?

Bringing people together? Watching teams work successfully? Quelling conflict? Coaching others?

Ask yourself: What gets me out of bed? What do I love doing, no matter what anyone else thinks about it? When have I felt most alive?

WHAT ARE THE TIMES YOU'VE LAUGHED THE MOST?

Whenever I'm in a business meeting and I want to bring some levity to an anxious moment, I'll say, "Don't worry, I'll lead you through this—unless we're on a boat snorkeling." When my audience looks at me curiously, I tell them this story.

I grew up in California. I love the ocean and was constantly in the water. So when my husband and I were on our honeymoon in Aruba and the opportunity to snorkel presented itself, I was all in.

I was feeling extremely self-assured, so I decided I'd be the first in the water. There was a single ladder on that boat, and I was absolutely going to be the person leading everyone down it. I didn't even put on a life vest, my confidence in my skills was so high.

I jumped into that warm, wonderful, deep, dark blue water and swam off to check out the sunken German U-Boat we were there to see. I thought the view would be crystal clear and amazing, but it was pitch black and incredibly creepy. I could barely see two feet in front of me.

Then all of a sudden, a giant wall of fish appeared out of the darkness. It looked bigger than the Empire State Building to me. Somehow, I had it in my head that a giant sea creature would appear and drag me down into the depths of the ocean, never to return, and I started absolutely freaking out.

I popped up out of the water and grabbed onto the rope chain attached to the anchor for dear life. I was still terrified of the wall of killer fish, so I started crawling up the rope like a crazed monkey. My husband said my eyes looked like they were going to pop out of my head.

He kept yelling, "Drop in the water. You can't get on the boat that way!" but I ignored him and kept going. Of course, once I was at the top, I couldn't climb into the boat so I had to let go—into that fish-filled water again! With no rope to save me now, I tried to clamber onto my husband's shoulders. I was basically drowning him.

Whenever I or my husband tell that story, it always gets a great laugh. It's so embarrassing yet so funny to me all these years later, and I don't mind being the punchline of that joke.

Laughter creates bonds and connections unlike anything else. I definitely recommend sharing funny (and possibly self-deprecating) stories that show your lighter and more playful side when appropriate.

Ask yourself: What stories always make me laugh, every single time I think about them? What happened? What does it say about me? How can I use that story to make others feel more at ease?

WHAT WOULD YOUR TED TALK BE ABOUT?

If you had five minutes to prepare, what would you be able to give an effective presentation about? No matter the topic, you want to consider what this speech would say about you and how it might help you achieve your goals.

Personally, I would speak about one of two things.

If I were giving a TED talk right now, it would 100 percent be about brand building. This aligns perfectly with my goal right now, my why, which is to build my brand and company so I can help *you* build your brand and company.

In the future, I'd likely talk about entrepreneurship: how to build a successful business while balancing family life. My goal is to eventually run for office, become a professor, teach, and write another ten books, so this message would serve to help me achieve that. In both cases, I'd be sharing tailored stories to help me reach my goals.

If you're not immediately sure what your TED talk would be about, ask your spouse, friends, and others what they think the topic might be. That not only tells you what someone knows about you, but also where they think your expertise lies and what makes you different.

Your TED Talk would need to be about something you have a deep knowledge of and a passion for. As Gary Vaynerchuk always emphasizes (and I'm paraphrasing here), "Go to work, shut up, learn, and THEN start talking about it."

Once you determine the topic and goal, decide what stories of yours will help you get where you want to go.

Ask yourself: What would my TED talk be about? What would I say? What would people learn about me? How would it help me reach my goals?

WHAT IS THE BRAVEST THING YOU'VE EVER DONE?

The bravest thing I ever did was stay married when Gordon went to prison. It took such courage and conviction. The world was saying not to stay, but I did. When I said *for better or for worse* in front of the Lord, I meant it.

My decision has been worth every bit of struggle, but it was a struggle. If I'd listened to the naysayers—relatives, friends, community members—I wouldn't have a healthy nuclear family today. I wouldn't have my youngest daughter. I wouldn't have the business I have. I wouldn't be with someone I love daily. I wouldn't be able to write this book because I wouldn't be able to give you advice based upon experience. Lemons to lemonade through hard work.

You can see that in telling you the bravest thing I've ever done, I shared three or four stories about why that decision was worth it. Choose your story of bravery to highlight the lessons you learned and values you exemplified through that experience.

Ask yourself: When was I the bravest? What made me brave in that moment? Would others perceive my actions as brave? Did what I did work? Did it not work? Why and how?

WHERE HAVE YOU STRUGGLED? WHAT CHALLENGES HAVE YOU OVERCOME?

One of the greatest challenges I've overcome is building my business through the fire. When my husband first went to prison, showing up at networking events and holding my head up high was a struggle. But by continuing to show up—and displaying my integrity and authenticity time and again—I converted the doubters and gossipers into believers and brand ambassadors. (I also did the work and did it well—all those things work in tandem).

Challenges show what we're made of and how resilient we can truly be. I know there are worse things than having a husband in prison, but that's my story. For other people, it might be battling through migraines or watching their child beat cancer.

Almost everything comes back to fear: of failure, being found out, not having friends, having no legacy or no money. To be sure, other challenges are always coming, but knowing we've overcome big challenges in our lives helps us face those fears head on.

Your story here needs to include examples of how you persevered in the face of uncertainty, adversity, or risk, and ideally, that will help your audience identify with you. Such examples make you human and authentic, and will enhance your chances of establishing an emotional connection. You'll also want to reinforce that story through your social media channels (more on this in the coming chapters).

Remember, hard times give you an incredible opportunity to put your core values on display. Sharing stories about challenging situations creates another opportunity to authenticate those core values.

Ask yourself: Where do I struggle? Why? How do I overcome these challenges? How does this reflect on my character? How will this help others see me in my best light or be better able to relate to me?

HOW HAVE YOU RECOVERED FROM A FAILURE?

How you recover from a failure is far more important than the actual thing you failed at. My favorite stories are redemption stories. We all fail. Christ died for my sin and yours. His sacrifice means we all can have eternal life and a clean slate through faith in Him. You will have consequences, but you have the ability to grow through them and move forward.

Despite any challenges you've faced, you simply need to stay steadfast in building your brand and your integrity—brick by brick, day by day, moment by moment, situation by situation. Put in the hard work and persevere.

Once you're through the darkness, share with others how you recovered from your failure. Help them as they're walking through their own fire. Inspire others with your story of recovery.

When Gordon first went to prison, the naysayers came after me. Their message was: *Oh my God, I can't believe you're still with your husband!* After a while, though, they started thinking, *Wait a minute...is she actually getting through this? Did she actually do that keynote in front of all those people? Did that Fortune 500 company actually hire her?* Eventually, many of my critics became my fans.

Ask yourself: What challenges have I had to come back from? What lessons did that teach me? How was I able to make a comeback?

If you have a redemption story, I definitely want to hear it. I've lived my own, I see my husband currently living his, and I want to hear about yours—so write to me about it. Put it on LinkedIn, in the MODA Facebook group, or through Instagram. I'll share it if you want me to. You might be surprised to find that YOU'RE the unexpected hero people want to cheer on. Everybody loves a good comeback story!

WHAT WAS A HARD BUT NECESSARY CHANGE YOU MADE IN YOUR LIFE?

The answer is different for everyone. Maybe you moved to a different city and had to leave the neighborhood and friends you love so much for a different job opportunity. Perhaps it was deciding not to talk to certain people anymore because you realized they're toxic for you, even if that was a family member. We've all done hard but necessary things in life.

Although this is a story you might not share as often as some of the others, it's still one you should know. Sharing difficulties and challenging moments helps us understand and relate better to others. That kind of deep connection can't be beat.

Ask yourself: What are some of the hardest things I've ever done? When and how did I realize I needed to do them? How did that impact me as a person? What did I learn from these times? How did my core values shine through?

WHEN WAS A TIME YOU LOST CONFIDENCE IN YOURSELF?

Losing a contract, missing out on an opportunity at work, or being removed from a project are all things that impact confidence. Sometimes the huge roadblocks in life are the ones where we need to shift direction when we didn't even know we needed to. It is crucial to pause in those moments, reflect on who you know you are, and build back from there.

Losing or disappointing a client kills me—but I know who I am, WHY I do what I do, and believe with certainty I was created for a purpose. You will have moments of angst and fear and failure, but knowing you have a purpose ensures you move forward versus being stuck in the mud of despair. Confidence comes from knowing who you are. Making a mistake doesn't have to lower it.

Ask yourself: When did I lose confidence in myself? Why? What was the fallout of that? What could I do differently next time? What lessons did I learn from that experience?

WHAT EXPERIENCE DO YOU VALUE MOST?

We all have those defining moments in our lives that we remember forever. These teach us who and what really matters to us above all else. Mine your indelible memories for stories that will have the most impact on others.

Ask yourself: What experience would I not trade for anything in the world? What did it teach me? Why was it so memorable? Was it positive or negative? How did I change as a result? Why do I value it the most?

WHAT/WHO INSPIRES YOU MOST?

One of my greatest inspirations is my grandfather. As I mentioned before, he was sent to a concentration camp in World War II. He escaped, which is not surprising at all, because he has always seemed larger than life to me.

Once my cousins asked how he'd escaped, since he was locked up and guards were everywhere. My grandfather replied, "You just do it." It's like he was the originator of Nike's advertising campaign, and he 100 percent believed in the "just do it" attitude. I think about that often, and it never fails to inspire me. His experience makes me want to just do it, too.

The day I was giving my first big keynote (that I talked about in the introduction) and I'd found out Gordon was getting transferred to the maximum-security prison, thinking about my grandfather helped me through it. I thought, *Well at least the Nazis aren't going to shoot me. The worst that can happen is I fail. No one's going to kill me. It's going to be alright.*

Ask yourself: Who brings me inspiration? Whose example do I follow? Why do I hold them in such high regard? What qualities of theirs would I like to emulate?

WHO INFLUENCED YOU MOST?

Think about the people that have stepped in and changed the trajectory of your life. Consider the invaluable influence they've had on you. There is such a debt of gratitude to be owed to people like this.

These could be people whose stories you've read or watched videos about on YouTube and social media. I've been influenced by so many people I haven't met—I mention many of them in this book and am so grateful they share their stories. I now have the ability to share their stories as well, and continue to use their moments as moments of inspiration for others. This is how your story, your moment, your life becomes an incredible legacy.

Ask yourself: Who are the people who had a great influence on my life? Why did they choose to support me? What did they do to help me? What is it about that person that made them able to put their neck on the line for me?

WHO CAN YOU ALWAYS COUNT ON AND WHY?

If I don't work, I don't get paid and my business doesn't grow. Sometimes I'm running so hard, friendships get put on the back burner. I'm not as mindful as I should be about checking in.

Knowing how hard it is to stay on top of everything, I'm even more appreciative of the people in my life I can always count on who don't judge me for not constantly following up. They help make me a better person by showing me what a good friend really is. (See? There's that show, don't tell again!)

For instance, I have a friend of more than ten years who is the most loyal, amazing person. She walked through the fire with me, never left my side, and never once judged me. If I'm having a bad day, she can hear it in my voice. I can be talking about unicorns and sunshine, but she can still tell there's something wrong.

Our kids play soccer together. Whenever we see each other at practice or a game, she brings me a big bag of my favorite gummy bears. It's such a sweet, simple gesture that shows she's always thinking of me. I want to emulate her traits and characteristics and be this kind of friend!

Or consider this: When Gordon first left for prison, I was considered damaged goods. Many people did not want to work with me. A few clients ghosted me; some projects were canceled. And then there was Charles, the manager of the Dillard's I mentioned earlier in the book. He knew my story and took a chance on me anyhow. He let me host as many events as I wanted. Whenever I think about that rough time in my life, I think about Charles, and the entire staff at the store during that time, and how grateful I am for their support.

A person who walks through the fire with you is someone you know you can always count on. You are incredibly lucky to have in your life whoever offers you a hand, an ear, a leg up, a place to host events, a laugh, or a bag of gummy bears no matter the circumstances. These are also the kind of people you may want to borrow stories from whenever one of yours isn't quite a fit.

Ask yourself: Who is someone I can always count on? How do I know? In what ways do they show that to me? What have I counted on them for? What have they walked through with me?

WHAT CONVERSATION CHANGED YOUR LIFE?

Sometimes, a message hits you and has incredible staying power. Think about the times someone said something to you that impacted the trajectory of your career or life. This is a great story to tell!

For me, that conversation was one I had with Craig Becker, CEO of the Tennessee Hospital Association for two decades plus. To this day, he is a mentor, friend, and someone that I respect greatly.

What Craig said to me that day—and what he has said to many other people as well—was: *I give you permission to fail.* In fact, he almost encouraged me to fail, because in his eyes, that meant I was learning.

His addendum was equally as impactful. He told me: But if you're going to fail, I need you to fail fast. I need you to get up the next day and not fail again for a while. Then, fail fast again. The "fail fast" concept opened my mind up to a different level of creativity. By saying what he said, Craig allowed me to be the best I could be without fear. That is one sign of a great leader.

Today, I share that story with other leaders while I'm coaching them. I want them to give their employees a safe place to fail, because out of failure comes great innovation. Now the conversation that changed my life is changing other's lives, and the legacy lives on.

Ask yourself: What conversation has had a lasting impact on me? Who was it with and what made that message so powerful? What did it make me realize about myself, work, or life? Why did it resonate so strongly? Was it something I'd heard before, or was the information entirely new to me? How did it affect me going forward?

WHAT HAVE YOU LEARNED FROM A JERK IN YOUR LIFE, AND WHAT CAN YOU THANK THEM FOR?

Tony Robbins often says his parents weren't always the best, but he knows there's no sense in wasting time hating his parents. Instead, he thanks them for giving him their worst, because it created who he is today.

Ask yourself: Who was not so great to me but taught me a big lesson anyhow? What do I have to thank them for? How have the lessons they taught me made me a better person or changed my behavior as a result?

HOW DO OTHERS DESCRIBE YOU?

It's imperative that you know what other people are saying about you. As I've mentioned before, listening to how people introduce you is a good way to figure out what they think about you.

You can also ask friends, colleagues, and partners, "What's the most memorable thing about me? What's the thing that you think of when you think about me?" Once you know how people describe you, you can begin to tell stories that will highlight other attributes, if necessary. Confusion leads to lost opportunity. If people don't know something important about you, it's your job to tell them. So many assume their stories are well-known and that sharing them once is enough. WRONG. This is where we get into trouble—we stop sharing or assume too much. Don't do either.

Ask yourself: How do people describe me? How do I make other people feel? Do I tell a story with purpose? Do I ramble on? Am I prepared with the right stories? Do I know what people need to hear?

WHAT TYPE OF COLLEGE DEGREE DID YOU PURSUE?

Some of us didn't know exactly what we wanted to do in college. Others had a clear vision. How we end up on our respective careers can be a winding road or a direct path. The story of how you went from there to here is a great way to bond with others.

Ask yourself: Did I stumble into my industry or pursue my position doggedly? Does my college major relate directly to my work today, or did I start out on a different path? What did I think I wanted to pursue? How did I get here? What was the path?

WHAT IS YOUR COMPETITIVE EDGE? WHAT DO YOU OFFER THAT OTHERS DON'T?

No one else has the value or gifting that you have. I want you to start telling the world what special gifts you have to offer. Share those stories!

My competitive edge is not that I'm really good at branding—even though I am, and that's my thing. It's that I can walk in a room and see how everyone is feeling. I see the struggle. I see I the arrogance. I see the pride. I see the pain. I know how to bring all those people and emotions together to create a winning culture. That's my value add.

Ask yourself: What's my value add? Is it part of my actual job description, or outside of it? How did I cultivate this skill? How does it help me in work and in life?

WHAT WAS YOUR BEST WORK MOMENT?

My best work moments are when a client calls and tells me they landed the job, were given lead on a project, had the courage to talk with their boss, stood up for something that mattered even though it was tough, received a promotion and did the right thing. Those are the times I think, *This is why I was born. I'm so lucky I get to continue my purpose. I could die today and be happy.*

Your best work moment might be when you earned the promotion that meant you'd be able to afford your kid's college tuition. It could be an award or recognition. Or perhaps it was when you saw someone going through a hard time and instead of walking by, you said, "Know that I'm here for you," and lent them an ear.

You might be surprised to find that your best work moment is outside your actual work and job description. It may not have anything at all to do with your production or product. Often, it is about helping someone else.

Ask yourself: What was my best moment at work? How does that reflect my why and core values? What does it show about me and my unique gifting?

WHAT WAS YOUR WORST WORK MOMENT?

Think about the worst thing you've done, seen, said, or heard at work.

It could be that you gossiped, which kills a company, kills culture, and kills your reputation. Maybe you didn't have a good excuse for not attending work meetings, so you invented a reason. Or it might be that you said you completed a project but made someone else do it for you.

People confide in me about all sorts of bad work moments. I've heard it all, and I'm a safe place to fall. I'll treat you with grace, keep you accountable to the truth, and walk through it with you.

It's always a good idea to have a story about your worst work moment in your back pocket, because you never know when it might come back to haunt you. If the mistake was gossiping, perhaps your story about it becomes, "I have gossiped at work, and I realized the pain it can create. Integrity matters to me, so I make certain not to do that anymore." I have 100 percent felt this way. None of us are perfect.

You will only fall as far as your personal brand lets you. If you have a strong foundation—a brand you have built with integrity, consistency, and patience over time, you will come back from a mistake so much faster than if nobody knows who you are. We all make mistakes, but if you have people who can build you back up faster, you recover much more quickly. This is why having brand ambassadors is critical.

Even bad moments can be used for good. Your stories about regretful behavior can work to mentor others. You might share them in a group to teach a lesson. They might help your kids from making the same mistakes. Live and learn!

Ask yourself: What's the worst thing I've done, seen, said, or heard at work? What did I do to recover from that? How has my behavior changed as a result? Do I have brand ambassadors who can help me in difficult situations—people who really know me, can speak on my behalf, and share my brand narrative and story?

WHAT WAS THE BEST (OR WORST!) TEAM YOU'VE BEEN ON?

Sometimes, it can be hard to pinpoint exactly why a team ran so successfully or was a complete disaster. Think back on a time that you were part of an incredibly great or terrible team.

Keep going through the why. Typically, this gets you to a pretty raw place where you finally realize the ultimate answer. Maybe the real why was every time the leader of the group walked in, he had a grim and sour look on his face and everyone else knew they were in for it that day. The goal of remembering these things is to ensure you take what you have learned so that you can apply it to others. Leading requires experience—simple opinions based upon guesses are worthless. Remembering what made a team a disaster allows you to help another team be their best by sharing the stories of your experience.

Ask yourself: Why was that team the worst? Or, who made it the best? What did they say? What did they do? How did they act? What was their emotion? Was it how they ran it? Was it the inefficiency? How would I run things differently if I were in charge, or how would I incorporate the example that person gave me?

HAVE YOU EVER HAD A HORRIBLE BOSS? WHY WERE THEY SO BAD?

I've heard so many stories from clients about mean, bad, rude, condescending bosses/managers. Two gifts of having a terrible boss are one, you learn what not to do, and two, you can take that experience and share with others as you grow in leadership. Experiences are priceless—even the bad ones.

Ask yourself: What did they do? What did they say? How did they make me feel? What did I learn as a result? If I were a boss, how would I treat people differently?

WHAT IS SOMETHING THAT NEVER SHOULD HAVE WORKED— BUT DID?

Sometimes, making a Hail Mary pass can really pay off. It takes guts, calculated risk, and faith. Everyone loves the story of an underdog succeeding against all odds.

Ask yourself: When did I take a risk that paid off? Why did it work when by all accounts it should not have? What gave you the courage to take that leap? What were you thinking? What were you feeling? Who was encouraging you? Who was discouraging you?

HOW WAS YOUR COMPANY FOUNDED (WHETHER YOU ARE A BUSINESS OWNER OR WORK FOR A COMPANY)?

Countless people have come to this country with nothing, started from scratch, and built incredibly successful businesses. Countless entrepreneurs have mortgaged their homes to bet on their dreams. We love hearing stories like these. They inspire and spark something within us. They create a connection between us and those entrepreneurs and make us want to support their companies.

If you are an entrepreneur or business owner, the story behind how you took that leap can be an incredible one to share. Depending on the circumstances, it might show others your determination, ability to take calculated risks, perseverance, or innovation. This is the ultimate way to show, not tell.

If you work for a company, you can feel grounded and inspired by the reason why the company began, how it began, and the story of the founders. Then, you can share that story in person, on social media, with new employees—all to increase loyalty in that brand story.

Ask yourself: How did I make the leap into business ownership or to join this particular company? What gave me the idea and the courage to do so? Was it an easy transition or one fraught with bumps along the road?

THE LIGHT: BRAND STORIES RECAP

Storytelling is what connects and bonds us.

Stories grow out of your why, and must 100 percent authenticate it.

Stories are remembered twenty-two times more than facts.

Storytelling is effective for all types of learners.

Yes, you do have stories—everyone does!

Storytelling isn't bragging, it's SHARING.

Stories SHOW people who and what you are, which is far more effective than simply telling them.

Curating your stories carefully ensures people are seeing the qualities you want them to see in you.

Stories help you speak up for yourself and earn your worth.

Even tough times and "failures" make great stories—don't be afraid to share your trials and what you learned from them.

Stories build brand equity and authenticity.

Part Five

BRAND LEADER

"True leadership cannot be awarded, appointed, or assigned. It comes only from influence, and that cannot be mandated. It must be earned. The only thing a title can buy is a little time—either to increase your level of influence with others or to undermine it."

—JOHN MAXWELL

THE SPARK

Yes, You ARE a Leader

People who aren't in the C-Suite—whether they're straight out of college, in a mid-level support role, or don't do client-facing work—often say to me, "I don't lead anyone. I just do my job." But as John Maxwell tells us, 99 percent of all leadership comes from the middle of a company, not the top.

Chances are, you are already leading in some way, despite what you may think. Remember the janitor at NASA who proudly told President Kennedy he was helping put a man on the moon? He was a leader. No matter what you "do" as your job or where you are on the company ladder, you have that same capability.

The problem is that most people believe in the wrong things when it comes to leading. Title doesn't make you a leader. Position doesn't make you a leader.

You can lead by being at every meeting, on time, with a joyful attitude. You can lead by being an incredible communicator. You can bring teams together. You can be the one who puts the fire out on office gossip.

The act of leadership takes many forms, but there is only one way to define leadership—leadership is influence. Hard stop. I have called this brand equity for years.

You must build equity in who you are before you can lead. Jumping in, telling people what to do, being loud, controlling, or even rude makes you a terrible and uneducated colleague. Far from a leader.

Ask yourself: Why should people listen to you? What have you shared about yourself that has built your equity? Your value? Would you follow a stranger? I wouldn't. Neither should anyone. Think you're a leader? Do you have any followers? (For some of you, that was painful, but we are in this together. This entire book is the WHY, HOW, and WHAT of building brand equity so that you can actually have influence.)

You can also lead in areas of your life that have nothing to do with work. Leadership takes place inside of your home and community. I'm a soccer/volleyball/basketball mom, and one of my happiest places is at an event watching my kids compete and developing relationships with other parents. You don't have to be a senior vice president or on the director level to do any of that. We often forget that the same principles apply to leadership with our families—how we listen, speak, engage.

Besides, I've met people with incredible titles who couldn't lead their way through a marked trail in my backyard. Zero brand equity. Titles don't make someone a leader, and neither does work product.

Many people are incredibly efficient and hard-working. They get to work early, leave late, and don't waste time talking when they're in the office. But all that—while admirable—still doesn't translate into leadership.

You might be thinking right now, *No honestly, I really don't lead anyone. I don't even have an assistant!* Here's what I have to say to that: you don't have to command an army of people to be a leader. Many people think they aren't a leader because they're new, inexperienced, or don't know enough. This simply isn't the case. It's time to toss out the preconceived notion that you're not a leader. Turn around and look behind you. You may find you already have followers!

> If you're alive, you're leading something, somewhere—and the first person you need to lead is yourself.

This is why the first four chapters of this book were so important. Having a solid why and core values are the foundational pieces to becoming a leader people will CHOOSE to follow versus someone they *have* to follow. Why? Because it builds your brand equity—without equity, nobody SHOULD listen to you. Which would you rather be?

> Shout-out to John Maxwell: John, I've read all your books and been following you for years. Thank you for all of your insight and leadership. I'd love to be on your podcast, meet you, coffee?

THE FUEL

Leaders Are Confident

Early in my career, I often worried that I should somehow know everything about my client and their industry the minute I walked through their door. As a result, my confidence would quickly plummet. I'd question why I was doing what I was doing, if I was in the right place, and whether I was marketing my services appropriately. After all, who was I to tell people what to do?

With every successful project in every new business sector, I began to realize that learning about my clients' niches and their people, cultures, and challenges would come gradually—and that I was ALREADY the expert in the room when it came to coaching and branding. That's why they'd hired me!

I'm now completely confident when I walk in, no matter what the industry or issues facing them. I know my purpose, but I also have the experience, so my confidence is untouchable. It can't be swayed because one way or another, I will find a way to figure it out.

Good leaders always know the one or two things they are without a doubt experts in. They have incredible confidence because they know why they were created. They always have something to fall back on—a solid personal brand foundation.

Purpose gets you back up the same way Buster Douglas rose to his feet time and again despite the pounding he was taking from Mike Tyson. His mother told him that she knew he would win before she passed. Her belief in him added to his purpose, and gave him the confidence he needed to deliver on that promise. Remember, Douglas was a 42-to-1 underdog heading into his fight against Tyson—he wasn't supposed to beat Tyson.

If you're thinking Buster's feat was purely physical, you have it wrong. It was his MIND that allowed him to achieve what seemed impossible. When your mind says I *know my purpose*, your heart comes to believe it, and your body naturally follows. You keep going, putting one foot in front of the other, until you reach your goal. You're confident that you are on the right path, so you stick with it no matter how rough it gets.

This is why knowing who you are as a leader is so important. It's why you can't skip over why you do what you do. Without that, you will be easily swayed by others who may try to take you in the wrong direction. To lead effectively, you must have confidence in yourself, your gifting, and abilities.

Still, none of us is perfect. As a leader, there may be moments where you make the wrong decision, take a brand hit, or get thrown under a bus. Knowing your purpose and having confidence in your expertise helps you recover from mistakes faster and with more grace. Even more than that, every time I took a chance, succeeded, forged through a fire, and led with grace and strength, I gave people one more reason to follow me, believe in me, and most importantly, trust me.

LEADERS ARE CONSISTENT

Can you imagine General George Patton coming in acting one way one day, and then a different way the next? That would not inspire the troops' confidence. We can learn so much from Patton and apply his tactics, strategies, and leadership example to business.

Patton's leadership style can be best summed up by his quote, "Do everything you ask of those you command." What does that mean? Lead by example, do the work, know your business, get into the mud with your teams when needed, as often as needed. He finished by saying, "No good decision was ever made in a swivel chair."

Remember the Battle of the Bulge? (If you don't know what this is, you should. History is essential in being able to lead into the future. But I digress.) Patton had the incredible ability to instill trust into his troops. Consistency of behavior is a key factor in creating trust. Turning the tides during this key time in the war is considered one of the top military strategies of all time—but at the time, it was considered audacious, and some said, impossible.

As a leader, Patton had built equity in his leadership ability, but he also trusted his teams implicitly. So he not only was able to convince his leader, General Eisenhower, but he was able to get the buy-in from his troops. Without leadership equity, none of that would have happened.

Why don't people trust everyone and anyone to run with a good idea? Lead a group? Take over a project? Leadership equity. Brand equity. Weak personal brand. See how everything is tying in together?

Patton is an example of brand equity at its finest. I often say, "Would your teams follow you into a war?" His troops literally did—and what happened? Countless lives saved, Germans caught off guard, key victory. Everyone above and below him trusted his leadership and knew his decisions would always be incredibly sound. His consistency helped win the war.

Consistent leadership is as important for companies as it is in the military. Inconsistency leads to an unstable work environment, which leads to uncertainty and stress. I know we're not sitting in a foxhole in the middle of battle, but people need to be able to count on you the same way soldiers counted on the General. Your behavior must reflect the same kind of consistency he did before you can be trusted with important decisions that impact a team. The words used to describe you need to be the same whether they come from your friends, family, boss, a stranger, or employees.

Consistency is critical to effective leadership, but it can be extremely hard to put into practice (especially consistently!). This is why you have to put measures in place that ensure you'll show up in the same manner, time after time. For example, as I've mentioned before, I work out five days a week whether I want to or not—and let's be honest, many days I'd rather not. The reason I exercise is to be healthy and fit. But I'm able to exercise CONSISTENTLY because I put gym equipment in my garage. If I had to drive fifteen minutes to and from the gym and then spend another hour working out, it might never happen. I'd decide to be with my kids instead and poof, my commitment to fitness and health would fly right out the window. Because I can walk out into my garage and be finished working out in half an hour, I have zero excuses.

By creating a home gym, I set myself up for success. I made an intentional choice. I knew that in order to lead others, I had to be consistent in my own life. What can you do to consistently set yourself up for success in your own life?

Ask yourself: Do your team members know what they are walking into every day? Or do they tiptoe into the office wondering what type of mood you're going to be in? Why does that matter? When people know what they are walking into, they don't waste time focusing on emotion rather than focusing on their job.

LEADERS ARE APPROACHABLE

I recently worked with a young woman who'd moved up in her organization very quickly because of her incredible intelligence and superior job performance. The minute we met, I instantly loved her. The people who worked under her were a different story, though. They all disliked her wholeheartedly. Honestly, they couldn't STAND her.

I was so confused about the disconnect. This woman was brilliant. She had vision. She loved her team and only spoke well of them. She seemed to know their goals and what they needed in terms of coaching and training. One of the distinct differences was that she opened up to me immediately—showed me her heart, personality and shared pieces of her life. She hadn't done the same with any members of her team—they only knew the boss rather than the human. Common mistake.

When I talked to her people, they all told me, "Yes, she's smart. Yes, she gives us the right things to do. Yes, the work is great." What they didn't reveal was why they disliked her so much. I was at a loss.

I decided to hang out for a day and see if I could find some answers. It only took me twenty minutes to figure things out. When team members came into her office, she didn't smile or greet them. She wouldn't even fully look at them. So they'd stand there thinking, *Should I talk?* and stutter and stumble through whatever they needed to say.

When she'd finally turn her chair around to give that person her full attention, her face hung in a way that gave the impression she was incredibly annoyed. (Have you ever heard the term resting b*tch face? That's exactly what was happening here.) By the time she was able to say her catchphrase—which was an awkward "As you were saying?"— they would be completely flustered. Was it a good time to talk, a bad time to talk, or did she hate them?

It was honestly painful to watch. I thought, *Surely this must be a one-off thing*. But no—it happened all day long. I watched her lead a meeting where she repeated the exact same behavior.

After everyone else had gone home, I said to her, "Wow, you've clearly had a day, judging by the look on your face!"

She stared at me, eyes wide with surprise. "What do you mean? I was thinking through things. Sometimes if I'm looking at someone I get distracted, so I don't always make eye contact because I want my thoughts to be cohesive and give people all the details they need to do their job well."

It turns out, her greatest fear was letting her team down. As a result, she was always overthinking things and trying to prepare for what might come next. Her intentions were good, but her actions came off horribly rude.

We worked together and it was a pretty easy fix, frankly. Her team eventually ended up liking her, but not before she had a Come to Jesus talk with them where she had to admit, "This is what I was doing. This is the impression I thought I was sending. Will you guys forgive me?"

Because her behavior changed drastically after that, everyone did. We built out her team, gave them all the training they needed, and every- thing turned out beautifully. The department ended up growing by over 20 percent the next quarter and becoming incredibly successful. If I hadn't been there, would the team have succeeded? Would she have been promoted as a partner? Probably not. Why? Nobody was willing to talk with her about it. Sometimes you have to lead by having a tough, transparent, and loving conversation. Sometimes it works out, sometimes it doesn't, but at least you tried.

As a leader, being approachable and receptive to others is an absolute necessity. You can't say you have an open-door policy and then not turn your chair around when someone comes to you with a question. You have to be aware of your facial expression and ensure you look welcoming and interested in what they have to say. You need to have a vocal tone that inspires and motivates. Even more than this, leaders are constantly aware of their actions and how they affect others.

Great leaders encourage interaction and leave others feeling inspired and motivated, not confused or scared. Stay aware, show you care, and make people feel like you appreciate their presence. Leaders either have this naturally or develop the muscle of self-awareness, which falls under the umbrella of emotional intelligence (more on these later).

The ability to see how behavior—every move, body movement, eye contact, vocal tone, choice of words and more—impacts an organization.

LEADERS ARE EMPATHETIC

Want a superpower? Develop and learn how to authentically deploy empathy. Without empathy, failure is certain. Some would argue this IS the secret to leadership.

How else do you know that the person you are trying to reach is actually reached? When you're negotiating or selling, how else do you really understand the desires of the person on the other side of the table? Build and nurture a team? Eventually love those you lead?

Empathy is what allows you into someone's life, psyche, and eventually their heart in a way that simply being smart or helpful never could. It's easy to forget because we all get so caught up in our own stresses and fears, but I truly don't know if a greater trait than empathy exists.

Empathy can be defined as:

1. the ability to understand and share the feelings of another;
2. the capacity to understand or feel what someone else is experiencing from within that person's frame of reference versus your own; *or*
3. the ability to understand another person's experience, perspective and feelings.

Can you put yourself in someone else's shoes?

When you're empathetic, you have the ability to put yourself in someone else's shoes and see all sides of situations. You must assess how THEY feel in THEIR shoes—not how YOU would feel in their shoes. Big difference. You pick up on other people's emotional cues. You can speak the truth into any situation while still giving people a safe place to fall.

An empathetic leader isn't one that says, "Oh, you're right. I understand completely," because someone's emotional. Empathy is not about right or wrong—it's that you're taking the time to see, hear, and feel what's going on. Empathy is what allows you to understand the why or emotion BEHIND what someone is saying (especially on social media these days) instead of wanting to squash them for having a different opinion.

Some people think kindness is a weakness and that being empathetic means you're not being a leader. Often, I'll ask clients, "Why don't you care about your people?" The answer is usually, *I do, but I can't show them. I'm their boss!* They think leaders have to be hard—sometimes to the extent of being rude—to make people see and follow them. Nothing could be further from the truth! Side note: If you learned from a former boss or manager that style of "leadership," you learned wrong. Unlearn those terrible traits or you'll fail like they did.

Empathy actually INCREASES your efficacy and value as a leader. An empathetic leader who has a little less knowledge is going to be a thousand times more successful than the most intelligent jerk on the planet. Kindness garners loyalty in ways nothing else will.

Empathetic leaders foster differences, understand we have different ideas and perspectives, and recognize others' strengths and weaknesses. While you don't need to know all the nitty gritty details of everyone's life, you certainly do have to be able to put yourself in that person's position in order to lead them out of any rabbit hole they've dug themselves into or to push them toward the next goal they have.

There's plenty of data to support the importance of empathy in business. According to *Businessolver's 2017 Workplace Empathy Monitor*, empathy has a direct impact on employee productivity, loyalty, and engagement. This report found that 77 percent of workers would be willing to work more hours, and 60 percent would actually accept a slashed salary in a more empathetic workplace.

Still more data backs up the importance of empathy: 80 percent of millennials and 66 percent of baby boomers said they'd leave their current job if their office became less empathetic; 92 percent of HR professionals note that a compassionate workplace is a major factor for employee retention.

In the popular *Harvard Business Review* article "What Makes a Leader?", Dr. Daniel Goleman isolates three reasons why empathy is so important:

- the increasing use of teams, (which he refers to as "cauldrons of bubbling emotions");
- the rapid pace of globalization (with cross-cultural communication easily leading to misunderstandings); and

- the growing need to retain talent.

Leaders with empathy are always more successful. I don't have a specific statistic to back that one up, but I do have experience. If you've ever worked for an empathetic leader, you know exactly what I mean. You do more for them. You're more loyal to them. You feel safe spreading your wings with them.

Being an empathetic leader enables you to build better teams, which in turn builds better companies. Empathy benefits everyone: employees, leaders, companies, and maybe even the entire world. And on another note, the more empathetic you are, the more people open up to you, trust you, and come to you with all things. Once you get to know people, you have the ability to discern their gifting, see how it fits into the workplace, build their gifting, and create immense value for your team and for their lives.

LEADERS HAVE INTEGRITY

Dwight Eisenhower once said, "The supreme quality of leadership is unquestionably integrity. Without it, no real success is possible, no matter whether it is on a section gang, a football field, in an army, or in an office." (Fun fact: a section gang is a crew responsible for maintaining a specific segment of train tracks.)

As a leader, your actions, treatment of others, and even your thoughts must always reflect the highest level of integrity. No amount of brilliance or brand equity can make up for a lack of it.

I have had so many people tell me about their lack of integrity: I cheated on my books. I lied to my boss. I misrepresented things to the board. I gossiped. I never apologized for what I did. (That's a big one). I listen with empathy, and then explain that lapses of integrity often arise out of fear. Fear of not being enough, fear of being "found out," fear of not succeeding, or even not succeeding fast enough. Fear does not create a filter that encourages integrity. I always encourage them to come clean and fix the damage they've caused themselves or others.

Most people have lapses of integrity because they think they aren't enough, so they feel like they have to lie about who they are, what they have, what they've accomplished, and how they do their job. Others have lapses of integrity because they are so afraid of transparency—they avoid conflict like the plague—and aren't rooted solidly in who they are. If I screw up with a client, in a company, wherever, I say, "I screwed up and here's my thought on fixing this" rather than lie. Others might make up something to tell their bosses why or even blame others. Integrity breach!

Integrity breaches are easy to have and most of the time they start as seemingly small cracks. But you get enough cracks in your foundation and BOOM, no integrity. Reputation done.

A loss of integrity is the hardest, most painful thing to come back from. The consequences reverberate for years and possibly a lifetime. If this is something you struggle with: stop, drop, and roll. Seek help from friends, mentors, or other professionals. Don't do anything else until you figure out how to repair your broken filter. In the end, the legacy you leave through integrity is greater than any amount of money you could ever earn.

The path I've taken enables me to tell you that integrity is more important than anything in the world. I can't repeat it enough: You were meant to live your purpose WITHOUT HAVING TO LIE ABOUT IT.

That's sticking to your values. That's understanding why you do what you do. That's knowing who you are.

LEADERS ARE READERS

People who are crushing it personally and professionally never stop learning. They study what other leaders—business leaders, thought leaders, personal development leaders—are saying and doing to gain a wider perspective. Success comes from maintaining a continuous flow of information and truth into your heart.

This is big. Truth isn't subjective. Always check your sources. Don't believe anyone simply because they are an expert. TEST EVERYTHING.

Reading is the best way to learn and explore different perspectives. Of course, you can spend eight hours a day on your phone flipping through social media and reading comments (versus engaging, which you should be doing, which we'll get to in Part Eight)—but imagine if you took the next six months to read the books, articles, data, and studies written by industry leaders instead. How much more you would know versus scrolling Facebook and watching people fight about politics?

What you read and study is who you become, so it's important to filter what you're putting into your mind. Spend your time in the most productive, positive manner possible.

What does that look like on a daily basis? I advocate using the five-hour rule. That's when you commit to reading an hour a day, five days a week. Warren Buffett, Richard Branson, and Mark Cuban all practice this method. Keep a running list of books you want to read and prioritize them based on what's happening at work, with your team, and in your life.

In his book *Rich Habits: The Daily Success Habits of Wealthy Individuals*, author Thomas Corley found that wealthy individuals rarely watch television, and consume books voraciously. Whether listening to audiobooks or reading them, the goal is self-improvement. According to productivity expert Choncé Maddox in *Business Insider*, the average millionaire reads two or more books a month.

As a leader, wisdom is incredibly important, and voracious reading (or audiobook listening), is one of the greatest differentiators you can create. People who know more lead more effectively. It's as simple as that.

I'm headquartered in Nashville, so one of the first things I always ask my local clients is, "What have you seen lately in the *Nashville Business Journal* that sparked your interest?" Staying up to date on the local business journal, knowing who the leaders are in your city, following them on social media, and reading what they're reading is critical. You need to be current and well-informed, especially if you're in the C-suite and don't have as many personal mentors as you did earlier in your career.

Another favorite question I ask is, "What's your favorite John Maxwell book?" If you're not familiar with his work, I encourage you to start with *The Five Levels of Leadership*. In it, Maxwell talks about positional leadership. All too often, people come into a company with a certain title and number of reports automatically thinking, *I'm rocking it. I have a name.* The thing is, they haven't yet established their brand equity and value. They simply have a title, and that's it. Don't let that be you. Be a true leader (who is a reader!). Share the best books and articles with others. Be the one who wants everyone else around them to succeed.

Some people have blinders on and only see what's going on within their own company. Effective leaders know what's going on locally as well as globally. They follow industry and business news as a whole. This allows them to be versatile in conversation.

You must be able to discuss matters with anyone in the world at any time. I often tell people my heritage is Serbian and get a glazed look. Then I say, "You know, there was a war over there in the early 90s that the US took part in." Still nothing. Know your history. If not, you look ignorant.

A huge part of being a leader is Constant and Never-Ending Improvement (CANI), as Tony Robbins terms it. Reading and learning as a means of constant and never-ending improvement helps you stay in the know and turn on a dime. Things are shifting so fast in the world today, and you must be able to shift as fast or faster. The key is to keep your mind growing—because if you're not growing, you're dying.

> Shout-out to Tony Robbins: Tony, I want to share with everyone what an inspiration you are! As I listen to other leaders and consultants, I can always hear your words through them (and I am 100 percent in this category). Constant and Never-Ending Improvement (CANI) is one of those concepts everyone needs to know and implement in their lives, so thank you for that. I'm grateful for the time and effort you've put into coaching others, because it has been life-changing for so many. I will fly anywhere in the world to meet you at any time—say the word!

LEADERS FOCUS ON BRAND

Brand drives everything.

As a leader, your brand either reinforces or undermines the company brand. That's why it's so important to know your core values and use them as a filter for everything you do. There's so much more opportunity within your reach when your values uphold the corporate brand.

Jack Welch, former CEO of General Electric, said, "Good business leaders create a vision, articulate the vision, passionately own the vision, and relentlessly drive it to completion." To be a great leader like him, use the corporate or company 'why' to encourage, inspire, drive passion, and create a unified culture. You must also SHARE why the company is moving in the direction they are moving, as well as the strategy and action plan to achieve that goal. This keeps everyone moving in the same direction.

It's your job to remind them, *Brand is how we share our message and get work. Brand strength is what helps us win in the market.* It's also your job to enforce and hold your team accountable to the corporate values and get their buy-in, which increases loyalty and resolve when working through your values every single day. Instill, infuse, and exude the corporate, company, firm, or association brand to your team, over and over again.

This is how you lead a team. This is how you encourage them. This is how you create consistency in the marketplace. If you have team members acting outside of these attributes, the brand starts to weaken and crack. People outside the company can see those cracks, whether you realize it or not.

You might say, *Well, I work in finance. I don't really need to know the values of the company.* This is completely untrue. If you're a CFO and you're giving a quarterly report on Zoom or you're having a conference call with your investors, use the company core values—for instance, integrity and compassion—to deliver that message. You must project your company's values in every situation, from the certainty of your information, to your tone of voice, to the way you write and email. It's all the time, never-ending, can't sleep on it—brand is alive in all things.

How will you know if you and your team are successfully reinforcing the company brand? If you're landing clients because people love to work with your team (or, if you're not outward facing, when other departments in your company love to work with your team). And when that becomes the case, you'll have the opportunity to skyrocket to the top of your company.

LEADERS LEAD WITH LOVE

John Maxwell advocates leading with love. People work harder and longer for leaders who are loving rather than fear-provoking. I know some of you reading this right now are cringing at the thought of using the word love in a business context. You might even find yourself feeling prideful about being the hammer dropper at your company. But remember that leader who once told me it was okay to fail, but to fail fast? I felt this reflected his love and faith in me, and I've never been more able to be creative or efficient. Maybe fear isn't the great motivator you thought it was.

I once worked with a woman who was incredibly tough and intimidating but held the entire company together. She had an encyclopedic knowledge of all its ins and outs. If you had a question, she had the answer, whether it was, *Is our gardener coming on Tuesday? Did we meet revenue goals in 1984?* or *Where are the paper towels kept?* That was her gifting, and people relied on her so much, they were terrified of what might happen if she ever became sick or left.

HOWEVER—the people who worked for her feared her. Because she knew every detail of absolutely everything, she would give others a hard time when they didn't. In all her efficiency, she forgot about the value of empathy, compassion, and love. How much more could have been accomplished if she'd shown kindness to people? How much better communication would her team have had? What could her legacy have been then?

Innovation and efficiency happen when people are full of joy. They produce more and better-quality work under a benevolent reign than a dictatorship. Love is always the answer. Developing relationships; loving those you lead; growing loyalty, influence, and ultimately the business.

Don't let the word love sway you or become "cheesy." You can still be the boss and hold teams accountable. But do you really want the best for the people you are leading? Your filter, even when chastising, should be love first.

> When leaders love, nothing is ever about themselves—it is always about others.

If you stop loving your people, stop leading.

LEADERS INFLUENCE OTHERS

Warren Buffett has built his leadership and brand equity to a level where people take notice of what he has to say. If he walked in the room right now, we'd all sit down and listen, whether we agree with him or not. We'd do the same for most presidents, generals, and Fortune 500 CEOs. Why? Because they have influence.

Tony Robbins says influence is the greatest power we can have. As a leader, you need to build and use your influence for the greater good. When you know the why of each of your team members, it becomes easy to exert your influence in a positive way, showing people how to work for the benefit of the company while simultaneously growing personally and professionally.

Paying attention to purpose enables you to steer people—to influence them—in the direction of their goals. You can add an activity to their life, responsibility to their job description, or share an opportunity that is 100 percent aligned with their why. For instance, you might encourage someone to serve on a nonprofit board or invite them to join a committee at work. If I know somebody lives to provide for their family and another lives to be seen/known/revered, how I influence them to reach their goals is night and day.

If you don't know what gets your employees out of bed in the morning or only know as a means to check it off the list, that's a bigger problem. I want you to take a step back and recognize this as an accountability moment. Have you taken the time to invest in your people and understand their goals?

Your influence—and how you use it for the greater good—is the ultimate form of leadership. Find ways to spark joy and lead your team to their dreams.

When you are able to bring joy into someone's life that you lead or work with—even amidst the worst moments—this is leadership at the highest level. I coached someone who was extremely creative and very talented as a writer. He could maneuver from selling a story to sharing a story to changing how it was written to appeal to specific audiences and so on.

This man had worked for years at a company that told him he was not worthwhile. It made him second guess all of his talent and gifting. I was able to figure out pretty quickly he had not only been treated poorly, but his old boss was an idiot and didn't see the gem he was. I didn't have to teach him much and allowed his talent to be freed.

I knew he needed the joy of being on a team that gave him the freedom to be creative, a safe place to fall when sharing ideas, and a loving yet direct way of helping him shift gears. He is now the head of a successful division at his company and leading others with empathy while bringing joy everywhere he goes. He needed freedom, space, safety, and recognition. Once he had that, he flew.

LEADERS ASK FOR FEEDBACK

When I was in my early twenties, I didn't think about other people as much as I should have. I'll never forget the day a friend sat me down and gave me some hard to hear but incredibly valuable feedback. She said, "I love you, but you're a terrible friend."

Her words had the effect of ice water being thrown in my face (which was good—I needed it and it's certainly how I learn). Before I could reply or get defensive, she continued, "You often say you'll be here when I invite you over, and then you don't show up. You promise to call and the phone never rings. You always have an excuse, but you never do what you say you're going to do."

I thought about it and realized she was right. The problem was, I WANTED to say yes to everybody and every invitation. Unfortunately, that often meant I was overstretched and, as a result, I was letting people down left and right. I was like the leader who never turned her chair around when her team members came to talk to her—I had good intentions, but my actions came off as horrendously rude.

Though it was hard to hear, I truly appreciated my friend's feedback. She delivered the truth with grace, and it salvaged our relationship when she could have written me off. Without her strong words, how many friendships would I have torched before figuring out the problem was me?

How willing are you to hear this kind of feedback? I'll never forget the time a CEO asked me to sit in on a meeting with one of the leaders of his company. He felt I could offer different perspectives and provide additional insight to the conversation. The second the CEO started to offer feedback to this leader, he started to fight back.

Well, it's the team.

Well, it's this project.

Well, this person hasn't done a very good job.

The leader offered excuses and even some lies, not accountability.

With his team's permission, I'd written down everything they'd said about him as well as things I'd observed myself. I told him, "This is the reality you're faced with right now, and you have a choice. You can take all of this transparency and push it away—but eventually you'll be fired or your team will quit. Failure is inevitable with the path that you're on."

He looked like he might be about to start defending himself again, but then nodded. I continued, "Or, you can choose to listen to the feedback we've given you, take stock of your leadership skills, and grow through this. We can't say you're not good at your job because technically you are. But we can certainly say that you're a really poor leader. It's not going to be easy, but I will walk through this with you. Otherwise, I imagine you'll be replaced. That's it." Long pause.

It was a "step back" moment for him, and he eventually made the right choice. He took in the feedback, made changes, and became a much stronger leader. Can you do the same?

Even if you're at the pinnacle of your career, it's good for you to take stock of where you are now, because it likely isn't the same place you were in five years ago. Ask your colleagues and team what they really think. Be willing to hear some hard truths along with the praise you'll surely receive. I really can't count the amount of times I meet with someone who believes people think one thing and it is nowhere near what they really think. Leaders know. Period.

I'm not talking about doing an online DISC 360 or StrengthsFinder here. I'm talking about doing your own 360. Do you have a process for your employees to let you know how you're doing, what they're thinking, what they're worried about, things you can do better?

Many clients tell me, *Oh, my employees would never do that.* (And the reverse, *Oh, I could never tell my boss what I really think.*) As a leader, you have a decision to make: is my team going to practice transparency and value candor or not?

Giving people room to provide honest feedback benefits everyone— you, your employees, and even the company as a whole. Leaders who don't want to hear it and push things under the rug deal with a lot of turnover and unhappy staff. Leaders who consistently listen to feedback, take accountability for their actions, and communicate both successes and failures are the ones who win.

Ask yourself: do you know what people really think about your leadership skills? It's a big deal. Without candid feedback, you won't rise above your current level of growth. The best course of action is to ask, listen, learn, and adapt.

I worked with the leadership of a manufacturing company once. I was brought in to talk about brand, communication, emotional intelligence—all of the personal branding things—as well as training on the values and vision of the company. The leaders (executive suite) told me repeatedly that they loved their people and the feeling was mutual. I thought, "Great! This certainly makes training and buy-in much easier."

But the minute—and I mean the minute—I walked in, I was ambushed. The employees started to tell me everything wrong: the lies they were told, how overworked and unappreciated they were, the lack of communication or respect they felt. PHEW! Talk about Pandora's Box being opened.

I listened. I told them I wasn't brought in for what they were discussing but that I would create a line of communication. The leadership in the company was shocked, so I took a huge step back and started with training the executive team. A year later, the ship was finally righted. It's crucial to be AWARE of what your teams really think.

LEADERS HELP OTHERS BE THEIR BEST

John Quincy Adams once said, "If your actions inspire others to dream more, learn more, do more, and become more, you are a leader."

I recently worked with a company where I met a bright young woman who was being overlooked by others. She was fresh out of college and working as an assistant, and I quickly realized she had a gift other people weren't seeing. We talked quite a bit, and I was able to help discover her talent and gifting and map out a plan to align those with her job. She recently sent me a text that said: *Thanks for helping me find my why and giving me the inspiration to go for my goals!*

Messages like hers are what make my job so rewarding. Sure, I delivered on marketing and branding for that company—but I also helped a young woman find her why. The company now has a loyal and hardworking employee whom they don't have to worry about leaving, and I was able to deliver on the very reason I was put here on earth. What a win-win!

Part of being a leader is helping people to be their best—by honing in on their purpose, working to build their brand, and making sure others see their value. If you don't know these things about your employees, your company will miss out. According to *Entrepreneur*, companies that invest in personal branding initiatives have employees who are 27 percent more optimistic about the company's future, 20 percent more likely to stay at the company, and 40 percent more likely to believe the company is more competitive.

In other words, when people are not only working for a paycheck but also a purpose, they want to stay there for you. You experience less turnover (and the high costs associated with it). The trickle-down effect is more than you can possibly imagine.

A lot of people don't realize they have a gift. Your job is to help dig that out and point out what it is. Perhaps it's, "When you speak, the team listens—because they know you have integrity, empathy, and consistency." It's not enough to simply promote people based on the easy and most visible thing (which is normally a work product). Find out what value your people bring besides what they "do" as a job. That's where the magic lies.

I once worked with a man who was incredibly high-performing and passionate about his work. He was a strong leader in his industry, but an incredibly weak one when it came to leading his team. Growing his people, recognizing what their needs were, giving them the training they needed, and communicating with them was not something he'd ever given much thought to. When we worked together, I asked, "Who have you grown up? I know you're big on creating opportunities for your team, but it seems like you're not big on growing them."

The team felt like they were under a mushroom and he was the cap covering them.

Being a good leader is not only about doing YOUR job well. It's about growing others and giving THEM the opportunity to be the best they can be. Helping your people build an authentic personal brand is one of the best ways you can accomplish this goal.

LEADERS MENTOR AND SPONSOR

Mentors are teachers who devote their time and resources helping others grow. Sponsors promote others, speaking out on the behalf of people they believe in. True leaders do both—they mentor AND sponsor.

I've frequently been asked to mentor others, and have been blessed by people's compassion, time, and experience when they mentored me. When you identify someone you think could benefit from your talents and wisdom, ask to mentor them. Be forthright in your communication. Tell them directly, "I see something in you, and I want to help you grow and add to your success."

It's your job as a leader to help others rise as you once did. When I work with corporate clients, I often identify several people I'd like to mentor even after my consulting work there is over. I continue our relationship, offering up wisdom when I think it's necessary and staying in touch as a resource.

Great leaders lend their time, attention, and voices to helping others get ahead. They bring others up as others brought them up. Who are you doing that for?

LEADERS DELIVER TRUTH WITH GRACE

Leaders are often required to make tough choices and have hard conversations, and that includes holding people accountable for their actions. Having a backbone is critical, but there's nothing that says you can't be empathetic while also holding someone accountable. Those two qualities are not mutually exclusive.

For instance, you can fire somebody with both truth and grace. You don't have to thrash and bash someone to deliver a serious message. You might say, "I understand how you were feeling when you did that. However, you can no longer work here. I have no doubt you're going to learn from this and will reach the pinnacle of success at a new company."

As Pastor James McDonald says, truth without grace is brutality. Humiliation is not a communication strategy. It only reflects poor leadership.

Rehearsing your strategy and knowing how you're going to begin and end the conversation before jumping in is always a good idea. Set a goal of discovering how you can help people in the moment. You may share advice or a story that helps get your point across. Take into consideration this person's life, goals, and how they are going to react to what you're saying, and consider where they've been and where they're going.

Truth with grace is the best type of leadership. It enforces consequences while allowing others to maintain their dignity—and you, your humanity.

LEADERS DON'T TOLERATE GOSSIP

Gossip is the biggest culture killer there is. What you say—and what you allow others to say in your presence—is a direct reflection of your values as well as your leadership skills. True leaders don't gossip, and they don't tolerate it from anyone else, either.

And yes, I've done it. You've done it. EVERYONE has done it. The trick is, don't do it again. Let's get better as we get older. If you're still gossiping like you're in high school, deeper issues are beneath and you should definitely explore that!

Not only do you need to be conscious of what you SAY about people—you even need to be aware of what you THINK about people. Leaders keep their thoughts at the front of their minds at all times. As I've said before, the battle is for the mind every day. If you've already thought about it, your mind is taking over. You ask yourself, *Why did I think that?*

Those values we talk about? That is your filter. Before a word leaves your lips, ask yourself, do they represent each value?

At the same time, while you likely agree that you don't like gossip, are you willing to call people out on it? Let's say you overhear two colleagues talking about a third one. Of course, you don't want to turn around and be the third grader who says, "I'm going to tell the teacher on you!" But by not confronting it, you are tacitly approving of that behavior. Instead, follow up with the parties involved privately and let them know it's unacceptable: "Talking about our colleagues creates pain and distrust. I know that's not the person you want to be. I trust you won't do it again."

Leadership is tough especially in situations like this. But again, if you love those you lead and they know you love them, it is fairly easy to lead even with a tough conversation. If you haven't put the time in to love your teams, your advice in any capacity won't be heard as it should. It comes down to intent. If people know your intent, it makes leading so much simpler.

I once worked with a company where gossip started in the C-suite and trickled down from there. It seemed to be an ingrained part of the culture. The single internal team there that was kind, caring, and non-gossiping was referred to as the goody-goody group. As a consultant—even though I'd been hired to help with branding and marketing—I felt I had to address this situation because it was truly hurting the company. No one trusted anyone, hurt feelings abounded, and people were leaving.

As a leader, you have to be willing to confront this type of situation and create a line in the sand. Your brand must let people know that gossip is non-negotiable. Identifying and weeding out the company gossip is the quickest way to change a culture from negative to positive.

A gossiper is a culture killer. It doesn't matter what you say your values are, how amazing your brand guide is—if you allow it, even one time to go unchecked—you're unleashing an empowered culture killer. And now it's YOUR fault.

From this moment on, you have a choice: to not tolerate gossip in the workplace, or let it continue to insidiously bring down the culture. As the saying goes, one bad apple spoils the bunch. Good leaders know to hire fast and fire faster, and that includes the company gossip.

LEADERS FORGIVE AND FORGET

Some leaders have a hard time letting go of mistakes. But can you imagine someone bringing up one you made ten years ago? That'd be unfair. You've surely grown and matured in that time.

I've seen people hold others in a prison of their past mistakes without encouragement, and it doesn't help anyone involved. Everyone deserves the benefit of the doubt. As leaders, we have to allow our teams to make mistakes and then move forward once the situation has been addressed and rectified.

Stop focusing on failures. Use them as a way to teach others. For instance, I often talk about my husband's failure as well as my own to show others you can come out on the other side of mistakes even stronger than you were before—and that taking risks means you're also risking failure. This kind of authenticity is contagious.

Failure is a crucial ingredient for success. If you're not failing, you're not trying. When people fail—either purposefully or by accident—you can choose whether to fire them or not, but you don't get to choose forgiveness. IF you choose to keep them, then GROW them. Don't hold their failure in front of them daily. Who would get better or grow under the umbrella of constant shame? As Dr. Shawne Duperon, founder of the Project Forgive Foundation, said in *Inc.* magazine, "Forgiveness is a bold leadership skill. "

Let transparency and accountability be essential to your culture. Then forgive, forget, grow the person, and help everyone to move on.

THE FIRE

Kindness Breeds Loyalty

I once had a history teacher in high school who was so nice, I'll never forget him. I don't remember what I was going through in my life at the time, but one day in class I was so tired that I fell asleep on my desk. Instead of getting me in trouble, he gently woke me and told me to go to his office to take a nap, which I clearly needed.

After class was over—which I slept clear through—he woke me and told me to go on with my day. He never asked for an explanation or made me feel bad about it. Instead of seeing a child sleeping in his class and thinking, *How rude*, he simply thought, *Wow, she must be tired*.

I worked 10,000 times harder for him after that day.

One act of kindness garners incredible loyalty. Leaders should intentionally look for authentic moments to do that. When you're kind, people will work harder for you. They will follow you when you've shown you care about them.

Much later in life, I worked with a company where a beloved founder had recently passed away. Whenever he'd walk through the hallways, he'd ask how people were doing. He never broke eye contact as he was inquiring about people's parents, partners, and kids. He always listened with great respect to what they had to say.

Employees knew he cared. There wasn't that twinge of fear that sometimes accompanies talking to a company leader. The feeling was more like, *Man, I hope he stops at my door today!*

When this founder died, he left a big, gaping hole in the company. Employees still get emotional when they talk about him to this day. He was seen as the heart and soul of the company—all because he treated his employees with kindness and care.

Put some heart in your leadership. It pays dividends in loyalty and respect.

LEADERS ARE READERS OF PEOPLE, TOO

Great leaders know it's not only imperative to read books, newspapers, and articles—they also need to be able to read PEOPLE. Helping others navigate the emotional landscape of the workplace sets the tone for honest, open conversations while eliminating misunderstandings. Leaders who have honed this ability are better able to influence outcomes and change narratives for the better.

For instance, I worked with a CEO whose ability to read people was his greatest gifting. As a consultant who coaches on emotional intelligence, I'm usually the one everybody thinks is an oracle. Not this time. Within minutes, this leader knew what my insecurities were and where they came from, and how I was feeling at any given moment. His reading of me was so spot-on, it actually caught me off guard.

He even gave me the downlow on some of the people I'd be coaching during my contract there. In particular, he told me my empathetic yet direct personality would probably have a tougher time with one employee who always thought they were right and didn't like to be challenged. It was so helpful to know, and it allowed me to approach that person in a way that they could better understand and implement my suggestions.

Because this CEO was so attuned to what others were thinking and feeling, our meetings always ran smoothly. He always sat at the head of the boardroom table and observed people. If emotions were rising and making it difficult for the team to listen to one another, he'd step in and rephrase the point in different ways so other people could hear it. He seamlessly brought introverts into the conversation where they might have been otherwise overlooked. He kept extroverts from doing all the talking. As a result, people were calm and full of empathy. Nobody ever felt unheard.

The other key to his leadership was his ability to be transparent. He would say, "John, I can see you're reacting to what Sue said, but I believe she meant it this way." It was awesome watching him wade through emotions in real time, saving so much frustration and energy in the end. He believed in knowing people's intent and then sharing it with others. If someone said something that seemed rude but it wasn't the intent because they weren't as emotionally aware, he would help them by stating what happened and allowing the person to rephrase it. Hours and hours and hours of time saved.

You might be thinking, *That's all good and well, but it sounds exhausting and time-consuming.* You know what's more exhausting and time-consuming—not to mention expensive?—simmering emotions that make it difficult or impossible for your team to work together. Poor results because of hurt feelings and mistrust. Missed deadlines over a miscommunication.

If you spend enough time learning to read people, it eventually becomes second nature. You then teach others how to read their own emotions, along with other people's, by example. When you do all this successfully, the emotional tone of the office shifts, and both personal satisfaction and overall productivity soar.

KEEP CALM AND CARRY ON

Allow me to tell you a story: A woman was sitting in her house when a black snake slithered by her feet. She was deathly afraid of snakes, so she screamed for her husband. He jumped out of the shower, wrapped a towel around his waist, ran in the room, grabbed an old broom, and started poking around under the couch. Their dog was curious about what was going on and touched his nose to the back of the husband's heel. The husband then fainted, because he thought he had been bitten by the snake rather than sniffed by his dog. The wife assumed the husband was having a heart attack, so she ran to the hospital, which was a block away. Two EMTs followed her back to the house, and as they were carrying the husband out on the stretcher, the snake reappeared from under the couch. One of the EMTs became so scared, he dropped the stretcher and broke the husband's leg. Seeing her husband's leg broken, the wife collapsed on the spot. Meanwhile, the snake slithered quietly away.

The moral of the story is, of course, that panicking never solves anything. In fact, it often makes things far worse than they would have been in the first place. This goes double for leaders in the workplace. If you missed a deadline, you missed a deadline. If you missed a meeting, you missed a meeting. Panic will not change that.

Calmness is a strength that comes with experience. People are much more likely to follow a calm leader than a crazy person yelling in a microphone. Good leaders know the key to success is staying calm even in the most stressful of situations.

Whether you agree or disagree with Supreme Court Justice Amy Coney Barrett, she was amazing to watch while she was being grilled during her confirmation hearings. She repeatedly—and CALMLY—stated that her duty was to the law, and that she had chosen things that go against her personal beliefs because the law is the law. This incredible ability to stay calm under pressure comes from knowing exactly what she believes—integrity. When you act with integrity, it's easy to stay calm because the truth is on your side.

An African proverb says there are forty kinds of lunacy, but only one kind of common sense. Staying calm under pressure is using that common sense. It means you're more likely to make the right decisions. How? Use your values as a filter to breathe, take a moment to reassess a crazy situation, and then use those values to say the right thing and lead your team in the best direction.

Take a deep breath. Keep calm. And carry on.

LITTLE THINGS MAKE A BIG IMPACT

Joe Scarlet, former CEO of Tractor Supply, used to send me any column I wrote for the business journal with a personal note saying how much he enjoyed it. I was astounded how someone that important was willing to take the time to do that for me. My loyalty toward him skyrocketed because of this small but thoughtful act of kindness and recognition. Over time, I realized that was something he often did for so many, along with personal notes, emails, and even calls. Leadership at its best.

Another example: I know a woman who is on multiple corporate boards across the world. She's one of the smartest, and dare I say, coolest people I've ever met. Whenever I email her, she answers back within minutes. I am constantly amazed by her effort in that regard knowing how much influence, power, and importance she yields across industries. Her actions make me, and others, feel like the most important people in the world.

People who are at the pinnacle of success didn't arrive there by being rude. They reached that peak by writing notes. Sending columns. Answering emails at the speed of light when possible. The importance of kindness and common courtesy cannot be overstated.

As the saying goes, a rising tide lifts all ships.

THE HEAT

Leveling Up Your Leadership

Leadership is not only about hitting a budget, exceeding a revenue goal, meeting a deadline, or hiring and firing. Those are simply tasks. Leaders are more concerned about people—and when that's the case, revenue somehow follows. The budget always seems to be met. Goals are exceeded. Putting your time, effort, energy, and intent into developing others is where the rubber meets the road for businesses.

Remember Tony Robbins' edict of constant and never-ending improvement? It's something all leaders need to practice! So let's pause now to evaluate how you're showing up as a leader: where you're killing it, and where you could use some improvement.

Use your answers to the following questions to level up your leadership skills and help others fulfill their life's purpose. That's the ultimate leadership goal!

DO YOU LEAD WITH LOVE OR FEAR?

I once worked with a man who created an immense amount of fear in everyone he met. If you asked, people would say, "Oh no, he's fine," but that's only because they were terrified to speak out against him. The truth was, he was a gossiper and a culture killer. He yelled and fumed, was in everyone's face, and never had any data or experience to back up his work.

This man's behavior was in complete contrast to the CEO of the company, who was incredibly empathetic and caring. Every time he did something outrageously inappropriate, I'd expect the CEO to fire him. Instead...nada. It was so surprising, I actually used to wonder if he "had" something on the CEO.

Some leaders allow culture killers to stay in their companies because they perceive the performance is worth the bad behavior. This is never the case. Fear is no way to lead effectively. Love is. Which do you want your legacy to reflect?

Side note: Regardless of how "good" someone is at their job, if they kill your culture, you're dead in the water anyway. More than that, if you take too long to fire them, your culture takes years to fix. It's a mess. Hire fast, fire faster.

Ask yourself: Do I inspire others, or do I instill fear? Does my team resent me and work hard, or does my team love me and work hard? Would my team members be more effective and efficient if they felt more cared about?

DO YOU SPEAK FROM EXPERIENCE?

I know of several leadership groups where the only rule for adding to the conversation is that you must have experience behind the advice you're giving. That can be hard because some of us have thoughts, an intuition, or secondhand knowledge about situations we'd like to share.

But the truth is, experience trumps opinion every time. To paraphrase Gary Vee, put your head down and work for ten years before you say anything!

Opinion is hard to follow. You can speak from book experience but qualify the advice. It takes time to build experience—and once you have it, your value rises exponentially.

Ask yourself: When I offer advice, am I speaking from experience or opinion? Can you comment on something you have actually lived through? Something that you have seen firsthand? Been around firsthand?

DO YOU RESPECT THE COMPANY CULTURE?

Company culture is built over time. If you are new to a company, it's important to understand and respect that culture. Even if in your opinion it needs some tweaking, you need to earn brand equity and respect before working on changing the current culture.

People who walk in and try to immediately institute their own culture are dictators, not leaders. You need to take the time to get to know people as well as their history, goals, and vision before you can effectively lead them.

Ask yourself: What is the culture at this company? Is it working? Who is it working for? How does it encourage or discourage? How does it hold accountable or not hold accountable? How is it helping us to grow or keeping us from it?

DO YOU TREAT EVERYONE WITH THE SAME RESPECT?

Anyone who walks into your office—whether they are straight out of college and in an entry-level role or the CEO and founder of the company—deserves the same level of attention and respect from you. The standard you must rise to ensures you are giving the best of yourself to everyone, no matter what their title or "importance." Everyone is important, and no one person is better than another.

Ask yourself: Do I listen and pay attention to everyone equally? Am I reaching out to my team with the same frequency and interest as I am to my colleagues? Do I know and/or care more about people who are in a position to help grow my career?

WOULD PEOPLE JUMP IN A FOXHOLE WITH YOU?

It typically takes me less than ten minutes of conversation to know who I'd want in a foxhole with me if we were in a war. They have a certain calmness and presence about them that lets you know they're dependable, trustworthy, and good in a crisis.

COVID awakened many companies. The individuals whose brands won had experiences in life that showed they could lead when everyone else panicked. When you know who you are, you have a different way of walking through fires. You know there is always a solution, have the confidence to speak with great transparency, stay ahead of the crisis, and lead those that are in fear. Leaders are born through fire.

Ask yourself: Would I be the first choice to be in a foxhole with someone? How do I show that I am the right one to be there with them?

DO PEOPLE TRUST YOU?

Just as brands are built brick by brick, so is trust. It takes time and a lot of storytelling. You don't need to know your team's deepest, darkest secrets, nor do they need to hear yours. However, knowing what they have been through personally helps you to know what types and frequency of communication will enable them to trust you.

Over the past ten years, I have had to regain my ability to trust people because of my trial. And like me, everyone's trust has been hurt at some point in their lives. As a leader, understand that people have different levels of trust based on their experiences.

Trust is earned. It's not a given. Your actions need to show people you are worthy of their trust before they will give it to you.

Ask yourself: Have I proven myself to be trustworthy? How? Do people trust me? Why?

CAN PEOPLE DEPEND ON YOU?

Earlier in this section, I talked about a super-efficient woman. People could depend on her to have an encyclopedic knowledge of the company, but what they couldn't depend on was her emotions. No one ever knew how she was going to be on any given day. She might be in a good mood. She might be crabby and short. She might be annoyed.

A good leader is dependable in both ways: as a resource for answers and guidance, but also in their demeanor. Consistency in how you show up in the world and treat people matters.

Ask yourself: Can my team depend on me? Am I showing my best self every day, despite whatever else may be on my plate? Am I providing my team a safe place to fall and even fail?

WHAT ARE YOU KNOWN FOR?

True leaders are known for more than what they do for a job. In 2010 when thirty-three men were trapped in a mine for seventy days, their foreman Luis Urzuà immediately took charge of the situation. He created maps of the mine, became an important resource for engineers working to help the rescue effort, and helped his men cope with the mental toll the situation was taking on them. His calm confidence ensured the entire crew made it out of the mine alive.

Ask yourself: What am I known for? Am I known for being decisive? Am I known for always meeting goals? For putting out gossip or supporting others? Does what you are known for match your gifting? Are you showing your best self at work in this way?

WHY DO PEOPLE COME TO YOU?

People most often come to me for advice on brand or getting through trials—and sometimes both. This is my gifting, my thing, what I do best.

Does your team follow you for whatever your special "thing" is? (It's surely not only *here's your deadline* or *here's your timesheet*.) The answer can tell you whether or not you are sharing your gift to the fullest.

Ask yourself: What does my team come to me for? Do people know what I do well, and the value I offer? Am I using my gifting to benefit others? Have I shared my story so people know when and why they should come to me?

DO YOU KNOW YOUR PEOPLE'S GOALS?

Knowing your team members' goals allows you to influence them in all the right ways, growing their careers and benefiting the company at the same time. From experience, the reason most people don't know others' goals is simply because they haven't asked. If this is the case, it means you don't care or know how to communicate—a problem that needs to be fixed. If you don't know the ultimate goals of those you lead or even those around you, how on earth can you influence them?

Leaders do more than tell people what to do, they lead them to their purpose. Once you know someone's goals, you can frame your "asks" in a way that tells them they are on the right path and not simply doing work for work's sake. Other times, you will realize that the goals don't match with the work, which is another opportunity to lead and encourage growth somewhere else—sometimes in a different role, different department, or even different company/industry.

Ask yourself: What are my team members' short-term goals? What do I know about their long-term goals? What are their personal and professional goals?

DO YOU DELIVER TRUTH WITH GRACE?

If you treat others in a way that creates mortification or humiliation, reduces someone to lowliness, or makes someone submit, you are not a leader—you're a tyrant. You can be truthful and hold people accountable without doing so in a hurtful way. As a leader, delivering truth with grace is an art you must practice.

Ask yourself: Am I kind or brutal when communicating the truth to my team members? Do I hold others accountable while still considering their emotional needs?

ARE YOU OPEN TO FEEDBACK?

I've already talked quite a bit about Ray Dalio's book *Principles* in which he emphasizes asking the right questions to get your team to give it to you straight. He admits that in his own career he had to ask for feedback, hear what his team members were saying, take stock, and then make drastic changes because he was doing so many things wrong.

Inc. magazine recently detailed the memo Ray's employees gave him, which said:

> Ray sometimes says or does things to employees which makes them feel incompetent, unnecessary, humiliated, overwhelmed, belittled, oppressed, or otherwise bad. The odds of this happening rise when Ray is under stress...The impact of this is that people are demotivated rather than motivated.

To be fair, they also outlined the positive:

> He has good intentions about teamwork, building group ownership, providing flexible work conditions to employees, and compensating people well.

Ray Dalio listened, reflected, and adapted his behavior when his people told him *you are terrible at this* or *your expectations are ridiculous.* As a result, his team was happier and more productive, and his company more successful as a whole. He gives us an incredible example of a leader who was willing to hear where he needed improvement.

Humble yourself. Know that there is no way you know everything. Listen to those around you. You must be willing to hear all feedback about your leadership.

Ask yourself: Do I accept feedback gracefully? Do employees have a way to give me that feedback comfortably? Do I make changes to my behavior as a result? How do I communicate those?

DO YOU USE ADVERSITY TO TEACH?

During COVID, many employees' confidence took a huge hit. I watched as some of the toughest, most determined executives crumbled. They thought their worth was based on the revenue they generated or their impressive client roster, and they felt demoralized when they no longer had access to those things. What far too many didn't understand was that their value is so much more than any earthly thing.

I wanted to tell them that adversity is simply an opportunity to grow. My fire, though terribly painful, was one of the best parts of my life. That experience is the very reason I can write this book—because I'm not only speculating from opinion. Most seasoned leaders have walked through trials, learned from them, and emerged victorious. Victory comes in learning, not in winning a battle.

As a leader, you need to use your experience to help your employees walk through any trials they may be facing. During a crisis, personal brands either rise or fall. Many leaders won't want their brand associated with a broken brand, but any brand that's strong can stand up for one that's struggling.

Remember the woman at the Nashville nonprofit who made it a point to promote my brand even as my husband was in prison? That's a leaders' leader. She never hesitated to say she knew me, have my back, or push me forward. She believed in me and wanted to see me succeed.

My brand is now at a similar place of strength because I've been through that fire. It is proven and consistent. My husband rebuilt his by leveraging mine. I'm absolutely fine with that, because I know my brand is solid, I believe in him, and I know who he is now.

The very purpose of going through trials is to help others who go through them after you. The knowledge you gain during a fire helps you set a stronger example for others. Your experience can help their experience to be less painful and traumatic, and can help them come through it more successfully.

> 2 Corinthians 1:4 says: He comforts us in all our troubles so that we can comfort others. When they are troubled, we will be able to give them the same comfort God has given us.

Ask yourself: How do I lead when others are experiencing difficult moments? Am I helping others walk through their trials? Am I willing to get in the mud with them or do I not want to be associated with their brand? Can I support others even through a breach of integrity?

DO YOU VALUE EVERYONE'S TIME?

I once waited HOURS for a CEO to show up at a meeting he'd invited me to. Turns out, he was shopping for patio furniture with his wife right across the street and didn't value my time enough to do that another time or reschedule. His decision made it seem like he thought his time was more valuable than mine, and it showed me a lot about his leadership skills (or lack thereof).

As a leader, it's imperative you understand your time is no more valuable than someone else's—everyone's time matters. Everyone has busy lives and full plates. No one person is more important than another.

Ask yourself: Am I prompt, or do I keep people waiting? Do I schedule meetings and conduct important conversations during regular work hours? Do I review work and give feedback promptly?

THE LIGHT: BRAND LEADERSHIP RECAP

You are already a leader, even if you have no direct reports.

Leaders are confident, consistent, and know their why and core values.

Leaders are approachable and aware of the message their body language, vocal tone, and facial expressions are sending.

Leaders lead with love and know that empathy and kindness breed incredible loyalty.

Leaders hold others accountable while still sharing truth with grace.

Leaders value and display integrity above all else.

Leaders read widely and know what is going on in their community, industry, business as a whole, and the world.

Leaders uphold their brand and the company's, and help others do the same.

Leaders encourage and respond positively to open, honest feedback.

Leaders know their main job is to help others be their best.

Leaders both mentor and sponsor others.

Leaders do not engage in or allow others to gossip.

Leaders move on from mistakes rather than holding them over people's heads.

Part Six

BRAND AWARENESS

"If your emotional abilities aren't in hand, if you don't have self-awareness, if you are not able to manage your distressing emotions, if you can't have empathy and have effective relationships, then no matter how smart you are, you are not going to get very far."

—DANIEL GOLEMAN

THE SPARK

Can You Read the Signals?

The term emotional intelligence (EI) was coined by researchers Peter Salavoy and John Mayer and later popularized by Daniel Goleman in his book *Emotional Intelligence: Why it Can Mean More than IQ*. EI means the ability to monitor one's own emotions as well as those of other people, to discriminate between different emotions, and to label them appropriately. It is one of the most important soft skills you can bring to the table.

Within EI, there are two main areas of competency: personal and social. As the name implies, personal competence is focused on self-management and internal emotional awareness. You demonstrate personal competence through the ability to accurately perceive your own emotions as they come up and behave in a positive manner as a result of this knowledge. Social competence is doing this same thing in relation to other people—acting appropriately and effectively based on your understanding of other's emotions, moods, and behaviors.

Emotional intelligence (EI) is also sometimes referred to as emotional quotient (EQ). There's slight variation in the meanings, but for the most part people are talking about the same qualities. I prefer EI, so whenever I'm not citing a study that specifies EQ, I'll use that term.

People with high EI—who know their own emotions and can see, feel, and hear those of others—hold the keys to success in life and business. Studies show:

- EQ is the single strongest predictor of performance, serving as the foundation for a variety of other critical skills such as time management, communication, and customer service. It is responsible for 58 percent of professional success, regardless of job category. (Source: "Why You Need Emotional Intelligence to Succeed," by Travis Bradberry in *Inc.*, March 2015.)
- The more emotionally intelligent you are, the more likely you will be a top performer. 90 percent of top performers score high on EQ; only 20 percent of low performers score high on it. (Source: "What Makes a Leader," *Harvard Business Review*, January 2004)
- There is a direct correlation between salary and emotional intelligence. On average, people with high EQ earn $29,000 more annually than those with low EQ. For each percentage point increase in EQ, a person can add $1,300 to their annual salary. This is true across industries, regions, and levels. (Source: "Emotional Intelligence—What Do the Numbers Mean?" by Joanna Trotta on LinkedIn, December 2018)
- When it comes to professional success and prestige, social and emotional abilities matter four times more than IQ. (Source: Feist & Barron, 1996 as cited in Cherniss, 2000)
- Seventy-five percent of careers get derailed due to a lack of emotional competency—for example, an inability to handle interpersonal conflict, provide adequate leadership during a crisis, elicit trust from others, or cope with change. (Source: The Center for Creative Leadership)

I encourage you to read the original sources to expand upon your knowledge in this area, but clearly having high EI makes you more successful. It allows you to adjust, be flexible, and respond quickly. It gives you greater self-awareness so you can accurately interpret what's going on around you. This contributes to a better workplace, environment, and culture, which means both you and your company stay ahead of the competition.

EI also allows you as a leader to encourage and grow others. Understanding signals from those around you—changes in body language, facial expressions, and vocal tone—lets you read a person's story even when they're not talking to you. You know what is most likely going on inside of them. You can give feedback using those emotions to help them make the right decisions or take the next best move (which is why it helps with negotiation and sales)!

EI comes to some people naturally. If that's not you, know that it is a muscle that can be grown. So put down anything else you're doing, go sit in a quiet space, and read this chapter. Then reread it, and reread it again, because EI is your differentiator and key to success.

Shout-out to Daniel Goleman: Thanks for all your research, dedication, and perseverance. You've done such important work and have been an incredible inspiration to me. I'd love to meet you one day!

THE FUEL

Developing Self-Awareness

Self-awareness means you're able to recognize what you're feeling and why you're feeling it, right when you're feeling it. It allows you to objectively evaluate yourself, manage your emotions, align your behavior with your values, and understand correctly how others perceive you. People with high EI always possess a high sense of self-awareness (which only makes sense—you have to understand yourself before you can develop an understanding of others).

With high self-awareness, you know how to unravel your emotions and not let them affect you negatively. You can accurately identify any feeling and use the right word to describe it. Are you actually angry, or are you frustrated, peeved, anxious, or even irritable? Word choice matters! Peeved is a much smaller version of anger.

When you're able to pinpoint what your emotion is and where it is coming from at any given time, you're far less likely to bring it into a business setting or your relationships. For instance, a client with high self-awareness recently told me, "I had a really disappointing conversation with our CEO. His lack of understanding of what's going on in the world is affecting our organization, and it has taken the joy out of me today." Her ability to explain her emotional state helped mitigate its effect on both of us. We could then have our meeting without it getting hijacked by her frustration and sadness.

People who react immediately and negatively have low levels of EI. They lack the awareness to understand their emotional triggers in the moment. During my trial, I used to wonder if someone was asking me a question simply because they wanted to know, or if they were questioning my integrity. By developing my own self-awareness, I am now able to pause, recognize that as a trigger of mine, and temper my reactions. Most people are not out to get others, even though our emotions might try to tell us otherwise.

Self-awareness is something you have to work at to master. It takes time and effort to immediately realize when you start feeling something differently than you're already feeling, and put the brakes on the fight or flight response that typically follows.

As my mother-in-law used to remind me when she was still alive, you can't control what other people do, but you can certainly control your own reactions. The ability to do this grows out of self-awareness. Checking in with yourself frequently—both personally and professionally—helps flex and grow this muscle.

Emotions are contagious. A happy person can have a ripple effect, rubbing off on everybody they come in contact with during the day. The same goes for anger, frustration, and misery. Which would you rather bring into a room with you?

LEARNING TO READ OTHERS

Have you ever walked into a situation and felt a certain vibe? That's a sign of high EI. This falls under the social awareness segment of emotional intelligence. Social awareness is your ability to pick up on emotions in other people pretty accurately, and also understand what is really going on beneath the surface: WHY are they happy, upset, uncomfortable, inflexible, and so on. People who have it are typically more sensitive to what's going on in a roomful of people. Without anyone saying a word, they're able to read the collective energy, emotion, and even the why of the emotion after picking up on some cues.

A while back, an executive brought me in to speak to a diverse group of employees about growing their personal brands. Most of the participants hailed from different countries and were not native English speakers, and the company culture was one of people working to work and never investing in themselves or each other.

As an ice breaker, I shared with the group my background of being 100 percent Serbian and my fluency in the language. I even taught them how to pronounce my maiden name—Ljubica (it used to get butchered by teachers at the start of every school year—super fun in kindergarten. Insert eye roll here, ha). This opened the door for them to share their countries of origin, names, and backgrounds. I also told stories about my kids because I'd heard people talking about theirs before the meeting started. The group started to warm up and began to trust me. They could see we were in this thing together.

Once I started coaching, I listened to the words people were saying and watched for the signals they were giving me throughout the day. For instance, at one point I said to a participant, "I can tell you're not feeling this exercise." She looked at me, eyes wide with surprise. "How did you know?" I explained it was a combination of her words, body language, and facial expressions. She was amazed because it was a spot-on assessment.

Another person there was what I like to call a challenger, so of course he wanted to challenge me and prove me wrong. He said, "I bet that you can't tell me what I'm feeling." I gave him an assessment based on what I'd observed: how he spoke, wrote, sat, talked, made eye contact, fidgeted, ate, and so on.

I told him, "I think you don't have experience in what you're doing, but you were put in this position because of these particular qualities."

He was dumbfounded, and asked me, "How did you know that? Do you know my boss? Did someone give you my bio?" Of course, that wasn't the case at all. I'd simply watched him and drawn conclusions.

I'm by no means an oracle, but human behavior is something I enjoy studying. I truly care about people and I've lived through trials that allow me to see different perspectives. A client once told me I should seriously consider adding applicant screening to my portfolio of services. She said, "Every time I've asked your opinion about a candidate, you've been 100 percent right, despite only having met them briefly." I do think it is my greatest gifting.

I grew my emotional intelligence muscle by listening to people tell me how they felt, and then watching HOW they told me how they felt. I came to recognize what changes in body language and vocal tone meant. I saw how both intertwined for every emotion thousands of times, which gave me what some people view as almost a sixth sense but in reality is simply high EI.

The fact is, everything people do and say provides an abundance of information for you to assess and interpret. You can start by becoming more aware of the signals people are sending you. Are they smiling? Frowning? What are they holding? Are things falling out of their bag? Are they disheveled? Walking on the hem of their pants? Are their glasses crooked? Are they hungry?

Or let's say you are meeting an executive for the first time. Do they get up or stay seated when you walk in their office? Do they smile or look stern? Do they have a place for you to sit down? What books do they have on their bookshelf? What pictures, degrees, and awards are on the wall? All these things show you their motivation, where their confidence lies, and what they value.

Having high EI allows you to accurately pick up on the emotions of other people, understand what is really going on with them, and offer assistance when needed. EI is what gives you the confidence to say, "Hey, are you okay today? This is what I'm getting from you. If there's some way I can help, I'm happy to do that." This helps you build rapport, loyalty, and influence. People think, *Wow, you really noticed me. You really care.*

When you have high EI, you are able to read others well, which helps you anticipate and understand their reactions. It gives you a full picture of the human being in front of you.

Growing your ability to read other people, knowing what they are about, and understanding what they're going through makes you an exceptional judge of character. It means you are able to immediately find ways to relate, inspire, and lead. Sensing the motivations of others and seeing what lies beneath the surface is an incredible skill to hone in business and in life.

USING YOUR FILTER

No matter what you're going through at the moment—whether you are arguing with your spouse, experiencing a personal health scare, or enduring a trial—it's important for you to filter your behavior and reactions through your brand values. Those allow you to show up with the excellence, compassion, empathy, and integrity people deserve from you.

Part of the definition of EI uses the term self-management. This falls under the personal competence side of EI and is defined as your ability to use awareness of your emotions to stay flexible and positively direct your behavior. I have always taught clients to create, know, and use their brand words and brand values as a way to direct their behavior. It is not always easy to simply "stay flexible" and "be positive," but if you remember who you are using your own values, it makes it much easier. My brand words include excellence, truth, integrity, and compassion. So what does that actually mean? It means I'm going to use those words as a filter in every situation, no matter how difficult that may feel in the moment.

Case in point: I recently put a friend who is a recruiter in contact with a client. It seemed like she hadn't worked very hard on the referral, so I called her and said, "You aren't doing what I know you can do and normally do." I explained to her that my client was frustrated and my brand was going to take a hit because I gave the referral. My friend's response was that my client seemed terribly desperate and inauthentic, and that made it feel difficult to get behind them 100 percent.

Because I knew my friend well, I could see her filter was cracked in that moment. My filter allowed me to directly and honestly address the situation. I told her, "I hear you, but I know you pride yourself on your integrity and being black and white. I see a crack in that right now. If that's how you feel, you need to tell my client the truth and cut them loose. There is no in between. Either you get on board or you don't—you can't settle on being in the middle and only sort of helping, because that lacks integrity."

It's always a good idea to have an end goal in mind when having tough conversations like this one. My goal that day was to stay faithful to my brand words, help rectify the situation, and continue to be friends even though we were having a bumpy moment. It worked.

My friend agreed with my assessment. As a result, she offered my client an apology for not being able to help them more and refunded their initial investment. In an email later that day, she told me although my message had been hard to hear, accountability was very important to her and she was grateful I'd reminded her who she was.

So was it hard for me to say all that to a friend? Yes, but my filter has my brand words on it, and I keep those words in front of me in everything I do. I know integrity matters more than anything to me, and that I value empathy and honesty. (You can be both empathetic and truthful at the same time—they are not mutually exclusive.) My filter helped me know and do exactly what I needed to in that situation.

The next time you find yourself in a difficult situation at work, take a moment to pause, REMEMBER WHO YOU ARE (did you hear Mufasa's voice talking to Simba from *The Lion King* like I did?), and use your core values as a filter for your next words, thoughts, and actions. When you know who you are and that you are living your purpose, it makes it easier to manage emotion and continue on. Nobody can take your purpose from you or "make" you react outside of your filter.

Keeping your filter words in front of you at all times means you can always communicate who you are on your best day. Self-awareness is at the very core of EI, and is what helps you stay true to your brand.

ASSUMING INTENT (DON'T DO IT!)

I've often found myself in situations where people say, "Can you *believe* what that person said?"

It's usually not at all what I heard, so I ask them to clarify. And then comes this: "Well, maybe that's not what they said, but it's what they MEANT."

Assuming other people's intent is a stunning weakness, and I want you to avoid this trap at all costs. You might be thinking, *Isn't that emotional intelligence?* but the answer is no. Emotional intelligence is discerning how you and other people feel WITHOUT assuming negative intent. Being able to put the puzzle pieces together in order to figure out the why is vital for successful moments even amidst tough moments.

Many arguments start because someone incorrectly decided what the speaker actually meant. One person might say, "I don't agree with that idea." But instead of taking that message at face value, the other person starts thinking, "Oh yeah? You only want my job. You're saying that because you think you're better than me. You want me to look stupid."

Instead of wondering what someone's intent may have been and allowing anger, frustration, and negativity to build, my suggestion in these types of situations is to simply speak up. Say, "This is what you said. This was my state of mind. This is how I took it. I wanted to share that with you because I want to have a good relationship with you and be able to move forward." In doing this, the other person knows you care enough about them to make yourself uncomfortable by asking the question rather than walking out fuming, assuming you're angry for the right reasons.

Most of the time, it's simply a miscommunication. When it's not, it's usually because someone was feeling insecure and having a bad moment. If the other person does not admit to a bad intent, move on. It's enough to have brought it to their attention with grace. When their response is that your hunch was right, you get to talk through it and be a person who shows an enormous amount of understanding and high EI.

I've sat in meetings where I've watched people get angry about a comment I know full well wasn't meant for them. I saw how the person took it in through a broken filter and twisted it to mean something it never did. When I'm coaching, I like to point out these moments. I'll say, "I think I saw your body language shift in a way that made it seem like that comment hit you wrong. I want you to know it was not intentionally meant to hurt you or make you look bad." Transparency is always the best policy. EI is something anyone can choose to focus on and grow—it simply takes intentionality and great focus.

People with high EI know their core values and always remember them in the middle of a conflict. That's how you win people over. That's how you build influence. You don't attack. You communicate openly and ask for clarification when you're unsure. At the end of the day—unless you're a crystal ball—you can never be 100 percent certain what someone else is thinking.

LEARNING FORGIVENESS

People often ask, *How did you forgive your husband for betraying your trust and hurting you and others?* It took a long time and more prayer than you can imagine. I truly struggled with it. I used to want him to say on repeat, "I know how much my actions have hurt you." After a while, I realized that's not true forgiveness and found it in my heart to offer him real absolution.

Side note: Something I am often asked is: how do you really forgive? Personally, I have experienced forgiveness of all of my sins through Jesus Christ himself. Understanding the level of forgiveness I have received and not deserved means that I, too, must forgive. Over the last decade, I have leaned on Dr. Tony Evans for mentorship, guidance, and Biblical teaching. I haven't met him—yet—but encourage you to listen to his daily podcast, follow him on social media and read his books. Truly one of the most incredible Biblical pastors of our time. He says that forgiveness is a decision we make to no longer credit an offense to an offender. He brings home the point that forgiveness is a decision; not an emotion. He continues by sharing that a qualifying measure of whether you have forgiven an offense is to ask yourself if you are still seeking revenge. If so, forgiveness has not occurred. When forgiveness occurs the delete button is hit, or as 1 Corinthians 13:5 says, "You keep no record." Mighty words for something that can be so hard at times. Okay, back to work!

Most people don't talk about forgiveness at work. I've certainly never heard a CEO say, "You're really going to need to forgive your coworker," but I think it should happen more often. I'd even go as far as to say it would benefit companies to offer forgiveness training. Like empathy, forgiveness in the workplace contributes greatly to a positive company culture.

I'm a big fan of forgiveness because I understand the value of letting go of baggage. So many people hold grudges—especially when they feel they've been slighted or are the subject of gossip—but the inescapable fact is that people are going to hurt you, and you are going to hurt them. Although these hurts are usually unintentional, it's hard to move forward when carrying the weight of unforgiveness.

If you've been hurt, you might think, *Someone inflicted pain on me, so I'm going to give them that back plus a little more. They should pay for what they did!* Pause before you go there, because really—how much should they pay? Who's in charge of deciding? How do you know what they're already paying in private? Forgiving someone doesn't take away your right to be righteously angry at what they did, but retribution isn't the answer.

Sometimes it's not even an apology people want—they simply want to be heard. Even if you're the one in the right, listening goes a long way. So many of us tend to interrupt, comment back, talk over, and generally don't allow someone we are frustrated with to finish a whole thought. Listening to the whole story without interruption, giving full eye contact, and then pausing before responding is a formula for success. Approaching the other person with honesty, strength, patience and creativity wins the day. Deliver truth with grace and then lovingly work toward reconciliation. If you've been wronged, FORGIVE. It's amazing how uplifting and freeing that can be for everyone involved.

If you're the person who needs forgiveness, APOLOGIZE. No one is perfect, and people forgive fairly quickly as long as the moment of hurt is recognized. The key? Apologize with contrition. You can hear and see the difference.

Sometimes people won't apologize because they're worried they'll get "caught." They hope other people won't know what happened, and an apology seems like it will only shed unwanted light on the mistake. Nine times out of ten, though, the jig is already up. Everyone knows, and they're waiting to see what you're going to do about it. Without transparency and apology, mistakes typically snowball. Then you're in the middle of a mistake avalanche!

You cannot run away from your mistakes. Not long ago, I told a client she was making a mountain in her office with everything she tried to sweep under the rug, and that everyone could see it anyhow. You can't pretend like it didn't happen, move on, and expect anyone to be okay with you.

If your mistake does get you fired, then so be it. Your conscience is clear. You'll leave with your integrity and the opportunity to go somewhere else with a clean slate. Whatever consequences may come, at least you've done the right thing.

People with high EI play offense on their mistakes. Don't let someone come to you when you mess up—go to them. Outline how you will avoid making the same mistake in the future, and then follow through on your commitment. Sincere apologies are ones that actually result in changed behavior.

It also takes an incredible level of self-awareness not to dwell on past mistakes. Emotionally intelligent people don't forget about their mistakes, but they do keep a safe distance from them. Failure is one of the best teachers, and each one puts you further down the path to success. Once you master this mindset, you can bounce back from mistakes much more quickly.

Remember, everyone makes mistakes. When you are the offender, apologize. When you are on the receiving end, accept the other person's apology. Then actively work to create a culture that both accepts and moves on from mistakes.

DEPLOYING EMPATHY

Empathy is one of the pillars of EI. It requires you to understand, connect, and care about others. Being empathetic shows people they matter to you, and that you're willing to help in whatever way you can.

Growing your empathy takes constant work, just like building your muscles at the gym, and the most important strength builder is LIS-

TENING. This requires NOT TALKING. Even if you relate or lived through the exact same thing, you don't have to say it at that moment. Yes, I've been telling you to share your stories—but they shouldn't be shared on top of others stories, especially when those stories are full of emotion. You can show people at a later point that you understand fully by sharing your story slowly. Sometimes listening is the ONLY thing you need to focus on.

I once heard someone talking about going to a facility for alcoholism. It was clearly a tough conversation, and it seemed to be the first time they had admitted this to anyone. I then watched slack-jawed as a third person butted in and started aggressively asking questions, talking about what they'd gone through, making zero eye contact, and only focusing on themselves. It was mortifying. Your sister's brother-in-law's cousin twice removed may have had a tough battle with alcoholism, but it isn't about you. SHHHHHHHHHH! Put yourself in the other person's shoes, but do it quietly.

According to a recent study, 90 percent of employees believe empathy is important in the workplace, and eight in ten are willing to leave an employer who isn't empathetic. (Source: 2019 Businessolver *State of Workplace Empathy*).

I once worked with an executive who was so unkind it almost took my breath away. The first time I witnessed it, I thought, *Surely he must be having a bad day.* But then it kept happening, time after time, in one situation after another. No one wanted to work for him. I'd heard from many people how nice he was personally, but if that were true, he was two entirely separate people—an arrogant, mean, rude one in the office and a caring father, husband, and friend outside of it.

The greatest executives I've had the honor of being around, on the other hand, are warm and kind. They don't rule with an iron fist, gossip, or ignore their teams. They create a culture of caring and transparency, and get rewarded for it with incredible loyalty and productivity. People love them and are beating down the doors to work for them.

Which would you rather be known for: an iron fist or a kind soul?

And what would you rather have: employees who can't wait to leave, or ones who can't wait to come work for you?

The answer is clear. Empathy wins every time.

HAVING HUMILITY

> *"Pride goes before destruction, a haughty spirit before a fall."*
> —PROVERBS 16:18

People often become extraordinarily prideful once they achieve financial success and earn an impressive title. It's almost as if they forget about everything that helped them get to that level. Pride makes people blind to how they are acting and how others are feeling. It takes away their ability to be emotionally intelligent and socially aware.

I've seen "leaders" (using that term loosely here) walk into conference rooms and not even acknowledge the human beings sitting in the chairs. Their pride tells them they are so important that saying *hi* doesn't matter because the people in the room have to follow them. Maybe, but they certainly don't want to!

As the Lord tells us in the Bible, pride comes before the fall. When those same leaders walk out of the room with arrogance and pride, their employees say things like:

"If I have to work one more day for that person..."

"Who do they think they are?"

"We know you don't care about us, but you can at least say hi."

"Is it Friday yet?"

"I wish our old CEO was here so I could give that jerk a piece of my mind and stick up for us."

People with high EI have humility—the opposite of pridefulness. In fact, Merriam-Webster defines this as "freedom from pride or arrogance." When you're humble, you have a sense of calm because you are confident in who you are, you know your purpose, and you have a genuine care for human beings.

It's not only about how you feel, either—a recent study concluded that humble leaders are far more likely to delegate and innovate. This results in higher performance, less turnover, and an improvement in employee satisfaction. (Source: "Do Humble CEOs Matter? An Examination of CEO Humility and Firm Outcomes," *Journal of Management*, 2018)

Why then is humility so hard to find?

Unfortunately, it is frequently misconstrued as a "weak" brand attribute. We've been tricked into believing people who are humble are easily bulldozed by others and aren't willing to stick up for themselves. Some even think the word humility means having a low opinion of oneself or one's skills—which couldn't be further from the truth.

"Humility is not thinking less of yourself, it's thinking of yourself less."

—C.S. LEWIS

Avoid pride. Stay humble. Leave a lasting legacy of love.

ELIMINATING OVER-TALKING

Many people are not aware of how much they talk, and over-talking absolutely crushes conversation. In an effort to relate, over-talkers actually push people away.

So how can you tell if you're over-talking? Watch the nonverbal communication of the person with whom you're speaking. Are they looking away? Not engaging with you? Showing other signs of frustration? Typically, those signals mean they are not invested in your story or you've overstayed your welcome in a conversation.

Whenever I feel I may have talked too much, I'll change the topic and start asking questions to get the other person re-engaged. A recent Harvard study showed that asking people three questions and then listening to their responses makes others perceive you as more caring and understanding. (Source: "It Doesn't Hurt to Ask: Question-Asking Increases Liking," *Journal of Personality and Social Psychology*, 2017) No one likes a conversation hog!

I have a friend and colleague who is a chronic over-talker. She and I have developed a system where I give her nonverbal cues to stop this bad habit in its tracks. I'll shake my head slightly at her or make a hand signal for her to be quiet when she starts taking over a meeting or room without being aware of it.

People with high EI recognize the importance of LISTENING more than they talk. So the next time you're trying to bond and relate to someone, stop talking about yourself. Instead, get curious and start asking questions about them. Listen to their responses and ask some follow-up questions. The result is you'll be better liked and thought of more highly.

GETTING RADICAL

Radical candor is a term popularized by Kim Scott, former tech executive and author of *Radical Candor: Be a Kickass Boss without Losing Your Humanity*. In it, she teaches a method of providing feedback that is "kind and clear, specific and sincere." This concept is what I refer to as radical transparency and delivering truth with grace.

Most companies don't encourage or accept radical transparency, which leaves many people who would rather not speak the truth for fear of being fired or disliked. I've had clients tell me, "I don't want to stir the pot," or "I don't have time for drama." The truth is, you don't have time for turnover, lack of leadership, or the drama caused by your inability to be transparent.

People with high EI have the ability to be transparent. Direct and honest communication empowers people and encourages engagement. It also breeds an incredible amount of loyalty.

People with high EI know that accountability and grace can coexist. You can deliver truth and be loving in your message while still enforcing a consequence. For example, I once worked with a woman I had become close to, and she neglected to tell me something crucial I needed to know to do my job well. I am incredibly sensitive to people withholding information, and my reaction typically is, *If you don't tell me the truth, I'm done with you.* Remember my trigger?

But as I said earlier, having high self-awareness means not only recognizing what you're feeling, but why you're feeling it. Because of my experience, I knew I was more upset than I should have been in that moment. I also realized our relationship was more important than my hurt feelings. So instead of being angry, I decided to give it to her straight.

I called her out on her omission, allowed myself to be vulnerable in explaining how it made me feel, and accepted her eventual apology. Using radical transparency in that situation allowed us to remain friends. Without it, our relationship would have been over.

Sometimes, radical candor means calling out the elephant in the room. I recently had a meeting with a man who was being so rude, I had to say, "This seems like it's a bad day for you. Would you rather not engage right now?" That gave him an opportunity to apologize and reschedule for a better time.

This kind of truth-telling should simply be called "transparency," but that's not the world we live in today. It is still radical to have conversations where uncomfortable truths are plainly stated. To keep both your brand and company strong, work toward developing a culture that accepts and even expects truthful yet loving conversations and watch morale and productivity increase.

> Shout-out to Kim Scott: Thank you for being a kick-ass boss and showing us all how to not forget our humanity.

AVOIDING EMOTIONAL OUTBURSTS

We are all human, and sometimes showing emotion can be a great way to bond with others. REACTING emotionally, on the other hand, is the quickest way to keep people from wanting to be around you. Emotions can drive behavior and overwhelm our ability to function at our best.

For example, I once had a meeting with someone running for a political office. However, the meeting was not about politics. I was there to consult on marketing and brand at the company the candidate worked for, and I happened to be acquainted with this person's political opponent. Since I wasn't helping with the campaign and didn't know the opposition exceptionally well, there was zero conflict of interest. Truth is, I didn't even realize one was running against the other at the time. But none of that stopped this person from coming out of the blocks hot at me.

First, they wanted to know how I knew the opponent. When I started to tell them, they said they didn't care anymore and completely stopped talking. Shocking behavior. Rude and unnecessary. Everyone else at the meeting was incredibly uncomfortable, and their opinion of this person dropped.

I kept my cool because fighting anger with anger is never the answer in a work environment, and I had a great deal of respect for the other people in the room. I also didn't take the political candidate's beef with me personally because they didn't know me. I did feel awful for them, though, because a reputation is built slowly and lost quickly. They definitely lost it that day!

If only this person had deployed their EI, it would have been an entirely different situation. We could have talked off the record. I could have answered any questions with integrity and respect. Instead, the rest of the meeting didn't go well, and there hasn't been an apology or even a recognition of their behavior since.

Lashing out is a sign of low EI. It shows everyone that you don't consciously recognize how you feel. A better way to deal with an emotionally-charged situation is to discuss your feelings and use facts to work through it.

Allowing your emotions to take over is truly one of the worst mistakes you can make in business, so don't bring your baggage into work for other people to hold. Things go downhill fast when you lose touch with your emotions. You can be angry and share your frustration while still looking for common ground and remembering we are more alike than different. Communicate with candor, grace, and strength instead of letting emotions take the reins.

ACING INTERVIEWS

Even if you are happy and fulfilled at your current job, I want you to start preparing for future interviews right now. Waiting until you're ready to change positions, the company closes, or you get laid off only makes the process that much harder.

In today's age of social media (which we'll get to in more detail later in the book), it's important to realize people are already putting together the pieces of your story before they even meet you. I recently coached a client who had basically never used her LinkedIn profile. One of the first things we did was change her cover photo and develop a great story in the about section so interviewers would have a positive first impression of her.

Another client told me, "I'm not on any social media platforms, so I don't think anyone could find out anything about me on the internet." I did a little sleuthing and his old Myspace profile pic from when he was a teenager popped up on Google. It was so inappropriate! Unless you want people to find out about your embarrassing phase in junior high, you must take control of your narrative.

While interviewers are busy researching your background prior to your meeting, you should also be researching theirs. The goal is to look for clues that will enable you to connect quickly and effectively. Act like a detective when it comes to putting pieces of someone's life together to determine how to relate to them and build a relationship with them. It always pays to go the extra mile.

Check where they went to school and what hobbies they may have. For instance, my husband went to Chapel Hill. If I see someone else did too, I'm going to borrow my husband's brand and tell them we bleed blue when I meet them (because we do). Connection points are key to bonding.

It's also a good idea to identify and steer away from any topics that might make your interviewer uncomfortable (and no, I'm not only talking about religion or politics here). For example, I could tell by readily available posts and pictures that the person interviewing one of my clients had a real pain point with her children. I advised the executive—whose brood was full of extraordinarily athletic over-achievers—not to talk about the successes of his kids unless the interviewer specifically asked him. I told him he could talk about being a family man, but that's where the conversation should end on his part.

He said, "You're kidding me, right? They're my kids! I bring them up because I'm proud of their accomplishments." I told him, "That's the last thing you want to do. It's going to crush her." He thought I was crazy, even as I explained to him why I believed that conversation was a landmine that he didn't want to step on.

Months later, he called and admitted I was right. The interviewer—who later hired him—had opened up about the difficult situation with her children. There was no way he would have landed the job if he'd told her what superhuman kids he had.

Another thing you need to research before heading into an interview is the corporate culture and company brand. My first question to potential interns is, "What did you think of the video on our homepage?" If they haven't watched it yet, they've lost before they even tried to play the game. If you're competing for a job at Amazon, be sure to study their fourteen leadership principles and have stories prepared to show you're aligned with those values.

When it comes time for the actual interview, it's obviously crucial to show up on time and be dressed appropriately. But to interview successfully, you also have to create a bond with the interviewer. Of course, experience and education matter, but finding common ground and developing a rapport go a long way in making you more memorable, likable, and likely to be chosen for the position. Most people are simply not prepared for this part of the process.

Here's my best piece of advice for the interview: DO NOT talk about what you've done for the first five minutes, period. Focus on your vocal tone. Pause. Listen. Be lighthearted and transparent. People want to know who you are and connect first before the informational exchange begins.

Once you do start to share your experience through stories, watch for body language shifts and listen to vocal tone changes. The goal is to read the person's reactions while you're talking. If they seem to be enjoying your story, draw it out a bit longer. If it seems like you're losing them, change up how you're telling the story or cut it short.

It's important to have different versions of your story and to be able change how you're telling it on a dime. When talking to someone data-oriented, try beginning with an interesting statistic. When interviewing with a creative person, try painting a visual picture of what you're talking about. Be sure to vary your tone, cadence, speed, and the way in which you listen and bond based on your audience's verbal and nonverbal cues.

When you tell a story differently, does it mean that your message changes? No. But does it change the way in which you communicate a message, and how everyone receives it? Yes.

I'd rather have you focus on HOW you tell a story than WHAT story you're going to tell. This is why practicing your stories is so important. If you talk about the 8,000 accounts you won and how you grew revenue by fifty bajillion dollars in a bored, monotone voice without looking at the interviewer or allowing them to interact with you, you're never landing that job.

I often hear younger executives say, "But I'm really smart. Why do I need to go through all this?" I hear you, but people don't have a crystal ball to see how smart you are, so you must follow these steps in order to help them get to know you. If you've never done this before or didn't realize it was a must for getting ahead until now—that's okay. Nobody was born knowing how to interview. You're simply setting yourself up for opportunity.

We are all created for a purpose. We all want to be seen, appreciated, and valued. And beyond all that—we all want to work with people we can relate to and like. That's why, when you're able to connect on a personal level, you're going to ace that interview.

NETWORKING EFFECTIVELY

Networking is not about YOU sharing YOU. It's about reading a room, learning about others, connecting, engaging, and bonding. I want you to network like your life depends on it.

Networking is not instantaneous. It's about developing relationships and actually caring about the people you're meeting. Just as you build a brand brick by brick, connections are built over time.

When you first get to an event, get a read of the room. Watch what other people are doing and saying. Stay open and approachable. Don't let fear stop you from joining in on the conversation.

Ask questions and then listen. Try to pull as much out of the other person as you can. Focus more on them than yourself. I find most people simply want to talk and hang out. They're not jumping right to, *Hey, let's do business right now.* I don't even tell people what I do at most networking events. I'm there to listen.

In the same vein, avoid the nervous habit of oversharing, especially at networking events. If you find that you're taking up 40 percent or more of a conversation with new people, check yourself before you wreck yourself. You don't want to be branded as someone who lacks awareness.

When you find moments of connection, feel free to tell a story if it seems appropriate. Do so fast and efficiently. Have your stories prepped and ready so you don't miss your opportunity.

If there's one person you connect with in a networking room of five hundred, that's enough. Meeting ten quality contacts in a single meeting is an unrealistic goal. Don't be the person whose eyes are darting in every direction while talking to people. All that says is, *I'm waiting for you to shut it so I can go find someone more important than you.* That's a poor representation of your brand. Everybody is as important as the next person, and they should feel that way when talking to you.

File your connections away in your mind for after. My post-event notes always include what people were wearing, what stories they related to me, and which topics we discussed. I always follow up with a note on stationery that features my husband's family crest, expressing how nice it was to meet them. I talk about what we bonded over—I'll say *good luck* with your pregnancy, new job, or exciting project. I sign the note with my first name, then slip a business card in behind it, almost as an afterthought. I seal the envelope with wax to add a personal touch.

More important than what I DO when I'm first forming a relationship with someone is HOW I maintain the connection. My actions are all about building rapport. I'm not trying too hard, but I still go the extra mile by showing I care.

If there was someone in the room I didn't get a chance to talk to, I write them a note as well. In it, I might cite a piece I read about them in the business journal and mention that we'd attended the same event. Nine times out of ten, they respond with a phone call or an email. In fact, the CEO of one of the largest companies in the world recently had his assistant call to set up a time to talk to me. He said in all of his years, he never received a note where somebody didn't want something from him and that he appreciated it so much.

Networking is simply bonding. I'm often asked how I landed my biggest clients, and the answer is that I built a relationship with them over ten years of networking. When they had a need I could assist them with, they knew to call me versus someone else.

Networking is not about you, it's about: *What can I do for others? What can I do to help? What can I share?* So show up, and show the best of who you are. Don't try to sell—just relate. Build connections, one networking event at a time.

Stats Don't Lie

There's incredible data available that shows how EI benefits both individuals and companies. If you weren't sold on how important displaying high EI is up until now, this should convince you to start growing those muscles ASAP. For everything from more money to greater influence, EI is your key to success. According to the data:

- Seventy-one percent of employers say they value emotional intelligence more than IQ in their employees. (Source: Careerbuilder)
- A forty-year study of PhDs at UC Berkeley showed that EQ matters 400 percent more than IQ as a predictor of who will become the most successful. (Source: Joseph Cerny, Dr. Maresi Nerad)
- At Pepsi, managers with high EQ outpaced annual revenue targets by 15 to 20 percent while managers with low EQ came in below targets at that same percentage rate. (Source: PepsiCo)
- When a Fortune 500 Company in Texas wanted to reduce turnover in their salesforce, they decided to try switching from a personality-based screening to an EQ-based one, as well as implementing an EQ training and development program. This increased retention by 67 percent in just the first year, adding an estimated $32 million to their bottom line. (Source: "The Importance of

Emotional Intelligence in the Workplace: Why It Matters More than Personality," hr.com, 2005)

- By adding an EQ-based screening, a large city hospital lowered the turnover rate of their critical care nurses from a whopping 65 percent to just 15 percent over just eighteen months. (Source: "The Importance of Emotional Intelligence in the Workplace: Why It Matters More than Personality," hr.com, 2005)

- According to a study of Fortune 500 CEOs, technical knowledge only accounts for 25 percent of long-term job success. People skills are responsible for the other 75 percent. (Source: Stanford Research Institute International and the Carnegie Melon Foundation)

- A study of forty-four Fortune 500 companies conducted by the Hay Group states one study found that people in sales who display high EQ bring in double the revenue of people with average or below average EQ scores. (Source: "The Importance of Emotional Intelligence in the Workplace: Why It Matters More than Personality," hr.com, 2005)

THE HEAT

Staying Connected

EI is all about understanding feelings, connecting, and bonding. There are many less educated and experienced people who do far better in life than those who had straight A's and are off of the IQ scale. Being the smartest one in the class isn't the only goal anymore—having high EI is.

When you first start to grow this muscle, it may feel like a lot of work. That's absolutely right. But if you work on EI repeatedly, it will grow into a habit and eventually, simply become who you are.

Don't get overwhelmed. Do one thing at a time. Brick by brick!

ARE YOU AWARE OF HOW YOU'RE FEELING?

People with high EI can recognize what they're feeling and why. Journaling what you're feeling throughout the day can help you learn to pinpoint your emotions.

Ask yourself: Am I doing frequent self-checks? Can I determine what I'm feeling at any given time? Do I know why I'm feeling what I'm feeling?

DO YOU REACT EMOTIONALLY?

While authentic emotion can be a great way to bond with others, being emotional is not. Usually, this type of reaction is out of proportion to—and possibly not even related to—the actual situation. Responding in an emotionally charged manner is a sign of low EI, so avoid being the person who does this.

Ask yourself: Do my buttons get pushed easily? Do I get offended easily? How do I respond when this happens? How can I learn to react less strongly?

DO YOU KNOW HOW TO SAY NO?

Some of us say yes knowing it will make us feel overwhelmed and anxious. When you know how you're feeling at the moment, it becomes easier to say no in a way that doesn't offend anyone. When you can do that, it means you've mastered radical transparency.

I used to answer yes impulsively all the time, which led to anger, resentment, and an incredible level of burnout. Now that I'm really aware of how I'm feeling, NO comes much easier. I say no a lot these days: to groups, boards, clubs...I have two girls at home, and as a working mom, any yes needs to be worth taking time away from them. The result? I'm happier, more content, and live with fewer regrets.

Ask yourself: Do I feel pressured to say yes—even though I know it will make me stressed and unhappy? Am I willing to say no? What would it feel like to say no instead? Can I tell someone no without offending them?

DO YOU KNOW HOW TO DISCONNECT?

In today's world of 24/7 access to everything and everyone, it's important to take time off the grid to enjoy nature, solitude, and our in-person relationships with others. Getting away from technology and into the world has huge benefits, including lowering stress levels and increasing gratitude. Put your phone down and lift your head up. The world is beautiful if you take the time to see it!

Ask yourself: Do I put boundaries around when I'm doing work? Do I feel the need to answer emails and texts immediately—even late at night and early in the mornings before I begin working? Do I spend every waking moment looking at a screen? Does my partner or child complain that I don't pay enough attention to them?

DO YOU ACTIVELY WORK ON RELATING TO OTHERS?

People with high EI know how to listen far more than they talk. They ask questions and get to know others. They look for bonding points and places to relate.

Ask yourself: Am I hearing other people's stories? Do I work to find connections? Do I share my stories intentionally to create a bond with others?

DO YOU GIVE WITHOUT EXPECTING SOMETHING IN RETURN?

When you have a high level of EI, your goal is to build stronger and deeper relationships with others—which means you are intentionally and consistently thinking about them. This leads to giving without expectation, which leaves an enormous impression. I know a leader who gave his people cash for Christmas in two amounts: one amount as a gift to the employee, the other equal amount, for the employee to give away to someone else they thought needed it. That showed huge heart, and people loved him for it.

Ask yourself: Am I willing to help others without reservation? Or do I expect something in return?

DO YOU HOLD GRUDGES?

Carrying the weight of unforgiveness is stressful—it can even make you physically ill! Remember, you can be righteously angry that some-one did something and still offer them forgiveness. There can be consequences along with true grace.

Ask yourself: Am I being unforgiving with someone? Am I holding a grudge? What would it take to forgive that person? How would letting go of my grudges benefit me and them?

DO YOU ASSUME INTENT?

Thinking you know someone's intent—and getting angry as a result—is a stunning weakness. No one is a mind reader, so we can never really know what people are thinking. This is why it's so important to ask for clarification when you're unsure what a comment or action that hit you the wrong way actually means.

Ask yourself: Do I assume other people's intent? Do I think I know what they're *really* saying? Is that always negative?

DO YOU OVER-TALK?

People with high EI know listening is far more important than talking. Over-talking kills a conversation faster than anything else. Asking questions yields far better results than being the person TMI-ing a group.

Ask yourself: Are people looking at me? Are they engaging with me? Am I allowing them to speak? Am I taking breaths while I'm talking? Does the other person seem frustrated? Are they looking away from me? Am I looking at them?

THE LIGHT: BRAND AWARENESS RECAP

Emotional intelligence (EI) is one of the most important, if not the most important, soft skills you can bring to the table.

Statistics show that people with high EI are more successful and earn more than those with low EI.

High self-awareness is a quality people with high EI possess.

People with high EI can read other people well and understand their emotions.

Using your brand filter to manage your reactions and emotions is a sign of high EI.

Empathy, humility, and forgiveness are hallmarks of people with high EI.

Over-talking, pride, and arrogance are signs of low EI.

Radical transparency empowers people, gives them clarity, and increases loyalty.

Interviewing successfully is not only about experience and education, but finding connection with your interviewer. Spend time doing research on the company as well as the people you'll be speaking with, then practice the stories you're going to tell to prove you're the right person for the job.

Networking with EI is all about bonding and creating connections, not selling yourself or your business. Follow-up is key. A nice handwritten note goes a long way to cementing a new relationship.

Companies who value EI are more successful, more profitable, and seen as better places to work by employees.

Part Seven

BRAND MIRROR

"You cannot climb the ladder of success dressing in the costume of failure."
—ZIG ZIGLAR

THE SPARK

Putting Your Best Look Forward

Almost twenty years ago, my business took off when I began fashion consulting for a NASCAR driver. It wasn't that he'd been dressing WRONG, necessarily—it was that his clothes didn't reflect who he really was off of the track. Because his image didn't match his brand, he wasn't attracting the right kind of attention.

I watched as a fashion stylist dressed him on a photoshoot and thought, *WRONG*. With every outfit change I would think, *STILL WRONG*. My internal dialogue consisted of, *Terrible, ill-fitting, yikes, he hates that outfit but won't say anything, this person has no idea who he is or she wouldn't have picked these outfits, yikes again, and STOP*. Finally, I said, "STOP!" and MODA was born.

Since then, I've worked with thousands more people to ensure they are presenting the best version of themselves to the world every time they walk into a room or log onto a Zoom. High-level executives up for C-suite positions, managers who are ready for the next step, young professionals taking a new step into the world, and countless others trying to ensure their image reflects who they are on their best day and represents their personal brand at all times.

It's my job to help others convey a consistent professional image—in words, actions, and appearance—that's authentic and true to their personal brand. This can mean jeans, suits, blouses, and even shorts—but the RIGHT jeans, the right suits, the right blouses, and even the right shorts. It's not about the type of clothing, it is about the piece of clothing representing the best you.

I cannot stress this enough: the way you present yourself can literally change the trajectory of your career and life. For those of you who are behind the scenes in your companies, your image matters as much or more. Your clients are internal: colleagues, managers, associates, and business acquaintances. You never know who knows who, and your image might be the only way people know you.

I've seen hundreds of people passed over for promotions and more fulfilling jobs because of easily correctable fashion and grooming mistakes, and I've witnessed doors fly open for people who upgraded their image. For example, one of my favorite clients used to get on the elevator with the CEO of her company every morning, and in all that time, he'd never ONCE said hello to her. I helped her redo her wardrobe, and the very first day she wore one of the tailored, well-fitting, colorful outfits we'd put together, guess what happened? Yup. The CEO greeted her with a cheery, "Good morning. How are you today?"

Of course, what she wore didn't change who she was. Her new look simply helped reflect the person she had always been on the inside. Since she started consistently presenting an image that says *I'm professional, I'm ready to work, I care about this company, and you can count on me,* she has been offered big breaks that likely would not have come otherwise.

If you're thinking right now, *God created me perfectly and I'm beautiful on the inside no matter what I wear,* know that I heartily agree. I believe we are all fearfully and wonderfully made, and that God does not make mistakes with our image. Unfortunately, we also live in a visual world, and the way we appear to others DOES matter. Believe me, this isn't about me trying to make you prettier or more handsome. That's silly and inconsequential. Instead, it's about positioning you to reach your highest goals by making sure you ALREADY look the part and are representing your best self every day.

Just as people aren't born knowing how to change the oil in a car, many of us have not been gifted the innate ability to know how to dress for success. If that describes you, don't worry! Everyone—no matter their size, shape, or age—can learn how to upgrade their image using their brand filter words. The sooner you start, the better.

Because when you look good, you feel good.

When you feel good, you produce greater results.

And when you produce greater results, you typically make more money and reach the career heights you've always aspired to.

As the saying goes, you never get a second chance to make a first impression. Let's get to work on making yours the absolute best it can be.

THE FUEL

Create Trust—
Don't Crush It

Let's say you're checking out two apartment communities to decide which you're going to live in. You pull up to the first and see flowers in the garden and beautiful landscaping. You walk inside the building, which is sparkling clean and smells like a spa. You're greeted by a professionally dressed leasing agent who proceeds to show you a spacious, well-appointed apartment with ample amenities. You can't sign the lease fast enough, right?

Next you drive up to the second place. The sign for the complex is falling; there are weeds as tall as you on the lawn, trash all over the ground, and the windows are grimy. What do you do? Most likely, drive by without even getting out of the car. You already assume the inside is as messy and unkempt as the outside and the management is not worth the money they get paid, so what's the point?

The way people experience your brand is similar to those apartment communities. Every moment—every single interaction you have with someone—is an opportunity to build trust or crush it. Either you're the inviting, clean, professional, well-manicured brand people want to associate with, or the trash heap dumpster fire people dismiss without a second glance.

I've met people who think, *I am the best at what I do for my company, I don't need to worry about my "look."* But then leadership tells me, "I see the value this person brings to the table and I'd like to give them a promotion...too bad I can't because they look like they don't know how to lead anyone, including themselves, out of a paper bag." Despite superior job performance, that person's image is currently telling their boss they can't be trusted with more responsibility—so they stay stuck right where they are. Sometimes your boss knows how incredible you are but doesn't think you can represent the company or even the department simply because they know people will assume things about you that probably are negative and untrue. Either way, you lose.

I think we forget at times that our image does not simply reflect our own personal brand, but it 100 percent reflects the image, brand values, and culture of our company. We know this already: if you represent your company well, have a consistent image, and lift the company brand—you WIN BIG. Companies know the personal brand of their employees matters as much as if not more than the products/services/goods they promote. You can have the best services in the world and the most educated people, but if the personal brand/image of the people isn't conveying that story, you lose to someone who might be less experienced but knows how to represent themselves.

You might be protesting right now, *But I'm so smart! People should see past my outward image.* I hear you, but I also want you to know your competition will crush you with that attitude. Time and again, I've seen people get hired simply because they looked more put together. They might not know as much, be as bright, or have equivalent experience—but they get the opportunity because they understand the importance of executive presence.

I've helped many clients over the years who didn't want to address their image but also acknowledged it was necessary. They've typically been angry the whole time that we worked together, but like clock-work, they call to apologize afterward because they've had an aha moment. They realize image actually DOES matter, and not only in the eyes of other people. Looking better also makes THEM feel more professional and competent.

Cultivating a polished appearance means you'll garner more trust and respect from others. You'll feel more confident. And above all, you'll be accentuating what God has given you, which is exactly what He wants us all to do.

SEND THE RIGHT MESSAGE

You can still represent your best self even in your most casual moments. I once ran into an important client while standing in line for the Star Wars ride at Disney World. Thankfully, I was wearing tailored linen shorts that fit well, a polished white tank I had inten-tionally tucked into the front of my shorts, and a wide-brimmed straw hat. Even while holding a three-year-old on a sweltering day at a giant amusement park, the impression I gave my client was consistent with my professional image. It said, *I am a woman who is put together and cares at all times.*

Of course, it doesn't always happen like that. I once walked into Publix at ten o'clock at night after working on the house all day wearing paint-spattered clothes and a messy (and not cute) bun piled on top of my head. Before I even went inside the store, I bumped into a business colleague and friend in the parking lot and had to apologize for how I looked. Hint: if you have to make an excuse for your appearance, you've already lost the game. I certainly wished I'd taken a second to put myself together before I ran out the door to buy milk that night (or at least hidden myself under a baseball hat, ha)!

In a world full of camera-equipped cell phones and viral videos, some-one is always watching. Every time you go out in public, there's always the possibility of seeing someone you want to impress. That's why everything about your image must represent who you are at all times—and I mean everything.

People notice different things. For instance, my husband cares about shoes and can tell whether soles are stitched or glued. Someone else might see how well a jacket fits, whether it hugs the shoulders or falls below them (this is a big no-no). Still others might focus on your bag, assessing whether it has loose stitching and falls open or is appropriately structured for the workplace and is in great condition.

I can't tell you how many times people have said to me, *Don't judge, it's casual Friday.* My response is that I'm not judging their clothes. What I'm trying to understand is how someone trying to grow in their career and bring opportunities to themselves can show up at work looking like they've just rolled out of bed. People who don't think twice about the image they're portraying send the message, *I absolutely don't know what I'm talking about. I'm faking you out right now. You shouldn't believe me because I don't even know how to put myself together.*

When it comes to fashion, people assume you're presenting a certain image on purpose. Wet hair, tattered hems, scuffed shoes, see-through yoga pants that have seen better days—they're all a distraction. They contradict your competence. People think you don't know any better, and that lessens the value of your brand.

Because small shifts can create big opportunities, fashion is one of those places it's so easy to win. Replacing the generic plastic buttons on a jacket with more expensive looking ones gives you a unique look that is more detail-oriented. The plastic buttons say *I'm as basic as my blazer* while the fancier ones announce *I care about my appearance and your business* to an audience that notices those things. For the men, wearing straight leg khakis or slacks rather than a pair with pleats and cuffs ensures you are not dating yourself. The others say, *I'm stuck in the 1980s*—or worse, *I've had these pants since the 1980s.*

When you pick up any piece of clothing, your mind should immediately start thinking about your brand words and values. Every pair of shorts, workout pants, slacks, or tennis shoes, every baseball cap or suit should represent those three to five words. Having one wildcard item is fine, but then you need to bring together a cohesive brand message with your other pieces. For instance, while the fun pair of cut-off jean shorts you wear to the soccer game on the weekend may not scream excellence, the rest of your outfit still can. This can be the most fun part about choosing your outfits!

There's nothing like being able to walk into a room knowing your image is sharing the right message. Make it a goal to always present yourself in a way that says, *I care about you. I understand the professional environment I'm walking into. I appreciate the time you're giving me.* You may be surprised at how much positive feedback you receive, not only in compliments but in opportunities.

DRESSING FOR SUCCESS

People want to associate themselves with people who are successful—it's as simple as that.

This is why my husband cannot stop wearing his UNC–Chapel Hill gear, because most people associate his alma mater with incredible success, hard work, and a great education. It is why children dress up as doctors and lawyers (or if they're like my daughter, authors) on career day at school. It's why we follow every move of superstar athletes and celebrities.

To get others to want to associate with you in this same way, everything about your presentation needs to be intentional. For instance, whenever I'm meeting with C-suite leadership, I am sure to wear a serious suit that sends the message, *What I have to say today is very important and you need to listen.* This gives me the confidence to walk in and get the results I need. There have even been several times I've driven halfway to a meeting and gone back home to change because my outfit didn't quite fit the bill. Ensuring I'm wearing the right clothes has always been a worthwhile decision in the end.

People often look at me and wonder how I can be consistently and appropriately dressed for every occasion with my hair done and makeup on (other than that time at Publix!). I want to let you in on a secret here: it takes as much time to put on a pair of ratty old yoga pants as it does to wear an outfit that fits, matches, and shares my message. It's simply a matter of being well-prepared.

During the pandemic, wearing "mullet" outfits on Zoom became a thing: people were dressed professionally on top and then had on old, stained yoga pants—or worse, pajamas on the bottom. While I can see the humor in that, in order to be your best, you have to be 100 percent put together at all times. This holds true even if you're the only person who knows it, because there is an enormous correlation between image and success. Cultivating a positive presentation gives people more confidence and exudes an aura of leadership. There are even studies that tell us the psychological boost that accompanies dressing well makes us actually perform better.

Whether you're still in school, only starting your career, or getting ready to retire, it's never too early or late to make a great impression. One way to do this is to mix and match colors and fabrics. This adds a pop of personality while maintaining your professionalism.

For instance, you might wear a nubby tweed jacket with matte slacks and a silky shirt. A navy blue suit with matte nude or electric blue shoes. A classic white blouse with a bright pink or emerald green jacket. No matter what fun color or fabric choices you make, the structure of your outfit needs to say *I'm here to work*. The pieces need to fit well and represent your personality.

Take the time to present the best of who you are no matter what the occasion. The goal of fashion is to set a standard of respect, professionalism, and proper behavior. Wearing a carefully chosen outfit that sends the appropriate message will always add to your success and never distract from it.

ACTING THE PART

Typically, people see you before they hear you. That's why it's so important to put passion and care into your visual brand. Your posture, eye contact, facial expression, vocal tone, body language, and overall demeanor can make or break the first impression others get from you.

It's critical to note here that you can have an impeccable presentation, but if your actions don't match your look, you're in for a world of trouble. As the saying goes, you can put lipstick on a pig, but it's still a pig.

Psychological Science reported that it takes one-tenth of a second to make a first impression. Nonverbal cues such as eye contact, voice inflection and tone, and body language and gestures are at the foundation of that impression. According to research, these nonverbal cues have more than four times the impact of words.

Our nonverbal communication constantly sends signals out to the world, so you want to ensure your body language matches the message you're looking to convey. I want you to imagine you are a walking, living, breathing billboard for your brand. Act accordingly at all times!

THE EYES HAVE IT

There is a plethora of research supporting the benefits of eye contact at work. In fact, one study from the American College of Neurology shows people are more positively perceived when they hold eye contact forty to sixty percent of the time. Of course, some people need more and some need less. For instance, I have one client who wants eye contact 100 percent of the time, which is far beyond what most people are comfortable having.

Use your EI to determine this situationally, and don't be afraid to experiment with it. The goal is to learn what works and what doesn't. If I have something important to say, I generally make my eye contact extraordinarily direct. Then, if I notice people are getting uncomfortable, I smile and look in a different direction for a second or two before re-establishing eye contact. This gets us all back on the same page.

Another thing to be aware of is whether your eyes are supporting your verbal message. You don't want to say one thing visually and another verbally. For instance, if your words are saying *I'm reliable and trustworthy*, your eyes can't be darting around the room. People will not believe your words but your eyes in that case, which indicate you are shifty and not to be trusted.

My advice is always to look at a person's eyes long enough to note the color of them when first meeting or greeting someone. Poor eye contact tells people you don't have time for them, are not interested in them, and that you think you're more important than they are—whether you actually mean that or not. Strong eye contact indicates interest and care. It can also tell people that you are confident.

Eye rolling is one of the most significant mistakes you can make in business and in life. It tells someone you do not appreciate or respect them. Research even shows that one of the strongest predictors of divorce is a spouse who rolls their eyes at their partner. I've been in meetings where someone looks out the window and rolls their eyes, thinking no one can see them—but it's right there in the reflection. Remember, eye rolling is never an appropriate response no matter what is being said.

Eye contact tells people you're confident and have high self-esteem. It makes people trust in you and your abilities. Be intentional, and it will become a natural part of the way you interact—a nonverbal cue you don't have to think about to successfully employ.

If right now you're thinking, Mila, how am I supposed to read faces, change my story, keep it authentic, make sure everyone's included, wear the right outfits, AND make meaningful eye contact ALL AT THE SAME TIME? It's too much! My answer is, I understand it's a lot. Take it one step at a time. Don't try to do everything at once. Try to improve 1 percent every day, and by the end of one year you'll already be 365 percent better!

TAKE A GOOD LOOK

Eye contact isn't the only nonverbal signal we give visually. It's also important to watch where and how you're looking at things. For instance, looking at the clock is a huge problem. It makes people think you are bored and uninterested in what they have to say. Always tell someone you have another meeting before you get underway so they don't think you simply want to stop speaking to them. If you need to check the time to ensure you're still on schedule, be transparent and say, "As I mentioned before, I have another meeting after this so I need to check the clock to ensure we're not going beyond our scheduled time right now."

In addition, looking at the ground sends mixed signals. It might tell people you're shy, unsure of yourself, not interested, frustrated, or thinking of something to say and waiting for the right moment to interject. Don't hide behind your eyes. Even if you don't agree with what someone is saying, you can still maintain eye contact, show respect, ask and answer questions, and have a great conversation. Be transparent in both your eye contact and your words.

PUT YOUR BEST FACE FORWARD

It's important to understand what your facial expressions are saying and how they're being interpreted, because facial expressions are easily misinterpreted. For example, you might argue that you're thinking or have on your "listening face," while others might interpret your expression as rude or unapproachable.

Some people think a straight face or even a slightly furrowed brow means people are going to take them more seriously. This simply isn't the case. What you have to say is no less important if you walk in with a pleasant expression on your face.

Studies show smiling is contagious. Research shows people can actually HEAR when you're smiling. You're going to win more people over with a smile than with a resting face that tells people you're not a nice person. Research from Penn State University has even concluded that people who smile appear more friendly, courteous, and competent.

Still not convinced? The benefits of smiling extend even further. The University of Kansas found that smiling reduces stress and lowers the heart rate. A study by the University of Cambridge demonstrated that smiling during negotiations can increase feelings of competence and trust by 10 percent. In short, there's no excuse for not smiling in business.

I've been told that my kid's friends used to think I was intimidating. I started thinking, *Either I need Botox to erase the scowl line between my eyebrows, or I need to smile more.* I came to realize my resting face sometimes looks intimidating, so now I try to be extraordinarily aware of that. Because of this experience, my advice to you is to ask friends, family, and colleagues for feedback on your body language, nonverbal communication, image, grooming, and fashion. You need to know what visual cues are telling people about you and adjust as necessary. Many clients I work with have one perception, and most of the time it isn't correct.

Keep in mind, it's a disconcerting disconnect when your facial expression doesn't match the message you're delivering. For instance, if you say, *This is exciting!* while you're rolling your eyes, people are not going to believe you. During the pandemic, I saw a business associate smiling the entire time she was being interviewed on TV about how many people had COVID and how the hospitals were becoming fuller by the day. Her face was saying the exact opposite of the message she was conveying! I think she laughs and smiles when she is nervous, but even then you have to be aware. It's important to align the way you look with your words, or you'll risk being seen as untrustworthy and begin to lack credibility.

Your emotions, body language, and facial expression all contribute to your brand experience. Being clear and consistent helps others instantly recognize you and pay attention to what you have to say. People want to know what they're going to get.

SOUND THE PART

According to a study, 7 percent of meaning is communicated through spoken word, 38 percent through tone of voice, and 55 percent through body language. This is referred to as the 7-38-55 concept, which proves you have the power to breathe life into a conversation or suck it right out based on your vocal tone and body language.

Let's go back to your brand words. If excellence is one, ask yourself: what does excellence sound like? I'd assume the vocal tone of excellence is genuine. Excellence would say so if they didn't know something. It would be enthusiastic, receptive, and responsive. Competent, confident, knowledgeable, and experienced.

There are different ways of saying the same words. Most of us have said to a significant other at one time or another, "It's not what you said, it's how you said it." You can say hello and it can sound like you're going to a funeral, or you can say hello and it sounds like you're going to Disney World. This holds true both in person and when speaking on the phone.

Pay attention to how your voice rises and falls when you speak. Those peaks and valleys indicate to people that you're interested in them or not. Understanding what your tone is saying and learning how to use inflection is key to establishing positive impressions.

HAND IT TO THEM

A strong handshake is a sign of confidence. You want your hands to meet all the way, connecting between the thumb and the pointer fingers. No one wants to shake someone's limp, clammy fingers—you're not meeting the Queen of England.

Some people have been bumping fists or elbows since the pandemic. That's fine and appropriate, and you can have fun with that. But if you are shaking hands, make sure it's a handshake people remember.

HAVE GREAT BODY LANGUAGE

Studies show body language can reflect your mood, emotions, and personality. This is why developing the self-awareness to know what your body language is reflecting at any given time and having the ability to change that on a dime is critical.

Maintaining posture is also key to your appearance. Studies show that slumped shoulders send a message of laziness and insecurity. Poor posture tells people, *Ignore me. In fact, don't even look at me.* People who are perceived as more confident stand upright, like a pencil. Their shoulders are back. Their neck is elongated. Did you know good posture even results in improved vocal tone?

In addition to standing up straight and proud, another body position that conveys success is what is often referred to as the power stance, where you position your feet slightly apart and keep your arms and legs uncrossed. This even changes the chemicals in your brain to make you feel stronger and more confident. I don't want you to get missed because your crossed arms make people think you are closed off, rude, or perpetually negative. No one wants to work with an Eeyore.

In meetings, make sure your hands are calm. Fidgeting, tapping, twirling your hair, or touching your face creates anxiety in a room and is unnecessary at best. People who are confident in what they have to offer can typically sit without fidgeting.

Above all else, do not pick at your fingernails, head, face, stains on your shirt—ANYTHING. I once showed up at an important meeting after giving my youngest a bottle without realizing I had a flaky milk stain on my lapel. After I noticed it, I immediately took off my jacket and laid it over a chair. I did not pick at it or let it become a distraction. Because you may not even be aware you are picking, try to remain conscious of your hand movements at all times.

Your personal brand can be decimated with one poor communication signal. Don't let that happen to you. Stay self-aware so your overarching presence is overwhelmingly positive.

GROOM YOURSELF TO THE TOP

Personal grooming is an area where you can make so many small adjustments that have a big impact.

Women: do you have peach fuzz on your face? If yes, get rid of that distraction with one of the many razors or electronic devices available at the drug store or online. As an added bonus, shaving your face makes makeup application easier and longer lasting.

And speaking of makeup: research by sociologists from the University of Chicago and University of California at Irvine showed that women who wear makeup to work get paid more (though an excess can be seen as unprofessional). Accent your favorite features but don't go overboard! Make sure your eyeliner is straight and your lipstick is not smeared before you get to work. At the very minimum, always put on under eye concealer, lipstick or lip gloss, and a quick coat of mascara before leaving the house or getting on a Zoom call. Going to a meeting looking like you've just rolled out of bed does not inspire confidence in others.

Both genders need to pay particular attention to overgrown facial hair. Do you have a unibrow? Wax or shave it, stat. Trim any long hairs that are coming out of the eyebrows, nose, or ears. Nobody wants to see a bush growing out of your face. It's not only unsightly, but it sells what you have to offer short because it's the only thing other people can focus on.

The hair on your head is as important as the ones on your face. According to a Harvard Research Study, more than three quarters of senior executives said "unkempt hair" detracts from presence. Wet, frizzy, or unkempt styles negate everything else you may have done right in terms of grooming and fashion. Ensuring your hair is done well every day is a huge differentiator.

It's also important to have nails that are clean and cut to an appropriate length. If you wear nail polish, have it on all ten fingers or remove it all. There's nothing that screams poor grooming more than having one fully polished nail and nine chipped ones.

Another thing to pay attention to is the condition of your clothes. It's imperative you aren't wearing anything stained or misshapen to the office, to a meeting, or on Zoom. Have you ever seen the Tide commercial where the stain on the main character's shirt has a mouth that talks? Or the one where the couple is on a blind date and the man's V-neck is actually a wrinkled, loose U-neck? Don't be that person.

Year-long research from *Marie Claire* magazine and The Center for Talent Innovation (CTI) showed the best way to become a leader is by looking like one. Leaders are polished, pulled together, and well-groomed. Paying proper attention to your entire appearance—hair, skin, and hygiene—can really pay off on your career trajectory.

The world is competitive. Always strive to be your best! Here are quick tips for creating a winning edge:

- Use mints after meals (especially if you smoke or eat something with garlic, onions, or other pungent food).
- Keep your fingernails well-groomed (and toenails if wearing open-toed shoes). If your nails are polished, make sure none are chipped.

- Ensure facial hair is freshly shaven, neatly groomed, and trimmed—this includes eyebrows and any hair on or in the ears, nose, and neck.
- Be aware of how you smell. Wear minimal perfume or cologne and avoid sprays that cover odors (some people are allergic to the chemicals they contain). Use deodorant and avoid cigarette smoke.
- Keep your pockets empty as much as possible to avoid tinkling coins or keys and bulges.

THE FIRE

Looking Good at Any Price Point

Back when I was still doing my fashion seminars, I used to hold up two shirts—one from a very high-end department store that retailed for around $375 and one from a chain store that cost $50—and ask attendees which one looked more expensive. More often than not, they'd pick the $50 dollar one. They'd say it was because of the look of the buttons, placement of the armholes, or how the material felt. Wrong!

The fact is, most people can't tell the difference between a real diamond and a cubic zirconia, never mind one brand of clothing from another. At the end of the day, no one's going to be able to say, *That fabric looks like it came from the dollar store* (unless it is pilled and stretched out). It's not the brand or price of clothing that matters, it's how those pieces fit and how you feel in them.

You can look great at any price point, and planning a wardrobe—even one for going to the gym—is not as complicated as it may sound. All it takes is purchasing pieces in complementary color families. For instance, you might get yoga pants in green, black, and gray. Then choose tops in those same families, perhaps a few shades lighter and some of them marbled. All these pieces can be worn together to create a polished look. What's more, you absolutely don't have to spend $150 dollars at Lululemon or $99 dollars at Athleta for yoga pants if you don't want to. You can look as good in the Old Navy brand.

For men, one of my favorite pants on the market is Bonobos. They have their own store and are also sold at Nordstrom. Even good old Dockers now offer well-fitting straight leg pants in performance fabric that fit multiple body shapes and types.

There are certain brands and styles that work for every age and body type. I've created an online video guide expressly for readers of this book that shows exactly what works best for every body type and price point. Join my *Forged by Fire* Facebook Group (https://www.facebook.com/groups/milagriggforgedbyfire) to find out all my tips and tricks!

FIT IS KING

Back when I was still working primarily in fashion, I dressed people of all sizes, from negative zeroes to multiple X's. I quickly realized that, regardless of your shape or proportions, there is clothing you can get straight off the rack that will fit perfectly (with perhaps the exception of hemming the pants, skirt, or sleeves). During my fashion shows, I would bring all types of models—tall, short, rail thin, stocky and sturdy, young, old, you name it—on stage to prove my point.

When it comes to fashion, fit is king—and what's appropriate is going to be different depending on the occasion and audience. Let's take jeans for example. One pair might say *I'm going to work* and another *I should be mowing a lawn*. The professional-type jean typically has a darker wash, no whiskering across the front, and is hemmed to the right length. You aren't walking on your hems and the rest of your outfit is professional. When women wear jeans, you should have on a great looking shoe: heels, flats with an almond shaped toe, a blouse or button-down, blazer, and hair and makeup done. The jeans are the "party," but you need to remind yourself and others you are still a professional.

Another good example here is men's polo shirts. There are professional polos, others designated for date night, and still others for golf. The main difference is in the fabric and cut. Golf shirts are usually made with shinier performance fabric and fit more loosely, while the date night and professional polos come in polished cotton and have a slimmer profile.

No matter the type of polo, the sleeves should stop at the mid-upper arm and you should not be able to grab a lot of fabric underneath your triceps when holding your arm straight out. The shoulder line should be ON your shoulder, not the upper part of your arm, and the armhole should be close to your armpit. From the armpit, the fabric needs to go straight down your body (or you'll look like a flying squirrel!). Pro tip: always make sure the collar sits flat by steaming or ironing it before wearing.

My best advice is to focus on getting the right cut of shirt for your body type, whether you're shopping at Dillard's, Nordstrom, Brooks Brothers, Men's Wearhouse, Target, T.J. Maxx, or Walmart. Try on different sizes and fits—relaxed/classic (I don't recommend these as they tend to balloon out from the body), regular/standard, athletic, and slim—to see what looks best on you. It may vary from store to store, so it's worth expending the time and energy up front to get the best results. I know many of you guys hate shopping, but try to have fun with it. You will find out very quickly what works for your body type.

While men need to focus on the correct fit of shirts, I find women tend to need to pay more attention to pants. When working on image, I can't tell you how many pairs of slacks I've had to donate from clients' closets. Typically, the problem is in the rise and stride. The rise on a pair of pants is the distance from the crotch seam (between your legs) to the top of the waistband; this distance is important as it can influence where your waistline appears to be. If the rise is wrong, don't try to fix it—it won't work. You can hem pants and even tailor the leg width, but you can't fix a rise. If the crotch is too tight, it might be revealing. If it's too loose, the extra fabric gets in the way when walking and creates a sloppy appearance.

Pants should accentuate the natural shape and size of your body. Turn around and make sure there is no slouching in the rear end. No one wants to look like they're wearing a diaper. Also be aware that some fabrics stretch throughout the day and account for that when choosing the appropriate size. Try different styles and sizes to see what best fits your body proportions.

I've worked with people who want to buy sizes that are simply too big for them. When you wear bigger clothing, it does not make you look better—only bigger. No matter your size, your clothes have to fit your body.

THE HEAT

Show Them Who You Are

When my husband went to prison, I had to build us back up from nothing. Things were really tight financially. As a result, I learned how to dress on a budget—how to look like a million bucks but pay pennies.

When I went to visit Gordon on weekends, I made sure to both look and act like I was going to work. I always wore polished, tailored outfits that were confidence-boosting. I made eye contact with the guards in an intentional way, smiling when appropriate. I took a stance that conveyed, *You're going to check me in as fast as you can, because that is your job and what you're getting paid to do.* I signaled that there should be a level of mutual respect in all situations. Everything I did told the guards I was to be treated with respect and like a human being, and that I would do the same. I wanted them to know that I was a force to be reckoned with, despite having a husband behind bars.

If I can dress and act my best even in my worst moment, so can you. People decide who you are before you've ever said a word, so be intentional about how you present yourself at all times. Image matters, and you want to make sure yours is sending the right message.

WHAT DOES YOUR IMAGE TELL PEOPLE?

People make split-second decisions based on the way you look. It may not be fair, but that's reality. Every moment and every time you meet someone, you have an opportunity to create a lasting impression.

Ask yourself: Is this the image I want to present today? What do people think of me when they first see or meet me? Am I neatly groomed and dressed professionally? Have I ever lost a position to a person who was less qualified than me because of my image?

ARE YOU HALF-DRESSED?

To be successful, you need to do things 100 percent. That means making sure your clothes fit correctly and are appropriate for the occasion, your hair (and makeup, if you are a woman) is done, you are appropriately groomed, your shoes are polished, and your accessories scream professionalism. If only one of these things is off, people will notice and it will negate the effects of the things you did well.

Ask yourself: Is only the top half of me dressed appropriately when I am conducting business on Zoom? Do I take care of my appearance at all times—even when I'm going to the grocery store, gym, or amusement park? Do I choose outfits based on the situation? Do I generally feel I dress appropriately for the occasion?

DO YOU ADD A POP OF PERSONALITY TO YOUR OUTFITS?

Although you always want to look professional, you can also show parts of your personality through fashion at the office. Wearing a brightly colored heel with a darker suit or a jewel-toned blazer with navy or black slacks is one way to achieve this. The goal is to convey that you are serious about work while maintaining your individuality.

Accessories can also highlight a more playful side of you. Bracelets peeking out from under a jacket can add an element of color or surprise. Watches provide polish and personality while conveying that you are detail-oriented, deliberate, and respectful of other people's time. Other ways to show your personality are by mixing and matching gold and silver jewelry, and wearing colorful shoes, jewelry, pocket squares, or ties. Don't miss this opportunity to be unique and memorable!

Ask yourself: How can I add personality to my work wardrobe? What bright colors personify my message? What pieces might I invest in to act as my "personal pop?"

ARE YOUR BODY LANGUAGE, VOCAL TONE, AND FACIAL EXPRESSIONS SENDING THE RIGHT MESSAGE?

You can look great and say all the right words, but unless your body language, your tone of voice, and the look on your face align with these, people are going to feel very confused by your image. Developing a strong sense of self-awareness and reading how others are perceiving you will go a long way toward helping you achieve the success you desire.

Ask yourself: Am I giving strong eye contact? Do I smile when I greet people? Do I always remember to offer a firm handshake or fun fist bump? Do my vocal tone and eye contact match my words? Does my facial expression go along with the emotional tone of what I'm saying?

ARE YOU WELL-GROOMED?

Any number of small grooming mistakes can equal a big distraction.

Ensuring your hair, nails, and clothes are well-taken care of is imperative to your image. Being your best is the key to success and feeling your best. Remember this isn't about impressing other people. This is about sharing your best self so that your gifts can be seen immediately without distractions or an image that detracts from what others should see.

Ask yourself: Have I shaved my face? Have I applied my makeup carefully? Is there anything in my teeth? Have I groomed my eyebrows and removed any unibrow? Do I have any visible nose or ear hair? Are my nails clean and trimmed to an appropriate length? If they are polished, are they ALL polished? Is my hair dry and styled?

THE LIGHT: BRAND MIRROR RECAP

Presenting a positive image can change the trajectory of your career and life.

Your image should be authentic and true to your personal brand.

Though we are all wonderfully created by God, we live in a visual culture where image matters.

Everyone can cultivate a polished image on any type of budget.

Your image either creates trust or crushes it.

It's important to send the right message with what you wear and how you act.

Nonverbal communication matters! Look people in the eye, greet them enthusiastically, match your facial expressions and vocal tone to your message, and maintain good posture.

Good grooming begets good impressions.

Clothes must fit well to maintain a successful image.

Part Eight

BRAND SOCIAL

"To question the power of social media in society is to question the importance of sunlight on earth."

—ATANU SHAW, IN FORBES

THE SPARK

Social Media Is Not a Choice

Social media is how we communicate now. If you're not on it, you should just start writing on cave walls again.

Imagine someone is deciding between two companies to invest in. The first firm's CEO has a strong social presence, displays real thought leadership, and posts frequent videos. The second is nowhere to be found online. Since a whopping 82 percent of consumers say they are more likely to trust a brand when senior leadership is active and engaged on social media, and another 86 percent believe transparency from businesses is more important than ever before, it's a pretty sure bet the first company is going to get the investment.

When I first started in branding, social media didn't exist in the all-encompassing way it does today. Myspace had a moment and then faded into the background. Facebook was only used by college students at that point.

But then a few early adopters like Gary Vaynerchuk, who built a successful wine channel on YouTube, seized the opportunity social media had presented and ran with it. Soon, a wide variety of platforms like LinkedIn, Instagram, Snapchat, and now TikTok arrived on the scene, and the way products and people get promoted, viewed, and valued forever shifted.

Today, more than three billion users spend an average of 144 minutes scrolling through social media every day, giving us the opportunity to reach a mind-boggling number of people. Clearly, being online is no longer a choice—it's a MUST. And again, by the time you're reading this, these stats will have grown.

There are opportunities around every bend, things can change at any time, and people need to know who you are and what gifts you possess. Having a strong social media presence means you always have a solid brand ambassador base (people who share you, your company, your gifting, your brand), strong connections, and a story that represents all facets of yourself. It enables you to help others, lift your company whether you work for it or own it, build trust, and become someone people turn to in your field of expertise. It helps you pivot whenever necessary and avoid being overlooked.

For those of you who believe social media is not for you because it means you have to brag, "sell," or promote yourself in a cheesy way, I am here to tell you this is not the case. If you think it is only for people who are looking for a new job or career, that is also not the case. This truly is not about "fame" or grabbing onto some shiny new position—it's about creating lasting relationships and adding value.

I certainly wish I'd had the foresight Gary Vee did with YouTube. If I had been one of the first people to post a video after it was founded, how much wider would my reach be today? This is why I want you to jump into social media now. In the future, I don't want you to be thinking, "If only I'd known what a difference that could have made in my business and career!"

Whether you're a C-suite executive, business owner, entrepreneur, or fresh out of college, learning to successfully navigate social media is the answer to many of the challenges you now face or will face in the future. It is also about gaining influence in a world where the best way to have the furthest reach, and sometimes the most impact, is quite literally at your fingertips. Once again, it's about controlling your narrative. Where, how, and when you share your story impacts the way you are perceived (or not) by the world. With the right social media, you are ready for anything that comes your way.

Especially if you don't think you want to "do" social media, I want you to study this section carefully, experiment, and discover what the buzz is all about. All the information you've read, absorbed, and applied to your own brand in this book has fully prepared you to use social media to your best advantage. I promise, you are ready to present your best self to the world and start reaping the rewards that will return to you.

If anyone says differently, don't listen—there will always be the naysayer and the naysayer should not be taken seriously. In fact, learn to love the naysayer. Laugh at the negativity and let it fuel you, not hold you back.

Because the social media landscape changes quickly, this section will be continually updated in the *Forged by Fire* Facebook group (https://www.facebook.com/groups/milagriggforgedbyfire).

THE FUEL

Get Engaged

In previous chapters, we talked about how people decide very quickly whether you have anything to offer them when they see and hear you. So you probably won't be surprised to learn that the same holds true with social media. People are looking for stories, emotional connection, and important data that grab their interest and add value to their lives.

The point of social media is not to sell yourself online—it's to add value to other people's lives. It is also about engagement versus posting only. For people to follow and engage with you on social media, you have to follow and engage with them. It's as simple as that. When someone comes to your page and comments, respond. Start a conversation. Build a relationship. Help them understand why they should trust you.

Take the time to respond personally to anyone who wants to connect with you. Send a DM saying, *I really respect what you've done in your industry*, or *I loved your recent post about encouraging empathy in the workplace.* This is how you start to build brand and engagement versus having random followers who don't really know you.

Making a big impact on one person online is better than peppering a large amount of people with information and impacting none of them. When I was first starting out, any time someone asked me for an interview—even if they had one follower—I'd say yes. I spoke to all the networking groups I could. Nobody was too small when it came to sharing my brand. Today, that is still the case if I can make it happen.

Following, liking, commenting—this is how loyalty and trust is built online. When it comes to social media, engagement is the currency of success. Get engaged and get rich!

STAY CONSISTENT

Social media is just like every other aspect of branding—you have to stay consistent in mind, thought, engagement, tone, and emotion to be successful at it. People want someone who exhibits the same core values and principles in every post. They want to know what they're getting when you show up in their feeds. They want to know you will offer them some value, something they can learn or do immediately upon reading a post. Sometimes people know that when they go to your pages they will be encouraged, met with truth about hard topics, or inspired to do more and be better. Whatever it is, value must be shared.

You also have to post consistently. Frequent posts help you grow brand equity, value, or leadership. Sharing your message, co-branding with other people, reposting articles, and being a thought leader invites people to get to know you personally. This type of consistency creates trust, builds reputation, creates opportunity, and establishes your core values in all you do.

Even Gary Vaynerchuk says he doesn't post enough, and he posts more than anyone I've ever seen. I'd tell you to post twenty times a day if I thought that was a realistic goal, but instead I'll tell you to shoot for once a day to start if you haven't already. Frequent posting enables you to create new, meaningful relationships without filling your schedule with an insane amount of face-to-face coffee and lunch meetings.

Part of consistency is remembering to stay the course, even when you feel like things aren't happening fast enough for you online. When building your social media, it is important to remember that results are rarely, if ever, immediate. Every brand is built brick by brick, day by day, with consistency in action and communication.

You will inevitably fall, fail, have trials, and make mistakes. Welcome to the club! After you get up—hopefully quickly—you can keep going and start again.

This is where you can really stand out from the crowd. Your stability can be what people turn to you for in your industry, your area of thought, or your gifting. One day, someone will say, "I saw this incredible post..." about your project, column, blog, vlog, article, or experience, and the rewards will grow from there.

SOCIAL MEDIA MYTHS

None of the following are true!

- You can be an instant success with social media.

- You have to be on every social media platform to succeed.

- You're a lawyer, doctor, accountant, or other professional, so social media is not how you can grow your business.

- You can post anything—just post a lot, and your social media will be a success.

- You can't really tell if social media is working—it must be all hype.

- Social media is only for the younger generation—you are too old to get started and be relevant.

- You work in the background of your office—you are not client-facing therefore you don't need a LinkedIn.

LEVEL UP

Social media doesn't have feelings, loyalty, or concern about who your competition is. But it does give you the opportunity to communicate with a much wider audience than ever before, and this truly levels the playing field, giving smaller and lesser known brands more room to succeed. Instead of connecting with four colleagues at a local networking event, you can show up in the feeds of thousands of people you would never have been able to meet just by posting a valuable message and using the right hashtag.

One post viewed by one thousand people—what is that worth? And how long would it have taken you to be seen by that many in person?

It also helps people see that YOU are exactly who they need in this moment. For example, I recently received a referral from a professor at a large university that I had the opportunity to speak at a decade ago. She has continued to follow me online all these years, and when her friend needed branding help, I was the first person she thought of as a resource. She trusted me because of the information and value I've been sharing on social media all along and who she knew me to be.

Another speaking engagement was booked because the person in charge had been following me on LinkedIn for several years and had seen me speak to a small group in 2009. People think brand happens overnight but again, it happens brick by brick, one event after the other, one post, one column, one vlog, one interview, moving the needle forward daily. With social media, you can move that needle much faster.

Social media enables me to reach the most people most effectively by highlighting my gifting, offering my knowledge, and connecting authentically. It just takes time—which we all concentrate where we deem it most important. So where do I spend much of my work time? On social media.

I put my time into my marriage because I know that will create the best life for our family; my children because they're my greatest gifts and integral to my purpose here on earth; and my work, focusing on where I can add the most value to the most people in the most efficient way. My ultimate goals are to help others, build my brand, grow my business, and support my family.

Social media is truly the David that killed Goliath—and in this case, Goliath can be your competition. It gives everyone the same chance to be heard and seen, no matter how big or small, or how long you've been in business. To see big returns, you simply need to put the time and effort in. Then go crush it!

ELEVATE THE COMPANY'S BRAND THROUGH YOUR OWN

I'm often asked, *Does social media help grow brands from INSIDE a company?* The answer is a resounding YES. As an employee, you have the unique opportunity to help develop an audience for your company, organization, association, or corporate brand while moving your personal brand forward. Why? Because humans work for companies—and they are all ON social media, getting to know others THROUGH social media.

Personal brands serve to complement, build, and share corporate brands. In fact, statistics show that most people will go to an employee profile before a company profile. According to Sprout Social's 2019 Index, 45 percent of consumers said they were more likely to consider using a product or service if someone relatable—like an employee—posted about it rather than a business account. When companies post press releases or share about an award they won, it is typically pretty boring. But when an employee shares a press release and talks about what it means to them, WOW! Talk about immediate brand value.

Personal brands also help people outside a company see what goes on behind the scenes: The passion of the founder or executive teams. The concern the product developer has because they want the consumer to have the very best. The excitement of the sales professional when purchases help a business compete like never before. These are all stories that build brand loyalty, because they are PEOPLE-oriented messages, not PRODUCT-oriented.

When you have a strong personal brand that is building and sharing the company brand, your value to the company increases exponentially. You become priceless because you're speaking on their behalf. It's the ultimate win-win.

SHOW THEM WHO YOU ARE

During World War II, Winston Churchill frequently spoke on the radio, where his words and speeches engaged and encouraged the nation and the world. Volodymyr Zelensky, the President of Ukraine, has used video, image, emotional intelligence, storytelling, incredible communication skills, and social media to not only lead his country, but lead and influence the entire world. Both used the most effective media of the time to reach, influence, and reassure their audiences.

As a senior leader, businessperson or entrepreneur (or someone who wants to become one), you need to do the same. Being active and engaged on social media greatly enhances brand loyalty, equity, and trust. It allows you to lift up the curtain between the face of the brand and the people behind it. People get to hear your voice, learn the nuances of your personality, and bond with you in a different way than they might otherwise.

When you share yourself authentically, in a way that creates a good impression by telling real stories and being vulnerable when appropriate, people feel that you're trustworthy. When people trust you, you can pivot your brand in almost any direction. For example, Tesla goes to tequila, Dyson goes to desk lamps, Google goes from search to hosted email and so on.

When you have a strong brand and people know who you are, what you do, your gifting, and the value you add, you can cross industries, jump up a ladder quickly, be given more opportunities, pivot quicker than your perceived competition, and win faster.

> That way, your brand walks into the room before you do—and on social media, it networks for you even while you are sleeping.

Share the whole picture of yourself through social media. Bottom line, it gets you more opportunity. You don't have to be born with a silver spoon in your mouth anymore. Social media leveled that playing field and will continue to do so.

Want to succeed and be seen? GET SOCIAL.

GET IN THE GAME

When it comes to social media, the pandemic caught many people flat-footed. The companies they thought they'd retire from were shut down or downsized, and they were totally unprepared to be out in the job market again. They panicked because they didn't have content, followers, engagement, or thought leadership posted online.

If you, like them, feel behind the eight ball because you don't have a strong social media presence yet, I want you to know it's not too late. Study this section carefully, make a plan, and then start posting, engaging, and sharing. You can catch up.

First, it helps to know what platform or platforms you should post on. Which will give you the biggest reach? Where will provide the biggest return for your time investment? The answer is: it all depends. You have to find what works best for you and commit to it.

If you're an entrepreneur, you'll generally want to choose several places to become active on. If you're a business owner, you need to build your personal brand as much as the business. Your brands are linked regardless, and one should support and build the other.

My thoughts about a few of the platforms in general (you'll find specifics on each later in this section):

- Twitter is fantastic for establishing yourself as a thought leader and engaging with others. This is the engagement platform. On it you can find millions of "coffee shop" conversations. Find the right ones for you and jump in.
- Facebook for your personal brand can be the best way to become "friends" with business leaders in your community and share the whole picture of yourself. Facebook for Business is a fantastic marketing tool—if you actually use it and your market is open to it. Nashville, for instance, is still a Facebook town!
- Visual learners are hungry for content on YouTube. Statistic after statistic share how impactful video is and will continue to be.
- Instagram, Snapchat, and TikTok work well for engaging with EVERY demographic. I am currently working with a hospital system and selling them on the idea of using TikTok because it is necessary and getting in now is easier than later. All demographics are on all platforms, which is why this strategy is vital. Meet people where they are and share your message differently across platforms to do so. Don't miss the opportunity!
- And EVERYONE—regardless of industry, title, or length of time in the workforce—needs to be on LinkedIn. Absolutely, this is a non-negotiable. This platform isn't something you use only for when you need a job or a connection, it is the place to consistently share your story, expertise, experience, and personality so that when someone needs what you have, your content is right there for them to find and contact you before they call your competition.

Cultivating a strong online presence means you always have strong brand ambassadors. You don't get overlooked because you've highlighted your gifting and value. People know who you are and where to find you.

A strong social media presence is the best way to guard against the unexpected. It allows you to be seen so if things fall apart in "the real world," you have somewhere to land. Don't get caught in a tough spot like all those people in the pandemic—get online and get known.

SPEAK FROM EXPERIENCE

Even though I always understood the massive value of social media, I waited to present myself online as a thought leader until I was fully ready. I knew I had to BUILD my experiences before I could SPEAK from experience.

For thirteen years, I did everything I could to grow my knowledge. And then, when I finally became an expert to a degree, I started posting about branding regularly. I knew I had something of value to say, and I was able to say it with certainty. I now have a highly visible online presence, especially on LinkedIn, that provides value by highlighting my gifting.

While I want you to get out there and post, I also want you to know what you're talking about. If you're already an expert in your field, by all means share your thought leadership frequently and generously. Not yet an expert? No worries. Follow hashtags and keywords that are relevant to your business or industry. Co-brand with experts by reposting their content and adding your questions or commentary. Engage with their posts.

Keep growing and learning. Stay active online, but don't pretend to have knowledge you haven't earned yet. Your time will eventually come—you'll know when that is, and you'll be ready when it does.

KEEP IT REAL

There's nowhere to hide on social media. If there's a skeleton in your closet, some enterprising sleuth will come along and find it. Bet on it!

Still, that doesn't mean all is lost or that you should forget about putting yourself out there. If you've lived through a failure, social media can be an incredible way to play offense on it. Once again, it all goes back to controlling your narrative.

Whenever I'm working with a client who has made a mistake, we look to find another story that's similar to theirs. I then have them post about living and learning through the same situation as the well-known person we've identified as walking that same path. As I always say, we live through trials so we can help others who go through them.

Of course, I wouldn't suggest talking about failures every day, but being vulnerable and allowing a truly transparent moment can be extremely effective. None of us are perfect. We all make mistakes and fail. People are looking for authenticity, so when you're willing to share some of the ugly versus just the pretty, they begin to trust and relate to you more than ever before.

Be aware that social media is also something you'll probably MAKE mistakes on at one time or another. When that happens, your best bet is to apologize immediately. For instance, I was recently on Instagram and sent a message to a corporate client that was intended for one of my older daughters. While it was funny as a personal message, it was certainly not professional. The person who manages the corporate Instagram account I mistakenly sent it to is someone I trained, and she immediately came back with, *What on earth is this?* I called her, explained, and made a joke out of it, saying, *I obviously need glasses.* I now use this story to coach others. Mistakes can be very endearing if shared correctly.

The bottom line: don't let your past—or present—mistakes hold you back. Take control and play offense instead. People will respond to your honesty and ability to take responsibility for your actions.

BE INTENTIONAL

As a consultant, I'm often asked to help top corporations and small businesses make hiring decisions. They want to ensure the person has the right fit and skills for the position as well as a strong personal brand that resonates with the company brand, and are looking for me to review their qualifications. For most candidates, this type of review includes a social media audit. I'll walk into HR only to find an array of a candidate's Facebook, Instagram, Twitter, and LinkedIn posts printed out on a large conference table. I've seen qualified people missed because their LinkedIn profiles were dead profiles. People assume you don't know any better and are not knowledgeable about current market conditions. Don't stab yourself in the foot by having a dead or outdated profile.

For this and many other reasons, it's important to carefully consider the pieces of yourself you're putting out there. Make sure every post has the right context to go along with it. I know you have an amazing purpose, and that you're more than just one video, tweet, or picture—but you cannot let the world discern who you are. You have become the narrator of your own life and remain cognizant of how your story is being told.

For instance, before you start talking to coworkers about what you did over the weekend, you must first build a brand that tells them who you REALLY are—your why, purpose, and aspirations. That way, when you share the story of a particularly crazy time, they don't think to themselves, *Is this what she does before a huge presentation?* or *Is he going to go to the nearest bar after the convention when he should be networking with our vendors and suppliers?*

You need to paint a whole picture so people don't assume the worst. Then, if they see one post, hear one story, or even catch half of a story that seems a bit inappropriate, your brand will hold you steady in their minds. They know you can have fun, but they also understand you are serious when the situation calls for it.

I know I might sound like a little bit of a social media dictator here, but I'm giving you the rules now so you don't regret anything later. Is it fair? Probably not, but it's reality. If you want more freedom to share who you are, you must be intentional and aware of what you are posting now.

PICK THE RIGHT PICTURE

During the pandemic, Dolly Parton started a trend of posting four pictures meant for different social media platforms. A very buttoned-up Dolly wearing a professional suit and blouse with a bow at the neck was labeled LinkedIn; a well-coiffed but more casual Dolly wearing a black turtleneck was deemed right for Facebook; a black and white shot of a jean-clad, pig-tailed Dolly posing against a gritty wall with her guitar was slotted in for Instagram; and a sexy shot from *Playboy* was designated for her Tinder profile. The joke, of course, was how we choose to represent such different facets of ourselves depending on our audience.

Now of course, we all know Dolly is a genius, but she's especially on point with this one. On social media, profile pictures are extraordinarily important. They set the tone for everything else you do there. Your photo can either draw people in or make them keep scrolling, depending on how well you choose your shot. You can think of a headshot as the logo for your personal brand. This picture must be clear and taken from the chest up. In it, you should be wearing professional clothing (dark colors without patterns work best) and have your hair (and if you're a woman, makeup) done. Keep jewelry to a minimum.

As an entrepreneur or business owner, this matters more than many things you do. That first impression is huge. Again, professional is the key here: no grainy pictures, good makeup and hair, lighting, professional attire. That's not to say the picture has to be boring. You can have a waist-up shot as long as your face is really visible. Your hands can be crossed with one touching your chin. You can be sitting and leaning forward, both elbows on your thighs. And smile—you are not so important that you can't smile.

Carefully consider who you're trying to reach and post an appropriate picture for that particular audience. Make sure it wasn't taken at a party or cropped so it still includes someone's arm or half their head. Unless you're a veterinarian, keep your pets out of it. "Glamour shots" are also a no-no (if you're old enough to know what a glamour shot is, welcome to the club).

Yes, you absolutely must have a profile picture on every platform you join. It's fine if you don't have the budget for someone to take your profile pictures. Cell phone technology has come far enough that one taken in portrait mode will do fine until you can afford a great photographer (they are worth every penny). The amount of engagement you get when you have a picture versus when you don't is incredible, so just do it.

THE FIRE

The Basics of Posting

One of the most prolific and successful people I follow online runs a healthcare association. He posts about healthcare, leadership, empathy, seeing people's gifting and purpose, and bringing teams together. He's also a big fan of Patrick Lencioni, often reposting the author's content with commentary. I have never met this leader in person, but I can tell he has expertise in a wide variety of things by the way he's actively engaging with his audience. Looking at his profile, I can easily understand his platform and the value he shares. This is the goal!

So what should you post about? It all depends on what you want to accomplish and who you're trying to reach. Follow these steps to get a clearer picture of the content you need to start sharing.

STEP 1: DEFINE YOUR GOALS AND TARGET DEMOGRAPHICS

Determine your personal and professional goals over the next five to ten years. Ask yourself:

- Where do I want to be in five years?
- What narrative, if any, do I need to fix?

- Where do I have to be in one year to get to where I want to be in five?
- What do I need to change in the next ninety days to get to where I need to be in one year?
- What do I need to share to get to that one-year goal in the next 90 ninety days?
- And finally, WHO needs to know?

There's your audience. Goals—without them you're sunk and posting blindly.

Once you pinpoint the demographic you'll need to reach online, think about the kind of information they'll want to hear and how to best capture their attention. Having a plan and audience in mind is key to success on social media. For instance, when I'm working at two in the morning, I'll often take a picture and post it with the caption, *Hey, anyone else out there working with me?* The demographic I'm going for here is busy entrepreneurs. I never fail to get people commenting back, even at that hour. We bond over our businesses and what it takes to be successful—and how tired we can be at times!

People often think they can capture everyone with a single post, but that's absolutely not the case. Providing context is so much more important than just tossing out widespread content. A bunch of micro-focused posts are going to be much more effective than one sweeping, generalized macro post.

You want to directly engage with all the different buckets of people you're trying to reach. For instance, if you're selling life insurance, you might write one post for middle-aged women, another for men going through divorce, and yet another to families that have recently had a baby. The goal is to get their attention, make them feel understood, and offer a solution or even commiseration for whatever challenges they may be facing.

STEP 2: DETERMINE WHAT THEY NEED TO HEAR

It's your responsibility to find out what people need to hear from you to tip the scales in your favor. As you start brainstorming specific posts, it can be helpful to think of yourself as a teacher: What have you learned in life? Succeeded at? Failed at? The idea is to share your own wisdom through experiences and personal stories that build your value and help others learn from you.

I met with an entrepreneur recently who had by all earthly definitions "made it." He said, "Why social for me? Why now?" I questioned what he wanted his legacy to be—teaching others, building communities, some other takeaway about his experience and successes. Then I asked him, "Why aren't you giving away your knowledge online via blogs, videos, book recommendations, and podcast interviews?" And there it was. How he leaves a legacy is by teaching others on social media. New life was breathed into his heart.

The best posts create authentic moments of connection and promote bonding. For instance, I recently coached a client transitioning from one industry to another, and had her post the top thirteen things she'd learned over the past thirteen years in her current position. Some points were industry-related and others were data-focused. Some were successes and others were failures. Some had longer explanations and others only included short blurbs. The variety of information she shared and the different ways she did that reached a record number of people for her and created a high level of engagement. Get creative!

STEP 3: CO-BRAND FOR CREDIBILITY

Another great way to generate posts is by sharing stories from other influencers or data points from pertinent studies that have already gone viral—meaning, they've been seen and "liked" by thousands or even millions of people before. Adding a few sentences to your own post about how you relate to the content helps others see the original idea through your filter. Co-branding with well-respected centers of excellence like Harvard, Chapel Hill, and Stanford extends your reach and adds to your credibility, especially when you want to share data points.

For instance, I reposted a video from Mary Callahan Erdoes of JP MorganChase on LinkedIn. In it, she advised executives to do a deep dive and become the expert in a specific topic. I fully agree with this idea, so I wrote up a blurb about my own thoughts on it and shared it to my network. I used her brand to lift mine, and it created a lot of conversation and engagement on my page.

You'll know your social media is really starting to take off if people start reposting YOUR content and using your brand to lift theirs. It's always such an exciting moment when brands start to transition from being built to building others!

STEP 4: FOLLOW A POSTING CALENDAR

Once you've come up with some ideas of what you'd like to share, it's a good idea to develop a posting calendar. It might look like this:

- Monday: Motivation. This is a great time to share a story of your own, a lesson you've learned, or a lesson someone else has learned and taught you. Motivational quotes should not be daily, but when backed by a good story, they are always relevant, uplifting, and brand-building.
- Tuesday: Industry-specific. Be sure to tag others when sharing their successes, building a company post by resharing, or giving your take on an article in an industry publication.
- Wednesday: Learning/teaching moment. Post about something you've learned over the past year, the most salient points in a book you read, or an interesting fact you've recently come across.
- Thursday: Co-branding. Post a quote from someone with a strong brand, share a column from *Forbes* and offer your own insight, share a post from an industry influencer, or recommend a book that resonates with you on leadership or legacy.
- Friday: Inspiration. This can be something you share from your

own life or from someone else's. Sharing others' stories is a great way to build engagement. Share other people's posts and spend time engaging with them and building their brands.

Creating a structure for posting ensures you're including a variety of offerings for the different segments of your audience. It also ensures you will do "something." I love things to be more organic, but so many clients need an outline as a jumping-off point that will then hopefully lead to some spontaneous creativity!

And speaking of your audience: I want you to know that you can't serve the world. Not everyone is going to like your story, and that's fine. Just keep sharing. Stay true to your own message and the audience it relates to will flock to you.

STEP 5: GET CREATIVE TO EXTEND YOUR REACH

Here are some more specific ideas for reaching more people:

- Use trending hashtags in your posts, specific to each platform you're using (more on this in a bit).
- Layer a quote over a picture. This is much more effective than a static quote alone. You can find royalty-free pictures on many different sites including Unsplash and Pixabay.
- Post stories, whether captured on video or in a blog-type post. Stories are remembered twenty-two times more than facts.
- Repurpose your content from one platform to another. For instance, you can expand upon an idea you posted on Twitter by taking a screenshot of the original tweet, posting it as a picture on Instagram, and then writing a blog post to go along with it.

Maintaining an active presence, creating thought-provoking content, and being authentic and appropriately vulnerable is the best way to attract and build your social media audience. Believe it or not, using emotional intelligence on social media is vital! All that starts with one post, followed by another and another and another. Get started and keep going.

THE BASICS OF PROVIDING CONTEXT

The best way for people to start to know you and the value you offer is to provide context for all your posts. Blogging is the written version of this, and vlogging—a video blog or video log—is the visual and auditory version.

BLOGGING

When I talk about blogging on social media, I don't mean you have to sit down and write a thesis. I'm simply referring to your caption or story that goes along with your post. A social media blog can be as simple as a paragraph talking about why you shared a specific article from *Forbes* or *Becker's Healthcare Review*. You might expand on what you agree or disagree with in the original post, or how your work coincides with the article's content. You might even be able to show that you're innovative and ahead of the curve because you've already been doing what they're telling you to do for ten years!

A different example: I coached a man who grew up in Kansas. Scouring his potential employer's social media posts, I saw a blog about one of his interviewers being born and raised in the same hometown. It was a mind-blowing moment, and they ended up knowing a lot of the same people. When you give people pieces of yourself in your blogging, you can create incredible bonding moments like this. You will learn quickly how much smaller the world gets if you give a piece of yourself here and there for others to attach to!

VLOGGING

Vlogging is another great way to get in front of people. This has become an increasingly popular way to increase visibility and build online engagement. Vlogs are affordable, easy to digest, and a great way to develop rapport.

People really respond to being able to see and hear you talk confidently online. Here are some mind-blowing stats to convince you to start vlogging if you haven't already:

- The forecasts for video usage are through the roof. Data shows that by 2022, online videos will make up more than 82 percent of all consumer internet traffic—fifteen times higher than it was in 2017—and it will just keep growing from there. (Source: Cisco)
- Six out of ten people would rather watch online videos than television. (Source: Google)
- Viewers retain 95 percent of a message when they watch it in a video compared to 10 percent when reading it in text. (Source: Insivia)
- Social video generates 1200 percent more shares than text and image content combined. (Source: G2 Crowd)
- Ninety-two percent of users watching video on mobile will share it with others. (Source: WordStream)
- Video campaigns on LinkedIn have 50 percent view rates. (Source: LinkedIn)
- On average, people spend 2.6 times more time on pages with video than without. (Source: Wistia)
- Video increases organic search traffic on a website by 157 percent. (Source: Conversion XL)
- Seventy-eight percent of people watch online videos every week, and 55 percent view online videos every day. (Source: HubSpot)
- A website is fifty-three times more likely to reach the front page of Google if it includes video. (Source: Insivia)
- Eighty-five percent of consumers want to see more video content from brands. (Source: HubSpot)
- Fifty-nine percent of executives say they would rather watch a video than read text. (Source: WordStream)
- Seventy-two percent of customers would rather learn about a product or service by way of video. (Source: HubSpot)
- Including a video on your landing page can boost your conversion rate by up to 80 percent. (Source: Unbounce)
- Sixty-five percent of executives have gone to the marketer's site and 39 percent have called them on the phone after watching a marketing video. (Source: Forbes)

You can vlog from anywhere—I recently did one in the pick-up line at my daughter's school. Take out your phone, flip the camera, press record, and start talking. Good content trumps perfect production.

Video gives you the ability to communicate emotions more effectively. The most watched TED Talk ever has more hand gestures than any other, so speak in an animated manner using your hands. This helps others grasp what you're saying, relate, and buy into it more.

Use vlogs to document your journey. Share who you are, your why, purpose, and value. Discuss why you get up every day. People love to follow others—especially entrepreneurs—who are passionate about what they do. Get people excited about where you're going and take them along for the ride with you. They want to be a part of your success. And—big one—how do you make people feel when they go to your page?

As always, image matters. Always present yourself as a professional because people immediately buy in to you being a thought leader or they don't. In general, I suggest men wear a polo, button-down shirt, jacket, or any combination of those, and women wear a blouse or jacket. However, it all depends on your industry.

Vlogs don't have to be long to be effective. When it comes to inspiring viewers to action, videos less than two minutes long have the best engagement. Since data shows most videos are watched on mute, be sure to have captions whenever you can. Instagram puts them in there for you automatically if you choose to enable them, and there are several other captioning apps that will help you to be seen and heard. If you have the gift of speaking, my suggestion is to vlog at least once a week and post it on all your social media platforms.

You can add your vlogs to emails and post them on YouTube, LinkedIn, Facebook, Instagram, TikTok, Snapchat, and on corporate websites and intranets. In particular, YouTube offers a great platform and audience for your vlogs. In the US alone, 82 percent of people report using YouTube, making it the most popular social media platform. Worldwide, it boasts two billion logged-in active monthly users. Millions of people have YouTube channels, and over a billion hours of YouTube videos are watched daily.

NAVIGATING LINKEDIN

Clients often come to us for help building their personal or company brands—or both! They say they want to get into new markets, grab investor attention, create greater confidence, increase shareholder value, and exponentially grow their businesses. Yet at the same time, they'll say, *I just don't understand this LinkedIn thing*. This kills me! With more than 760 million total users in over 200 countries and territories, and 260 million monthly users—40 percent of whom are daily users—LinkedIn is an absolute must for any professional. (You may be reading this book at a time where those numbers have doubled—it will only keep growing!)

For example, I recently worked with a company that was seen in the marketplace as stodgy and old school because they weren't communicating well. They were losing people to their competitors because there wasn't any useful or updated information on social media—from either employees or leadership—about the workplace culture. I taught them how companies that are crushing it use LinkedIn to show what it's like to work for them. A "Life" page anyone?

After wrangling with some of the top execs about LinkedIn, I created a brand strategy that included posting guidelines, instructions on sharing culture, examples of winning posts that went viral in the region, and marketing plans for all locations that spoke to individual voices and so much more. They utilized these tools to showcase their culture, their employees, and the "fun" aspects of the business. Then I took the brand guide we created along with the social toolboxes and educated their employees on how to build and share their personal brands on their own LinkedIn pages.

They followed my advice and are now starting to be seen in a better light by employees, recruits, AND consumers. Their bottom line? Well, that's growing as well. The best part is that the one naysayer of the group is on board now, too (this after being rude, arguing, thinking they knew better, and lagging behind so far that employees started questioning the leader's ability to lead). What a win!

Another example: at an accounting firm I coached on marketing, one leader loved to connect—relational should be her middle name—so she had so many stories to use on LinkedIn. Her counterpart at the firm was the exact opposite, and told me, *I'm not going to share anything personal about myself. That's not what social media work is for.* To get his buy-in, I pointed out that many people responded to his direct manner of speaking. His way of getting to the truth is so fast and fearless, and that type of leadership and transparency of information was what he needed to show on LinkedIn. Both ended up building strong networks on the platform by using their unique personalities to highlight what they had to offer clients.

The best part of LinkedIn is that people WANT to find you there.

According to *US News & World Report*, 95 percent of employers use LinkedIn to find and vet potential candidates. This platform is one of the few ways you can advocate for career opportunities twenty-four hours a day, seven days a week.

Many companies now encourage employees to include their personal LinkedIn in their email signatures because it's a great way to share the company story. If you own a business, you definitely want your people to do this. If you're an employee in a larger organization and this isn't protocol yet, perhaps you can be the one to say it should be and put a feather in your cap as a result.

Gary Vee believes LinkedIn is now what Facebook was in 2012, and I agree wholeheartedly. This is where you need to be to grow your brand, value, and gifting. It's time to get on board if you aren't already there.

DEVELOPING YOUR PROFILE

As the most powerful networking tool in social media, LinkedIn requires you to present yourself as professionally as possible. The goal is to convey your why, what you are passionate about, and who your ideal client, job, or employer is. Maximizing your profile means maximizing your networking opportunities.

Photos

Data shows that LinkedIn profiles with photos get twenty-one times more views and thirty-six times more messages than those without, so you absolutely must include one in yours.

The cover photo is an often-underutilized space at the top of your page where you can place a graphic that shares a bit of who you are. If you're an entrepreneur, this should be the logo of your company, potentially overlaid with a larger picture in the background. Otherwise, you can use this spot to post a vision or mission statement from the company you work for, your values or value statements, a picture of your entire team with the logo and mission on top of it, or an event you're promoting, or borrow a quote that reflects your values. This sets the tone for your profile. Some Amazon employees have a cover photo with Amazon's principles—love it!

The Headline

This area, found right under your name, is one of the most visible parts of your LinkedIn profile. It is the fastest advertisement and biggest billboard (other than your picture) you have, and it should encourage people to stay on your profile. When you have a headline that works for the platform, you have more profile views which lead to more opportunities.

You now have 220 characters to tell people who you are. How do you make them memorable, eye-catching, and authentic?

Let's look at a few examples:

- Southwest: We run on Southwest Heart!
- Tractor Supply Company: Work hard, have fun and make money by providing legendary service and great products at everyday low prices.
- Tim Ferris: Bestselling author, human guinea pig. Experiments: tim.blog

Here are some ideas for you:

- Searching for brave minds to help us reimagine the healthcare industry (insert whatever industry works for your business here)
- Career matchmaker
- I usually don't stalk profiles—but if I do, it's most likely because I have an opportunity for you!
- Marketing ninja
- Nerd at heart, searching for answers in the lab

- Saving companies over $10.4M since 2015

Certainly, your headline can mention more than your title and company alone. Titles are different in different companies, and they don't tell people why they should keep reading. Differentiate yourself. Share the type of value people should expect to receive from you instead.

People can relate to measurable successes across industries, so include something about your experience and share some type of win. Did you drive growth, add 100K users, build metrics, and beat them? This is the type of information you want to put here.

Headlines play a large role in LinkedIn's search algorithm, and also carry weight when the platform itself is deciding which profiles to show for various search queries. Since LinkedIn is a search engine—like Google or YouTube—you need a headline that uses keywords. Don't stuff keywords, but use them authentically and easily when possible. Always focus on the ones that capture the most attention.

The About Section

This is where you can share your story quickly, but differentiate it by using your own words. Depending on the industry you're in, it may not have to be totally buttoned-up and can take a more personal tone. For instance, a CEO I follow shares that he is married with kids, loves a specific sports team, and has realized he is at his best when he knows his teams have everything they need. He also shares his why.

The head of communications for Southwest Airlines, Linda Rutherford, shares a personal and professional story that allows us to see a bit more of her instead of a title alone:

> *My dream in life was to work as a beat reporter for a major newspaper. While working for the Dallas Times Herald I had the privilege of meeting the wonderful people at Southwest Airlines. There was something about the People and the Company I couldn't shake. Turns out I didn't have to! I*

joined the Southwest Family as a Public Relations Coordinator in 1992. I now proudly lead Culture & Engagement and Communications & Outreach efforts across Southwest Airlines. I am privileged to work with the best People in the industry.*

Use the about section to help people get to know you a bit more. Offer career context, highlight your personality, and share a piece of your story. Use keywords to maximize SEO. Give people a reason to stop scrolling and want to link to you.

WHAT TO POST

Daily engagement on LinkedIn is key to getting noticed on the platform. Some ideas about what to post to your LinkedIn page include:

- Show videos that are positive, encouraging, and focusing on the good. People need and love leaders who inspire and motivate.
- Share an article and review it. Tell people why you agree—even better, tell them if you don't!
- Add a personal twist to something you know or do that adds value to your brand. How do you differ? Are you faster; do you know more or have experience the competition doesn't?
- One of my all-time favorite marketing experts, Neil Patel, had a post titled, "5 biggest SEO lessons I've learned over the last few years." This is easy—lessons learned that can add value to other people's lives. Share photos of your team, office, or meetings. Pictures always have a much better view rate than words alone. Tag other people in them and tell the story about what you were doing.
- Co-brand with influencers—people inside and outside of your industry that are making a statement. Share their thoughts, give them credit, and then say why you agree or disagree. Follow and engage with them. You can build bonds with anyone.
- Tell a personal story with a professional callback. For instance, I recently posted a picture of my husband and our two youngest

---

* "About," from Linda Rutherford's LinkedIn profile, https://www.linkedin.com/in/lindarutherford/.

girls when we were on a trip in Rosemary Beach to my LinkedIn. My caption talked about how entrepreneurs need to take a
moment to breathe every once in a while. This stayed on brand
while allowing me to share a bit more about my life outside of
work with colleagues. I was pleased to find it garnered a different
kind of loyalty and deeper level of trust. I recommend doing this
only once every month or two.

Shout-out to Neil Patel: You're a digital marketing force of nature, and
I would love to meet you one day!

USING HASHTAGS

Hashtags are the currency of LinkedIn. Use them to show what you're
interested in, and what other conversations you'd like to join. Your
profile offers hashtags you can follow.

I recommend using trending hashtags to create consistency online. The
goal is to engage more people and encourage your contacts to expect
specific content from you on specific days. Since daily engagement is key,
here are some hashtags to consider using based on the day of the week:

- Monday: #MondayMotivation #MotivationMonday #Marketing-
  Monday #MindfulMonday #MondayFunday
- Tuesday: #TravelTuesday #TransformationTuesday #TipTuesday
  #TechTuesday
- Wednesday: #Humpday #WisdomWednesday #WellnessWednes-
  day #WayBackWednesday #WineWednesday #WackyWednesday
  #WomenWednesday #WinItWednesday
- Thursday: #ThrowbackThursday (or #TBT) #ThankfulThursday
  #ThoughtfulThursday #ThursdayThoughts #TGIT (Thank God
  It's Thursday)
- Friday: #FlashBackFriday #FearlessFriday #FridayReads #Fol-
  lowFriday (or #FF) #FeatureFriday #FridayFun #FactFriday
  #FreebieFriday #TGIF (Thank God It's Friday)

Obviously you can create your own—but those won't help you initially to be found. Find the hashtags that are trending for your industry, business, and region and use those to begin.

HOW TO ENGAGE

Your goal is to have 500 connections on LinkedIn. Once you get to 500, the platform stops counting on your homepage. Five hundred or bust!

My advice as you begin is to accept everyone who wants to link with you unless they don't have a picture. The platform is about networking and sharing value, and even if you do not see an immediate connection with that person's industry or lane, you never know who else they know. If they do not have a picture posted, it's okay to ignore the request.

When you invite someone to LinkedIn or accept someone's invitation to do so, always follow up with a personal note. Say, *I really appreciate you accepting my invitation* or *I'd love to know more about what you do.* Sending a generic note—or worse, none at all—is a massive lost opportunity.

Make sure you "follow" some of the leading brands in your industry. Not only will this make your newsfeed more interesting, but you can also pick up plenty of great LinkedIn ideas and tactics by observing how they use this medium.

"Pin" a relevant article to your "featured" section each week or month. Change this out as often as you would like to. I recommend doing this once a month at a minimum.

NAVIGATING INSTAGRAM

With roughly one billion monthly active users, Instagram is where it's at!

It's important to come up with a personal branding strategy for sharing your expertise via photos, videos, and text captions on this platform. Some people like to read posts, others want to listen to you speak, and some simply want data and graphics. Your grid should include something for everyone.

Instagram has always been known as more playful and visually-based, but you also have to remember that most people are scrolling it on a phone. Profile pictures here need to make a big impact in a small space. I'd typically suggest using a smiling headshot here.

Instagram's bio is only 150 characters long. You'll want to use these characters to tell people what your brand is all about. Always add a link to your bio that directs people to more information about your recent posts or company.

Make sure the photos and videos you post are high quality. Pictures should be cropped well and in sharp focus. You can use Canva or Adobe Spark to easily create graphics to go along with your photos. Videos need to be clear. Titles are always helpful!

And while we're on the topic of video—use the Instagram Stories and Reels features. This is a huge missed opportunity if you don't. Not only does the stories feature allow you to group together stories of interest, but it also allows you to market to specific demographics.

Develop a daily posting schedule that takes advantage of when your audience is most active. Doing a search into your Insta Insights shows you when this is. I recommend posting one or two times a day to the platform. Be sure to like and comment on others' content to increase your following.

Using hashtags is another way to help others discover you and generate more followers. Be careful not to overuse hashtags because your content might then be mistaken for spam. A good range is five to twelve hashtags per post.

Here are some ideas of what to post on Instagram:

- Host a webinar, lunch and learn, or client event. Market the event on Instagram to specific groups with the goal of giving away tips to people who need your expertise.
- Take a picture and share some slides of what you are learning or teaching.
- Post pictures of books you're reading or events you're attending.
- Use quotes that match your brand values.
- Engage with people on your IG newsfeed by liking their posts or leaving a comment.
- Start a conversation by sending someone a direct message.
- Find and follow relevant people in your niche—if they like what you post, they might follow you back.
- Use engagement features such as "Ask me a question" or "Create a poll" in Instagram stories.
- Highlight certain stories you want to keep for longer than 24 hours in your IG profile.

NAVIGATING FACEBOOK

With almost three billion users, Facebook is still crushing it! Most individuals use Facebook daily, giving your brand maximum visibility. Across all age groups, 83 percent of users say they want to see key characteristics of a brand's personality on Facebook.

Some people I coach refuse to use Facebook, or refuse to use it for work-related reasons. But if you're not on there, you're missing a big opportunity. Despite a backlash from younger generations who often view Facebook as outdated, the sheer volume of people you can reach make it imperative to be on it—maybe even more than you already are.

In many cities—like Nashville, Austin, Atlanta, and Charlotte—Facebook is still one of the best ways to get to know other businesspeople. For instance, I am "friends" with many leaders in Nashville on Facebook. I share a different side of myself on the platform for my personal page, but with incredible intention. Whenever I go to an event, it never fails that someone will comment, "Your daughter has the curliest, blondest hair!" or "I've been watching your kids grow up!" This allows us to bond in a different way, and on a more personal level.

Every once in a while, I'll also repost something from my company page on my personal Facebook and share a bit of what it means to me. My goal is to give people a larger picture of my life. I want them to realize I love what I do for work, but that I'm also a wife and a mom, and I love Jesus.

To understand what interests other people, research what pages and groups your friends belong to, and pay attention to posts they share and comment on. In turn, like and comment on posts you can then use as topics of discussion—pictures of their children or grand-children, hobbies, and celebrations like anniversaries and weddings. Having this kind of awareness helps you bond quickly with others.

As with any platform, it's important to update and share your status regularly. Posting once a day is ideal. If you can't manage that, aim for posting at least three times a week. If you ignore your page, people will lose interest and forget about you.

Make sure your profile, and specifically the about section, is fully com-plete. Add in as much information as possible about your workplace, schools, and spouse here. Include a link to your LinkedIn profile and put your skills and interests outside of work on display. This allows others who want to know more about you to take a deeper dive or contact you directly to learn more.

On your personal Facebook page, you can be a bit looser and show more personality. My profile picture here is always of my family because I want to let people know what is most important to me. That being said, I am always cognizant that I am "friends" with business leaders and make sure to post appropriately as a result.

Obviously, business Facebook pages are open to all followers—the more, the better. My general advice about your personal Facebook page, though, is to keep it private. If you use Facebook only to see pictures of your grandkids or other family members, friend only people you already know and have a close, personal relationship with in real life. If you feel it's appropriate for you, friend specific people you want to connect with in your industry and business community. I take advantage of the opportunity Facebook gives me to befriend leaders in my area, but that may not be the strategy you want to take because it limits what is appropriate to post. Everyone has different goals.

Either way, jump in with both feet. Friend, share, and engage. Let people know who you are—your why, your gifting, and your passions.

TOP TIPS FOR FACEBOOK BUSINESS PAGES

For Facebook business pages, the most effective content comes in the form of videos, blogs, and curated posts that take existing content relevant to your industry and add the firm's brand voice and value to it. A great way to find high-quality content is to use the Facebook feature *Pages to Watch* to see what other top brands in the industry are talking about and sharing.

Some other suggestions for making your page a success are:

- Make the most of cover photos. Don't miss the opportunity to promote your business with eye-catching cover photos. People are interested in what you and your business look like, so give them the best impression possible. (Yes, it's fine to use the same cover photos on multiple platforms.) I'd prefer different ones, but don't overthink it. JUST DO. START.
- Pin the most important content at the top of the page. A pinned post is simply a regular post that you assign to stay at the top of your page so it doesn't get bumped down when you post new content. You can also use this space to share important news, showcase an amazing video, raise awareness about a current campaign, or anything else that will get people to engage with your

brand on Facebook. I suggest changing what you pin every week—once a month minimum.

- Link your page to other company communications and platforms. Make it easy for people you interact with on other social networks to find your Facebook page by linking to it in employee email signatures, company newsletters, and other channels. Incorporate Facebook like and share buttons on your website and on all blogs, vlogs, and newsletters so people can follow and share your page in one click.
- Make full use of the about section. Typically, the about tab is the first place people check for relevant information about your company. I recommend creating a video about your company's why to include here, and pinning it to the top of the page.
- Use keywords strategically. Keyword optimization is critical for social media marketing. Optimize your Facebook page by placing keywords in your title, URL, About Us, status updates, and other daily content. Keywords improve your chances of being seen in user searches, which means they will be more likely to find and engage with your content.
- Utilize Facebook Live. It is estimated that Facebook live videos get an average of sixty-four billion views per day. This is a fantastic way to increase social media engagement and get six times more interactions than regular Facebook videos. I recommend doing a Facebook Live monthly. Choose a different theme or topic each time, and be sure to add a personal element or story into it. Share value—don't sell. The goal is for you, your business, and your employees to become the thought leaders in your area.

NAVIGATING TWITTER

Total Number of Monetizable Daily Active Users: 199 million (according to the company themselves)

You can think of Twitter as a virtual cocktail party where a variety of conversations are all happening at once. The goal is to find out where your voice, gifting, experience, and advice would be the most helpful.

The most common reason people use Twitter is to learn about breaking news. This makes it a great platform for not only posting pithy content but also for sharing newsworthy articles and other relevant information.

Make sure you are speaking conversationally when you tweet. You will know it's working when people start talking back to you. If you read back your tweet and it doesn't sound like something you would say, or how you would say it, tweak it to match your personal style.

I recommend adding images to your tweets whenever you can. Original content is more likely to go viral with the right picture and hashtag. As with other platforms, reposting an already viral tweet with your commentary on it is also a good way to extend your reach.

Statistics show posting one to five times a day increases audience engagement dramatically. If you have several posts, blogs, content, and reshares, don't hesitate to share them on this platform. It's built for conversation and engagement!

Hashtags are critical to success on this platform. They are a great way to learn from others and improve your social output. Use hashtags to narrow down topics and find more specific conversations that are taking place and also be discovered. For instance, if you're an accountant or own an accounting firm, you might put #accounting, #accountinghour, or #bizadvice in a Twitter search. The platform then gives you potential profiles to follow, along with the latest relevant tweets, people, photos, and videos. Then, use these hashtags in your own posts as a way to lead people to your content.

Be sure to follow people in your industry. Their tweets can provide a wealth of information about their interests, needs, preferences. Engage by commenting, liking, and resharing their content. When you do this, be sure to tag them with an @ mention to drive traffic their way.

Here are some ideas for tweets:

- Retweets of other thought leaders
- Details of new publications or resources you have produced
- News items that feature your research
- Links to any blog posts you've written
- Thoughts on conferences you attended, tagging the featured speakers and people you met as well as using the conference hashtags
- Questions that invite feedback
- Interesting news items and photos you've found related to your experience, industry, or area of leadership
- Replies to other people's tweets
- Retweets of other people's tweets
- Funny memes that show your sense of humor (when appropriate)

NAVIGATING SNAPCHAT, TIK TOK, PINTEREST, AND
EVERYTHING ELSE WE DON'T EVEN KNOW IS COMING

Regardless of when you read this book, here is what you need to remember about all platforms: YOUR AUDIENCE.

1. Who are you trying to capture?
2. You aren't SELLING. You're sharing value—a part of yourself, your business, and personal story.
3. You are engaging with EVERYONE.
4. You are changing your posting strategy daily as campaigns succeed and fail.
5. You know how to make a good piece of content—whether a video, blog, or picture—to get somebody to be compelled to do business with you.
6. You are NOT quitting after one ad campaign didn't do well.
7. You KNOW what your audience needs to hear and are going ALL IN.
8. Don't make the mistake of thinking a platform is not for you, especially before you have researched or looked into it yourself.

NAVIGATING EMAIL

Email is still one of the best ways to communicate in business, but can it be considered a social media platform? From the perspective that you are sharing vital information, data, and value through it, the answer is a definite yes. Email is a great place to share your brand or story, sell a point, and show who you are.

When writing an email, your subject line should be clear and direct. Some examples are: Quick Question, Proposal Suggestion, or Meeting Date Changed. If the topic of the email changes, start a new thread rather than continuing to reply using the original subject line.

Take care to always include a greeting. This could simply be the recipient's name and a quick comment like *hope you are well*. Find a way to connect with the recipient to humanize your brand. Be polite before jumping into business.

Within the body of the email, consistency is once again key. Use only one space after a period and use exclamation points sparingly, as they can seem unprofessional and immature. Be cautious about using humor, and avoid emojis, memes, and pictures unless you're sure you can. Ensure that your signature and text are in the same font (and not Times New Roman—it's outdated).

And speaking of email signatures: I recently saw one that was an unclickable picture—meaning, you couldn't click the social icons or website link. It made the person who sent the email seem unprepared and unprofessional. Embedding your email address and social links into your signature enables people to research you further and contact you easily.

To avoid sending an unfinished or unchecked email, wait until you are finished drafting to add the recipient's address. Proofread every message for grammar and spelling before hitting send. A word to the wise: while spellcheck is a wonderful thing, it sometimes changes words to something you wouldn't want. For example, I recently wrote to somebody *one sec*, which was meant to be short for *one second*. I checked on my text later and saw autocorrect had changed it to *one sex*. I immediately texted again, *That was obviously unintentional.* We thankfully laughed about it, but I don't want you to find yourself in the same position.

People can feel what you're saying through email, so it's important to stay cognizant of the impact your words will have on the recipient. If you're unsure how your message sounds, send it to a trusted friend or colleague to double-check your tone. Better to spend more time upfront getting it right than having to clarify and apologize later.

If you send an email with great intention but it isn't read that way on the other side, stop what you're doing and pick up the phone. At the end of the day, nothing is more effective than a voice on the phone saying *I'm sorry*. Recognize the person's frustration. Thank them for letting you know how they feel. Everyone wants to be seen, valued, and respected.

And I'm sure this goes without saying, but I'll reiterate anyhow: Avoid *reply all* when responding to emails. The same goes for continually liking and hearting texts in a large group chat. Both are annoying and unnecessary.

Email is an extension of you. Your messages on it last forever, just like posts on other social media, and can be forwarded to anybody at any time. So of course, you shouldn't say anything in an email that's going to incriminate you, or that you wouldn't say to another person's face. Be professional and polite, add in a sprinkle of personality, and use it wisely for the best results.

NAVIGATING ZOOM

Being unable to meet in person posed quite a challenge during the pandemic (especially for those of us who are huggers!). It's hard to feel connected when you can't feel, see, or hear each other, and you miss out on bonding, banter, and brainstorming (not to mention that giant bowl of shared M&Ms). Having Zoom fill that void seamlessly allowed us to continue to connect in a personal way, and I'm so grateful for their hard work and service during that time.

The pandemic truly changed how we do business. Some companies decided to continue with the work-from-home model even after it was safe to return to the workplace. Others instituted a hybrid method of working several days in the office and several from home. As a result, Zoom is here to stay—so you need to learn how to use it to your advantage.

First of all, you HAVE to turn the camera on. That's how we bond and relate to each other. I know it can be tempting not to show your face, but it's a non-negotiable.

Put your laptop at eye level—use a stack of books if you need to. If the computer is too high, it will look like you're taking a selfie. If it's too low, people will be able to look up your nose, and nobody needs that view!

Be polished and always look your best. This gives you a different sense of confidence, self, purpose, and value. As I've said for years, *When you look good, you feel good. When you feel good, you produce greater results. And when you produce greater results, you typically make more money.* Don't dress like a human mullet—business on top, pajamas on the bottom. You would never go into a negotiation or client meeting half-dressed, so don't do that on Zoom.

Always use a ring light. These are inexpensive but add so much to your appearance. I bought the one I use on Amazon, and it has three different light settings: cold, warm, and warmer. Lighting is so important because it allows your audience to see you clearly, garnering more trust.

> Shout-out to Amazon: Thank you for giving us the ability to buy almost anything we need fast and at different price points. Shout-out to Jeff Bezos again: Thank you for inspiring us. You aren't perfect, but you keep on going. Ten-minute meeting at your office? Or I'll fly wherever you are!

Change your background based on who you're speaking to. For instance, I swap out the painting I display in my office depending on who I'm meeting with on Zoom. All of my artwork shows different sides of who I am authentically, but some resonate more with certain people than others. This all comes back to knowing your audience, and is akin to picking your outfit to match the dress code of a specific business or industry.

Look directly into the camera when speaking, because that mimics real eye contact. Use a strong voice and make sure you're not trailing off at the end of sentences. The goal is to appear confident, try not to interrupt, and discern the right time to interject your thoughts. Don't slouch, hunch, or sway your chair while speaking. Imagine there's a string running from your head to the ceiling to maintain proper posture.

If you are presenting on Zoom, practice your subject matter four or five times before the actual meeting. That way, you can focus on the audience reactions and body language rather than your notes. Learn to pivot, teach, and ask questions based on what you see and hear from them.

If you are the one scheduling Zoom meetings, leave time at the beginning so people can catch up and bond. Bring the quieter people into the conversation whenever possible, and gracefully shut people down who are talking too much.

> Shout-out to Eric Yuan, founder and CEO of Zoom: Thank you for being able to pivot quickly during the pandemic to bring people together and keep businesses afloat in a way we never perceived would become so important!

THE HEAT

Climbing the Social Ladder

You must have a robust social media presence to have an unstoppable brand. The two go hand in hand. Starting a business? Crush competition with social media. Building a company brand? Get online and show everyone why you're better than the rest.

We've all heard the stories of how people in the horse business said cars were not a threat. People in newsprint media said the internet was not a threat. People at Blockbuster said online movies were not a threat, and retailers said Amazon was a fad. You will become the same story if you do not adapt to social media.

Do a social media audit, decide where you're winning, and pinpoint places you might need to push harder.

ARE YOU JUST POSTING, OR ARE YOU ENGAGING?

You need to post and engage daily on social media. Full stop. You won't be seen otherwise.

Many people begin posting without a plan, followers, or any idea who they're looking to attract. They jump in feet first by commenting, arguing, and passionately spilling their guts, and then wonder why people aren't listening to them. My answer to that is: Would you follow, engage with, or trust somebody you didn't know?

Showing people who you are, building a following, and creating connections is the best way to succeed when using social media. Reaching your target audience by engaging with them on their favorite platform is how you win business, loyalty, and a strong following.

Ask yourself: Do I respond to every comment? Do I actively like and comment on others posts? Do I seek out leaders in my industry? Do I ask people to connect on various social media platforms? Am I accepting others' requests?

ARE YOU POSTING OFTEN ENOUGH?

At the risk of sounding like a broken record, daily engagement is a requirement on social media. Some platforms, like Twitter and Snapchat, need even more attention.

Ask yourself: Am I posting every single day? Do I have a posting schedule to keep me accountable and on track?

ARE YOU PROVIDING PROPER CONTEXT TO YOUR POSTS?

Know your audience. Share value with each segment. Knowing your audience helps you to know which social media platform you need to invest in!

Offering explanations around your posts is the best way to provide thought leadership on social media. Whether that means blogging about your thoughts or vlogging, people are looking for your ideas and particular take on the subject.

Ask yourself: Am I fully expressing my views on the subjects I'm posting about, and offering value to my followers in that way? Are my videos a reflection of who I authentically am? Would people seeing only one of my blogs or vlogs get an accurate perception of my values, why, and goals?

ARE YOU POSTING ABOUT A VARIETY OF SUBJECTS?

Remember how Kathie Lee Gifford always talked about her kids on her TV show? It was always Cody this and Cody that until it became almost a joke. Learn from her mistakes and try to stay measured in your coverage of any one facet of your life online. Overkill is annoying.

Ask yourself: Am I too focused on a single subject? Do I offer variety to my followers? Can I expand the focus of my content to reach more people?

ARE YOU PAYING ATTENTION ON ZOOM?

On Zoom, you need to be aware of how people are responding to your message while you're leading or speaking. When someone smiles, you can acknowledge it and say, "I'm hoping that means you liked that point." If you see someone's eyebrows go up, you might comment, "Are you on board with this? Your opinion, thoughts, and energy on this project are important to me." Body language holds all the clues you need to read your audience well.

Ask yourself: Am I watching my audience on Zoom carefully for clues on how they are receiving my message? Am I calling it out when I see a particular gesture or body language—a smirk, smile, or eyeroll—and asking for clarification? Am I practicing radical candor based on those observations?

ARE THE VALUES YOU DISPLAY ONLINE ALIGNED WITH YOUR CAREER?

It's important to authentically integrate the values of the company you're a part of, or are trying to join, into your posts. That way, when people research who you are, they'll immediately see your value to the company as well as your personal value. Telling the story of your care for clients and community in a way that can be shown, seen, felt, and heard helps you win.

Ask yourself: What values does my company (or the company I want to work for) display? Am I incorporating these into my social media? Can I be more aligned than I am now in my messaging?

ARE YOU LEVERAGING YOUR COMPANY'S BRAND THROUGH YOURS?

As an employee, you have the unique opportunity to lift the brand of the company you work for while leveraging your own. It works both ways!

For instance, I coached many people during COVID to build their brands from inside large corporations through LinkedIn. They weren't allowed back at work yet and therefore weren't getting to know their colleagues on a personal level—sometimes they'd never even met them in person. LinkedIn offered a great way to share pieces of themselves and connect with others when building in-person relationships was not an option.

Ask yourself: Am I reposting company wins on my social media? Am I acting as an online representative of my workplace? Can I do more to promote what I'm doing inside my company?

ARE YOUR POSTS APPROPRIATE?

Social media shows up in Google searches. Would you feel comfortable if your employer or a potential employer reviewed your posts? If not, you should probably start deleting now, and become more intentional and aware of what you put out there in the future. Give people an accurate picture of who you are by providing the proper context for every post and curating the best of who you are.

Ask yourself: Am I representing myself well online? Am I being intentional enough about what I post? Are my posts something anyone could look at without embarrassing me?

THE LIGHT: BRAND SOCIAL RECAP

Social media is not a choice, it is a must.

Whether you're a C-suite executive, business owner, entrepreneur, or fresh out of college, learning to successfully navigate social media is the answer to many of the challenges you face.

Social media helps you create value and develop connections.

Your posts should reflect who you are authentically, provide context, and be done frequently.

Consistency and engagement are the keys to success on social media.

Engagement is more important than the number of likes or followers you have.

The platforms you choose to be on depend on your goals and target audience.

Each platform has a different demographic, optimal posting schedule, and ways to engage.

Getting involved now is crucial—don't get left behind!

Conclusion

So many people think brand strength is measured by their successes. *I landed my biggest client. I brought in $500,000 this month. I won a prestigious award.* While it's wonderful to be recognized for your work, none of those things are the source of your strength. That comes from living your authentic truth. It comes from your resiliency and consistency in the face of any challenge.

I've seen even the toughest executives crumble under the pressure of trials. But guess who won't? You! If you've done all the exercises in this book and followed the advice I share here, your brand will be able withstand any fire.

You now have an unshakeable foundation based on your core values, stories, communication skills, emotional intelligence, and professional image. No matter what happens—a client questions your worth, you get laid off, your company closes—you're not going to break into a million pieces. Adversity is simply an opportunity for further growth, sharing, and connection. Your brand will hold you steadfast and strong.

Whenever things start to get hot, I want you to go back to your values and stories. Remember WHO YOU ARE. You have a gift no one else has, and unique experiences that allow you to help others. Use them wisely.

Though apps and platforms might shift, technology will evolve, and you may have to seek out different opportunities, who you are and why you were put on this earth will not change. Whatever the future holds, the brand you've built here will remain timeless and true. You're ready for anything.

THE SPARK: STAY IN ALIGNMENT

Of course, no one is an overnight success. If you don't see immediate results as you are implementing the tactics in this book, that doesn't mean your brand strategy isn't working—it means you haven't given it enough time yet. Be consistent and keep the faith.

It takes time for people to see you in a different light, but someone is always watching. People are looking at your LinkedIn profile, reading your emails, and watching your body language. They're seeing you beat deadlines and take on more responsibility. They're noticing and wondering if that's who you really are. This is true especially if you've made a mistake in the past, have never spoken up in meetings before, or haven't shown leadership until this moment. THAT'S OKAY.

As long as you're using your core values as a filter for everything you do, people will come to trust that this is who you authentically are. The world will eventually catch up with where you are now. Once they do, they'll follow you to all the great places you're headed in the future.

My greatest encouragement to you is KEEP GOING. Don't be discouraged. There may be a delay between your actions and people registering these changes. Brand alignment takes time. Stay the course.

THE FUEL: FIND YOUR TRIBE

When Gordon went to prison, I found out many people I thought were my friends actually weren't. It didn't matter to them that I hadn't done anything wrong. When I called one of them looking for support after the press reported the news, she said, "Yes, I read about it. Best of luck to you," and hung up the phone. I haven't talked to her since.

But then there were other amazing people who stayed loyal to us throughout the entire fire. Not one but two colleagues called to tell me the leader of a networking group I belonged to had gossiped about my situation, and they both let him know they weren't going to support that kind of behavior. Others sat with me in a courtroom while my husband went in front of a federal judge and US attorney.

Going through my trial made me realize how important having a tribe is. People who really know you and who you're striving to be can help hold you steady and strong no matter the circumstances. They're willing to put their reputation on the line to stand by yours. When life hits you hard, you need them for support.

A few years back, I worked with a client who told me, "I love to have fun on the weekends, and I think I'm pretty funny. But my office environment and boss are very serious, and I don't know what parts of myself to show, what parts to hide, and how to find my tribe at work." My advice to her was: You don't have to be the same all the time. Like onions, we all have many layers. We can be authentic to who we are in every single moment. Use everything you've learned in this book about EQ, social awareness, image, and body language to show people different pieces of yourself to start building a supportive tribe.

Anyone can be a part of your support team, even across continents and time zones. Although many in your tribe will be people you know through work or other parts of life, some you may only know virtually. For instance, there's a gentleman who lives in another country that supports me wholeheartedly on LinkedIn. We've never been in the same room, but he's always commenting on my posts and says he'll be among the first to buy this book.

No matter who is in your tribe, I encourage you to surround yourself with people who know you well enough to speak truth into your life. There's nothing more valuable than someone who is willing to say, "Hey, I see you going down a wrong path. That decision doesn't mesh with your value system or goals." Count on your tribe to keep you in alignment when you start to drift, and vice versa.

I now have one mentor who is very data-driven and takes care to point out my mistakes. I have another who is incredibly funny and guides me with humor. Yet another is an older woman who tells me about her life and regrets in an effort to steer me away from them. Each questions, corrects, and encourages me. But most of all, they remind me it's okay to be myself regardless of who I'm around because that's how I was made.

I can only assume that the people I thought were friends who bowed out of my life during the fire had decided their brands weren't strong enough to be aligned with mine, which they perceived as forever broken. Post-fire, some came back and apologized, wanting to be part of my life again. Others could never bring themselves to do the same.

All of this is to say, people you think are your tribe may leave or turn on you—but the ones who matter will continue to support you. Align yourself with those people. Support them as strongly as they support you in return.

THE FIRE: FORGET FAILURE AND FEAR

There's a saying that fear has two potential meanings: Forget Everything And Run, or Face Everything And Rise. I encourage you to choose the latter. Fear-based decisions are never in your best interest.

Fear wants you to think that you weren't created for a reason when you were. It makes you question your purpose when that is a God-given gift and cannot be taken away. It wants you to believe you don't have a choice when you always do.

I once worked with a songwriter who wasn't making money with her music, which made her question if it was truly what she was meant to do with her life. When I suggested she work at Walmart during the day to pay her bills and write songs at night, she looked at me like I was crazy—fear was telling her that would mean she was giving up on her dream. I reminded her, "You can work anywhere and still fulfill the purpose for which you were created. What you do isn't who you are."

And as long as you know that, your foundation can't be shaken. There isn't anything that can move you from where you're supposed to go. No matter where you are or how long you've worked, whether you were a huge success and now you're bankrupt, or you had an amazing opportunity and were then told you weren't right for a job, it's not going to change the trajectory of your life unless you let it.

That doesn't mean it will be easy. The world is going to test you. People are going to test you. Give yourself the tools and the armor necessary to move forward. Let your brand remind you who you are on your best day.

Do what you need to do to get grounded and get your mind right on a daily basis. I get up every day knowing that my mind is a battlefield and fear will try to creep into my thinking. To ensure I do not drift off my path, I read the Bible, listen to God's word, and go back to my core values.

Stay true to your core values and align yourself with like-minded people so you can grow strong in your foundation. Don't let fear of what others think of you affect how you act in any situation or make you drift from what you know is right.

There will come a point where you will be able to spread your wings and not be swayed by what other people think, say, or do. On your journey toward that day, you're going to fear, fail, get up, and improve. This doesn't mean you're not worthy of being heard. It simply means you are trying, risking, learning, and growing.

Fear not and *be not afraid* are repeated over and over in the Bible—let that give you courage. Be brave. God is always with you.

THE HEAT: NEVER, EVER QUIT

Establishing your brand doesn't simply happen. It takes EFFORT and PLANNING. Find the people around you who can change your life. Determine your own narrative. Push your stories out every channel. Especially now that so many people are working from home, this is the best way to ensure you'll be seen.

A personal marketing plan is a must to execute on your branding strategy effectively. Instead of wondering what you should do, it allows you to know exactly what you NEED to do. This means you'll get that post out. Send that one email. Find the twenty people in your niche that need to know who you are. Check, check, and check! Even executing a single thing a day can help. Keep the ball rolling.

There's an old tale about a woman trying to cross a river who, instead of putting the bags she was carrying on her back down, walked in the water with them and drowned. Don't do that to yourself. Drop whatever baggage is weighing you down on one side of the river, jump in, swim to the other side, and keep walking. Don't let the past drown you.

Revise and revive your brand by constantly strengthening and improving as you go along. Continue learning, growing, and finding new ways of doing things. Don't let the naysayers get in your head. Execute and allow history, merit, and experience to be your judge instead.

Whatever you do, don't quit. As Ryan Serhant from *Million Dollar Listing* says, "If the competition is gaining ground, wake up earlier."

There are more hours in the day. You simply have to be willing to put in the time.

You can't fix yesterday, so continue moving forward. Focus on today. What can you do NOW that will move the needle?

THE LIGHT: THE LORD

After all that's been said and done (and read and studied), are you still looking for your purpose? Trying to discover where you'll thrive and grow? Hoping to find the thing you'll enjoy doing that uses your passions and gifts for good?

This book was written to help you start that journey. It is your runway to finding your why by using your core values, reminding yourself who you are, and mining your life stories. And still, even those things may not instantly nail the answer to *here's why I was created.*

For me, it took going through a trial that lasted five-plus years to solidify my purpose. I eventually found it not because of what I did in business, but through who I put my faith in. In knowing Jesus, I found out who I am.

When Gordon was in prison, I realized everything was out of my control—yet I could still find joy, and so could he. Happiness comes from the earth and is fleeting, but joy comes from the Lord. I said to my husband recently, "You must have been afraid on that first day in the penitentiary where they threw you in solitary confinement with nothing but a blanket and a little bit of toilet paper." He replied, "Yes, but I also realized that even though I was there because I had done something wrong, my purpose didn't go away." That's Biblical. That's Scriptural. His joy came from knowing who God was, and who he was in the Lord.

When looking for my purpose, I didn't go to the Lord and say, Here's what I want to do. I want my husband to come home from prison. I want to build a self-sustaining business. I want two kids, one with curly brown hair and the other with curly blonde hair. I want to drive a white car. I want to live in this house on this street. I want to have these friends. God is not a wish-granter. Instead, I had to listen and learn HIS plan for my life.

Once I stopped asking for things and started asking who I am in Christ, the plan of my life started to unfold. I think the fire would have melted me if the Lord hadn't walked me through it. In focusing on Him, I started to see pieces of myself in different ways than before. I put my trust in the Lord—someone who's never left, who will never leave, who even in the most painful moments in life is right there with me.

In the Bible, it says God leans His ear down to His child who calls out his name. The more I grew closer to Jesus Christ, the more my gifting grew. Looking back now, I can reflect and say that I saw pieces of that gift before the fire. But the minute I started to truly believe, that's when my gifting exploded. He revealed things to me through scripture.

Once I was living His purpose and following Him, it was like all of a sudden, my eyes were opened. I could clearly see the leader in the room. The one who hadn't been heard. The one who'd been hurt. This empathy gave me the ability to help in a way that I hadn't before, and also the confidence to do so. That came straight from the Lord.

I understand this isn't necessarily what people want to hear—we all want instant gratification—but the honest answer here is, the only way to discover what you were meant for is by knowing Jesus, understanding what he's done for you, and hearing how he speaks to you. As the apostle Paul says in Ephesians, *We have obtained an inheritance, having been predestined, according to His purpose, who works all things for the counsel of His will.* The Lord wants to fulfill His purpose through us, just as we fulfill our purpose through Him.

This all stems from believing you were CREATED by God for a reason. Without that basic foundation, it's hard to find ourselves. Whenever you find yourself in a place of fear, look for your purpose in God's word. It's part of the journey. I know that may sound extraordinarily hard, but it's also wonderful and joyous. Read the Bible.

The Lord wants to know you deeply. Instead of saying, "God, here's what I want to do," try asking, "Lord, what is Your purpose for my life?" Because that is what you were created for, and in that you will find incredible joy.

I know some of you reading this right now are thinking, *Well, you had me until you started preaching.* I don't want to lose you. I don't want you to think that if you don't believe what I believe this book hasn't been worth reading. I simply know that my job is to share my story and glorify God in that broken story.

The Lord said, Anyone who listens to my teaching and follows it is wise, like a person who builds a house on solid rock. Though the rain comes in torrents and the floodwaters rise and the winds beat against that house, it won't collapse because it is built on bedrock. But anyone who hears my teaching and doesn't obey it is foolish, like a person who builds a house on sand. When the rains and floods come and the winds beat against that house, it will collapse with a mighty crash.

During my trial, I imagined that scripture coming to life so many times. I pictured myself standing on solid rock and letting the waves of insecurity, fear, doubt, shame, and guilt wash by me. I knew my feet were on cement that wouldn't crack. I knew my purpose could not be thwarted.

I know many people have made mistakes. Crushed their brands. Said the wrong thing. This is my message of hope to you: It doesn't matter what happened in the past. You don't have to be that person forever. God did not create you for that. It is okay to say, *What I have been is not what I will be.* God's protection is there for you regardless. His covering is strong enough to keep you safe. That is the promise for us all, and that is my greatest encouragement for you.

If this is the part of the book where some of you are thinking, *She is full of it* and *I cannot believe she went from business to talking to me about this*—it's still worth every word. I can't leave this year, this book, or this moment without getting to where all foundations should be made, which is on His rock-solid word. As Jeremiah 29-11 says, *For I know the plans I have for you, declares the Lord, plans to prosper you and not harm you, plans to give you a hope and a future.* To which I say, amen.

I now declare you unstoppable. Go forth and let the world know who you authentically are and why you were put on this earth. I'll be here cheering for you the whole time!

The Book Doesn't Stop Here!

I WANT TO HEAR FROM YOU AND HELP YOU. LET'S CONNECT!

LinkedIn: @modaimageandbrandconsulting

Instagram: @modaimageandbrandconsulting

Facebook: @MODAImageCnsltg

Forged by Fire Facebook Group: @milagriggforgedbyfire

Twitter: @MODAImageCnsltg

TikTok: @modaimageandbrand

YouTube: MODA Image and Brand Consulting

CPSIA information can be obtained
at www.ICGtesting.com
Printed in the USA
JSHW021012101122
32949JS00001B/2